BEHAVIOUR AT WORK

Advanced GNVQ

BEHAVIOUR AT WORK
Advanced GNVQ

Susan Curtis
Lecturer in Economics, Crewe & Alsager Faculty of Manchester Metropolitan University

Barry Curtis
Manager, Social Sciences, South Cheshire College, Crewe
Chief Examiner, NEAB 'A' level Business Studies

 published in association with

This book is for Laura and George

PITMAN PUBLISHING
128 Long Acre, London WC2E 9AN

A Division of Longman Group Limited

First published in 1994

A CIP catalogue record for this book can be obtained from the British Library.

ISBN 0 273 60399 X

10 9 8 7 6 5 4 3 2

Typeset by PanTek Arts, Maidstone.
Printed and bound in Great Britain by Clays Ltd, St Ives plc

The Publishers' policy is to use paper manufactured from sustainable forests.

Contents

List of activities and case studies

Element 15.3
Behavioural aspects of managing people which influence performance at work

Acknowledgements

The authors would like to thank the following for their help and contributions:

Simon Lake, Ian Little, Julian Thomas, Deborah Mallender, Neil Williams-Slaven, Peter Griffiths, John Spragg, Lorraine Phipps, Zoe McKinney, Thelma Appleton, Ollie O'Neill, Sue Winters, Jonathan Grint, Winifred Fryer, Mark Shenton, Brian Unger, Mark Rivers, Sheila Jenkins, Janet Gilford, Zoe Coupe, Richard Uli, Dick Bruggeman, Danielle Rossini, Nancy Seevers, Renee Loth, Mark Lindner, Mary Ann Parchim, Molly Waite, Rosalene Dietrich, Laura Fuesting, Sandy Massie, Rosie Collins, Anthea Beaty, Tracie Latham, Vivienne Walker, Nigel Fryer, Chris Hurst, Jane Henshall, Joyce Curtis, Peter Jones, John Priest.

Rolls-Royce Motor Cars plc; Lyceum Theatre, Crewe; Hallmark Cards, USA; John English Ltd, Smash Hits; Marks & Spencer plc, Hanley; Foden Trucks, Signal Radio, Countryside Graphics, Motorola, LoDan Electronics, First Chicago Bank, William Rainey Harper College, Allstate Insurance, *Management Today*, *Financial Times*, *Personnel Management*, The Body Shop, European Components Co Ltd.

> Please note the assignments included in this book are not part of the BTEC designed assignments published by BTEC which meet the full requirements of the BTEC specifications. They will however, provide opportunities for students to produce useful evidence towards the full requirement.

Element 15.1

INVESTIGATE FACTORS INFLUENCING ATTITUDES AND PERFORMANCE AT WORK

PERFORMANCE CRITERIA

1 **Factors affecting individual attitudes are examined**
   Range: nature of work, hierarchy of needs; organisational culture:
   norms, power, status, task, person, role; relationship
   within the organisation between functions and departments.

2 **Factors affecting motivation at work are described**
   Range: the personal needs, drives and aspirations which determine
   behaviour; theories of motivation: physiological, social;
   satisfiers/dissatisfiers; job enrichment, job rotation.

3 **Impact of monitoring factors on performance are investigated and explained**
   Range: Piece rates, measured day work, performance appraisal
   and performance related pay.

EVIDENCE INDICATOR

A survey to identify the personal attitudes of a small work group and the impact of motivation on their performance.

Factors affecting individual attitudes

Individual attitudes to work

An attitude is the way in which a person tends to respond to events, people and objects. Two people may have totally different attitudes towards the prospect of going on the same roller-coaster ride. One may have a positive attitude and be full of enthusiasm and excitement; the other may have a negative attitude and be terrified at the thought. These attitudes determine their feelings, thoughts and behaviour.

There are three parts to an attitude:

- feelings or emotions
- thought or knowledge
- behaviour (what a person does)

Attitudes are directed towards something a person has feelings and beliefs about. We have attitudes about work, school, other people, television pro-grammes – in fact, almost everything that we come into contact with.

Attitudes determine the way we feel about things, the way we behave and our beliefs about people and objects. Attitudes are not visible. The way people behave gives clues as to the attitudes they hold.

Attitudes help to shape our behaviour at work, as can be seen in Fig. 1.1.

Like the operative in Fig 1.1, many workers would have a positive attitude towards such a statement; they will be motivated and determined to achieve the highest production in order to win the money. Other workers, however, may consider that they have no chance of winning the production bonus, so their response will be different. Their negative attitude will reveal different thoughts, feelings and actions to the person with the positive attitude.

People have attitudes about parts of their jobs as well as the job as a whole. If Laura does not like working on Saturday evenings, she has a negative attitude towards this aspect of her job. Attitudes tend to stay the same if nothing is done

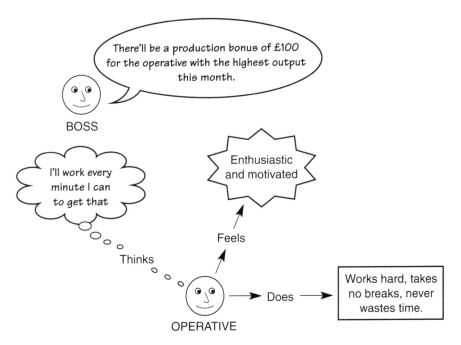

Fig. 1.1 Attitudes at work

to change them. If Laura's hours are changed so that she does not have to work on Saturday evenings, she will be happier and her attitude may become more positive.

Attitudes provide people with a basis for expressing their values. A manager who believes strongly in everyone working hard may consider subordinates lazy if they go home at the appointed time instead of working voluntary overtime every evening.

An understanding of attitudes is important in that attitudes help people to adapt to their work environment. When people are treated well by their boss, they are likely to develop a positive attitude towards management and the organisation. They will be more comfortable working for that organisation if they feel appreciated and important.

People's attitudes to their work are interlinked with their motivation to work. If they are well motivated they will be loyal to the organisation and work hard. They will need less supervision and be less likely to come into conflict with management.

Attitudes are affected by factors such as the nature of the work, individual needs, the culture (the way things are done and the structure of the organisation) and how the company is organised.

ATTITUDES QUESTIONNAIRE

Do you agree or disagree with the following statements?

	Agree	Disagree
1 We work to live, not live to work	☐	☐
2 I want a good salary, a sense of achievement and an interesting job when I go to work	☐	☐
3 I would never object to working voluntary overtime to help out at work if my boss really needed me to	☐	☐
4 You can have a good laugh at work	☐	☐
5 Going to work is like having a second home and family	☐	☐
6 Being a student for as long as possible is my aim in life	☐	☐
7 Once you start work, it's a long, long time to wait until you retire	☐	☐
8 I want to travel the world and live a bit before I settle down and find a job	☐	☐
9 Work is the best place for making friends	☐	☐

Now add up your scores:

1 Agree 1 Disagree 5	**6** Agree 1 Disagree 5
2 Agree 5 Disagree 1	**7** Agree 1 Disagree 5
3 Agree 5 Disagree 1	**8** Agree 1 Disagree 5
4 Agree 5 Disagree 1	**9** Agree 5 Disagree 1
5 Agree 5 Disagree 1	

How did you score?

Over 26?
You have a positive attitude towards work, and you believe it is something to be enjoyed and looked forward to.

Under 26?
You have a negative attitude towards work – perhaps you're not ready for it yet or you've had bad experiences so far. Don't let that put you off – there are plenty of different jobs to do and many different employers to work for.

Individual attitudes and the nature of work

The majority of people do jobs that they have chosen to do. Many people love their work and say that they would do it even if they did not get paid for it. Others feel that they need money to live and the job they do is the best they can get at the present time.

The nature of work has two factors:

1 The job content – the task, what has to be done to complete the job
2 The job context – the environment in which the job is done

1 The job content

There are many differences in jobs – people work outdoors, indoors, far away from home and others work inside their homes. Some people interact with others all day long, and some work alone with machinery or computers and never speak to other people. Some people have a great variety of tasks to do as part of their job while others perform the same task or movement all day long. Some people get a lot of exercise in their jobs, other get none. Some people do a great deal of travelling as part of their job while others stand or sit in exactly the same spot every day for years. The nature of work will be an important factor in shaping people's attitudes towards their work.

TASK

A. Think of people you know who work – do you know how they spend their day? Carry out a survey to find out what people do at work.

B. What would be your ideal job? What would it involve doing?

Technology

How jobs are done are affected by changing technology. Years ago, clerks would neatly copy out documents with a quill pen, but then the typewriter was invented and the job changed completely. Computers and word processors have again changed the nature of the work. Not only are different skills needed, but the work itself is different.

TASK

Ask some older people you know:
- How their job has changed while they have been doing it.
- Is it now a different job?
- Have they been trained in order to acquire different skills?
- How have these changes affected their attitudes?

Management attitudes

It is the responsibility of a manager to organise the work load. He or she may break each task down into small parts and give each employee one repetitive task to do all the time, or involve the workers more and allow them to decide how the work is organised.

People who work along mass-production lines may develop certain attitudes to work. To them, work may be important for the companionship or the money. If they are putting windscreen wipers on a succession of cars all day, packing boxes or testing batteries, they are unlikely to feel that it is an interesting, worthwhile job. Their attitude to work will have been affected by the way that the work is organised in their organisation.

Alternatively, people who have been able to have a substantial say in how they do their work, solved problems themselves or started new initiatives as part of their jobs, may well have different attitudes towards work than if they had worked on a production line.

2 The job context

Any job, such as word processor operator, factory operative or company director, will be affected tremendously by the industry and organisation. For example, the word processor operator will find his or her job very different if moved from a large hospital to a small estate agents. A shop assistant would find life very different in a small village shop after working in a city centre department store. The context or environment in which the work is done will affect the job itself and the person's attitude towards that job.

The flexible firm

Changes in contracts of employment are affecting people's attitudes to work. Traditionally, employees were given permanent full-time contracts so that they could work for an organisation all of their lives, if they so wished and they were needed. More flexible or non-standard contracts have been introduced by many organisations over recent years. People are employed part-time, on temporary fixed term contracts, or on a self-employed basis to a greater extent than ever before. The major growth has been in part-time contracts which are largely taken up by women. Part-time workers are useful to firms for busy periods, so that organisations can meet peaks in demand.

Employing workers on a temporary or self-employed basis costs less than permanent, full-time employees. The employer is not paying wages for people when the firm is not busy and also saves on employee benefits such as pensions. This lack of security will affect people's attitudes.

TASK

In groups, discuss the following situations:

1 You are employed on a temporary three month contract in your present job – what might your attitude to work be in the third month and how would that be affected by your employer telling you either that there was no chance of being kept on, or a good chance of being kept on?

2 You are trying to sell your skills to employers on a self-employed basis. You want them to contract work out to you in the same way as they might to a builder or window cleaner. How would this self-employed status affect your attitude to work?

3 You are employed on a part-time basis and do not receive full pay rises, pensions and other benefits which the full-time members of staff receive. You can only work part-time due to other commitments. Would your attitude to work be affected by the lack of benefits you receive?

Employment commitment

In 1992, over 3,000 people were asked whether they would stop working if they had enough money to live comfortably on for the rest of their lives.

In every category of job, the majority of people answered that they would continue to work. Professional and managerial workers were the most strongly in favour of continuing to work (*see* Fig. 1.2).

QUESTIONS

1 What conclusions can you draw from Fig.1.2 about people's attitude towards work?

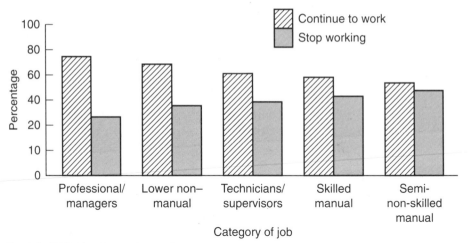

Fig. 1.2 *Attitudes towards work*

2 Why do you think people in managerial/professional jobs are more likely to want to continue working?

3 Would you wish to work if you had enough money to live on? If so, what job would you choose to do?

People talking about their jobs

Zoe

Zoe is a packer in a bone china manufacturers. The pottery comes from the kiln, is inspected for faults and then packed into boxes. Quantity and designs packed depend upon customer orders.

'Every day is different. It's nice to see the new patterns that they bring out. The time goes quickly as we are always busy. Most of us work in twos from one bench. Sometimes we get very big orders, it could be up to 500 dozen. Then we would have to share it between the ten packers. Also, some of the orders have to have bar codes on them.

'We pick up the trays of ware together and we help each other out if we are unsure whether it should be packed of whether it should go into seconds. There's always one of the bosses around we

Zoe – China packer

can ask if we need to. If there's a very small mark on the ware, they might let that go, depending upon how strict the customer is.

'We are selector/packers and part of the job is quality control. If there is a problem, we all discuss it so we do work as a team. There are ten of us and we share the work out equally. If not, somebody will start moaning.

'I don't think there are any promotion prospects here, although I wish there were – it would give me a goal to aim for in the future. It is a responsible job because we have the last say before it goes to the customer. People do it mostly for the money. I'm quite happy with the pay, although I have had no experience elsewhere. I have done lithographing as well when I first started here, but they were a packer short and they asked me if I would go on packing and I have been here ever since.'

Jonathan

Jonathan is a tyre fitter at a Tyre Distribution Centre. He repairs punctures and fits tyres, exhausts and batteries to both cars and lorries.

'I'm interested in cars basically. I've always been interested in cars. I enjoy working with the other lads. We have a good time, we all get on well together.

'They train you here. It's better if they train you than going to college. If I stay here for years I could become foremen and eventually assistant manager.

'You've got a lot of responsibility. Every job you do has got to be done right because people's lives are at risk. They rely on you. If the wheels come off, they're not going to be very happy.

Jonathan – tyre fitter

'The bad part is just the getting dirty. I'm a part-time waiter as well, so I have to get my nails dead clean every night after work. I'm washing my hands for about half an hour. I'm quite happy with the money here. I have been a part-time waiter ever since I was at school, I've just carried it on.'

Sue

Sue is a librarian. She mans the enquiry desk, information desk and reference desk on a timetabled basis. She also carries out stock revision. Sue works part-time, $18\frac{1}{2}$ hours per week. She was a group librarian before she stopped working to have a family.

'I like the enquiry work, meeting people, the variety of the work and helping people. The part-time aspect is preferable because that fits in with the family and other activities like playing tennis, but you miss out on what's going on. After a couple of days off things have changed and quite often you are not informed, though efforts are made to keep all staff briefed about any meetings or new developments.

Sue – librarian

'I enjoy being in a large library like this because it's a lot busier and a lot more goes on, and there are a lot more different enquiries. I enjoy being with a larger staff.

'Not being in charge doesn't bother me at the moment because it's better to come out to work than be at home all the time. I'm not particularly bothered about having extra responsibility at the moment. That may change in the future. Some things are frustrating because I'm not in charge and I can't do anything about things. That's something you have to accept.

'We work as a team; all the jobs overlap so we pick up from where someone else left off. We have to communicate with one another and on the whole I like the people here.

'There may be prospects for promotion on a job share basis, but there's nothing imminent at the moment. It's not a particularly responsible job, most of the responsibility is taken away. That's one thing that's changed since I've come back. The management structure has changed considerably. Areas like reference have a specialist and they're responsible for reference here and in the smaller libraries in the area and we're all responsible to them.

'Working Saturday mornings is awkward, being away from the family. I feel guilty, although I enjoy the work here because its busy.'

Lorraine

Lorraine is a marketing manager in a theatre. The main marketing role is to maintain a high profile for the theatre and to identify who and where its customers are and to meet their needs.

A high profile is achieved by promoting all aspects of the theatre. This involves the preparation and distribution of promotional materials which include the season's brochures, leaflets and posters. Another important vehicle is to obtain a high media coverage. Therefore, advertising schedules and campaigns need to be prepared, along with press nights, press launches and various promotional events.

Lorraine – marketing manager

Along with analysing customer information from the computer base, to ascertain who they are and where they come from, it is also necessary to identify their needs. This is achieved by preparing and distributing questionnaires and carrying out surveys.

Lorraine has worked in the theatre for two years and previously worked in a leisure centre.

'After working in a leisure centre for nearly nine years, I was very sceptical when I was asked to "look after" a theatre's marketing activities on a temporary secondment basis; the only marketing experience I had was co-ordinating and marketing the visit of the Royal Exchange Theatre when they visited the leisure centre. Working at the centre was like putting on an old pair of slippers; it was comfortable. But I decided that it was time to widen my horizons, so, armed with my pad and pen, off I went.

'It was all very alien to me at first, especially when I had the daunting task of actually having to liaise with another marketing manager. The little knowledge I gained in marketing through various college courses (especially the BTEC in Business and Finance when I took the marketing module as an option), along with hands-on experience, has helped me gain more and more confidence and now, only two years on, I no longer feel intimidated by meeting other professional people in the field of marketing.

'When I first came to the theatre it operated an antiquated box office booking system, which gave us very little or no customer data. However, within 18 months we implemented a computerised box office and administration system, which gave me the ideal vehicle to analyse our customers and to put marketing theories into practice. By enabling me to market customers to particular productions and to analyse their data (who are they and where do they come from?), my job was made comparatively easier.

'The most interesting part of my job (and I suppose the most glamorous), is that I meet all the stars. I used to think that was wonderful, but now it's an everyday part of the job. I organise press launches with them and take them to various radio stations if I have arranged an 'on air' interview. I also enjoy my liaison with the press and have formed very good relationships, which in turn is an aide to help me maintain a high media presence.

'The diversity of my role, given the staffing structure at the theatre, means that no day is the same. When the computers were implemented last year, I took over the role of systems manager. This meant that the general manager undertook the marketing activities for a few months and in his absence I oversee the general running of the theatre.

'Some days I do not even touch any marketing activities. Today I've got to organise new curtains for the auditorium, along with the fitting of new toilet seats in the ladies' loo. Since I implemented the computer system I oversee the box office operation, which again takes a great deal of my time. I've really had some laughs. Last year I dressed up as a goose (somebody chickened out!) for a promotional photograph for the pantomime; I have the photos to prove it!

'It's not always interesting and glamorous; it's a matter of all hands to the deck, especially during mail shot periods. We have, and it's still growing, 8,500 customers who we regularly mail. So, it's a matter of rolling up your sleeves and stuffing envelopes.

'We feel that the most important employees at the theatre are those in the front line, especially the box office assistants. Marketing is quite global. It covers what the usherettes are wearing – every aspect of the theatre. We keep the staff fully informed of future productions and changes in working practices. We hold many staff meetings. I have regular meetings with the general manager, when we update on each other's activities. Again, these are really time-consuming although it's important that the left hand knows what the right hand is doing.

'There are special productions such as the pantomime I'm organising now [July] and the launch of the new season in September. We're having an event outside the theatre with local radio coming along and some dancers from the local dancing school. I oversee all group bookings, look after special requirements, organise buses for old age pensioners. I was frustrated yesterday because I couldn't get the new till for the front of house programmed into the computer; it nearly went through the window!

'We have a very diverse programme with 27 productions which have to be marketed – from Hamlet to Ken Dodd. Each Production Company thinks you're just marketing theirs, and they get in touch and ask you what you've done about their particular production. I'd love to be able to market one production and put all my heart and soul into that. Everything is happening at once and I don't like the demands made upon me; I can't put everything into delivering them.

'My personality goes with the job; I enjoy meeting people. If you're not outward going, you wouldn't survive in a job like this.'

Ollie

Ollie is an air traffic controller at an international airport. His job entails controlling the aeroplanes coming into and going out of the airport, to within 40 miles of the airport. Aircraft landing, taking off and taxiing on the runways, are also given guidance. Even when the aeroplanes are not near an airport, they are being controlled and guided by the airways controllers at the London Air Traffic Control Centre. Once an aircraft is released by the airport, the airways controllers deal with them *en route*, including flights abroad.

Ollie – air traffic controller

'There's a great deal of job satisfaction. You have to be able to think three-dimensionally, think quickly – even when you've decided upon a particular sequence of events, you may have to change at a moment's notice if the situation demands it. Being able to do that on a daily basis gives a great deal of job satisfaction. Safety comes first with everything, but you can also save aircraft fuel and people's time by using your skills.

'It's very much teamwork. There are five controllers on a shift, and there's lots of liaison between different positions in this airport, plus liaising with other controllers at other airports, the airways controllers, the pilots and our assistants who feed us information. The airways controllers ring you up and agree a level, a time or a position to hand the aircraft over to you.

'We're constantly problem solving, juggling the little private fliers around and trying to integrate them into the schedule. It's like playing a good game of three-dimensional chess. There are breaks, you're not doing it all the time. The quieter moments give relief from the pressure. When it's busy, it makes the adrenalin flow. After a busy time, you get a buzz from it, you feel as if you've resolved problems.

You have to up your work rate significantly in a short space of time. You're always thinking three or four moves ahead and when you've completed a busy period, you feel on a high.

'You're constantly taking to people. There's nearly always something to do or somebody to talk to. You cannot work in isolation, you have to be a teamworker. They're a good team and they make some wonderful cups of tea. You get to use the better, more advanced technology.

'The downside of it is that it mostly involves shiftwork. It can be anti-social, I have missed the children's parents' evenings at school and sports days because of the shifts. Although, you can do your shopping when no-one else is shopping.

'Also, you're piggy in the middle trying to satisfy the requirements of pilots not wanting to be delayed and trying to comply with a system which has to take into account many, many other pilots. Some pilots, although not many, think they're the only one in the sky.

'But, apart from flying the aeroplane myself, I wouldn't want any other job. It certainly has its moments.'

QUESTIONS

1 What sort of attitudes have the people talking about their jobs got towards their work?

2 Which people are the happiest in their jobs?

3 What parts of their jobs are people dissatisfied about?

4 How are people's attitudes affected by their work environment?

5 Besides the money, what do people get out of working?

Management attitudes and the nature of work

Management attitudes towards workers will shape how work is organised. Last century, and in the early part of this century, managers believed that firms operated to make a profit and the workers' part was restricted to doing a job to enable this to happen efficiently. A manager saw the worker as an economic unit, a part of the production process, which should be instructed on exactly what to do, and hired and fired as necessary. Machines were purchased to help make a profit for the firm, management made the decisions about when and where and how they should operate, and the same went for people. It was an engineer's view of individuals as interchangeable parts and it affected how employees were treated and how the work they did was organised.

During this century, it was realised that workers were more than 'just a pair of hands' and were capable of a greater contribution to the firm than pressing the same button all day. Organisations have widened their view of their responsibility to their employees and have tended to concentrate more on meeting the needs of the whole person than they used to do.

To summarise, management thinking has tended to focus on employees as:

- machine-like workers, only interested in the money
  OR
- unique, individual people with different interests, needs and motivations – prepared to work as a member of a team and contribute to the organisation

These alternative views of people's attitudes have shaped the way that jobs are designed and the way in which people are paid.

The machine-like worker

Here the worker is seen as someone who is not capable of contributing to the managing of work, and so is instructed to carry out work in a particular way. The task is broken down into small operations, so that the worker carries out the same repetitive job all day, every day. The worker is paid according to the output he or she produces, i.e. piece rate. For example, in a chocolate factory, it may be the job of one worker to check that all chocolate bars are the right shape. This method of breaking the work down into specialist components is sometimes called 'division of labour' and is often referred to as 'Taylorism' (after F W Taylor) or 'Fordism' (after Henry Ford).

The participative worker

Here the worker is seen as someone who is capable of contributing to the work, and he or she is part of the decision-making process and encouraged to think up new ideas, solve problems and be far more committed to the organisation. For example, workers may be split into teams to discuss what went wrong with their work yesterday and how to put it right. They may design new procedures for an office or devise a job rotation scheme for their own part of the factory. The participative worker needs less supervision because he or she has more control over his or her own work.

The view of a worker as a non-thinking machine whose work should be one repetitive and restricted task, is symbolised by the work of F W Taylor and Henry Ford. The alternative view of a worker as a thinking whole person who can contribute to the organisation originated from the Hawthorne Studies.

F W Taylor's 'Scientific Management'

Frederick Winslow Taylor was born in America in 1856 and was trained as an engineer. While he was working at the Bethlehem Steel Works, he observed how tasks, such as shovelling coke, were carried out. He experimented with different shovel sizes and measured daily outputs. Taylor designed a method of working using an exact shovel size which would be best for the job and which allowed for rest breaks. When Taylor's method of doing the work was used, output increased by nearly 400 per cent and wages increased by over 60 per cent. Costs were reduced considerably over a three year period as the number of workers needed fell by over 260.

The unions were not happy with Taylor's innovations because apart from the job losses, the wage rises were not equal to the increases in production. The employers gained more from the new methods than the workers. There was also resistance from management because they were used to being in charge of whole workshops, whereas Taylor believed that every worker in an organisation should only perform a single function. He devised a system of 'functional management' under which each worker would be responsible to around five different foremen, each controlling one small aspect of the job.

The principle of studying work and designing a 'best way' of doing the work was called 'Scientific Management'. Taylor's ideas were so successful at increasing production and caused such a lot of interest throughout America that they were tried out by other industries, although not always with happy results. In 1912, there were labour troubles at Watertown Arsenal, Massachusetts, caused by an attempt to apply his principles. As a result of the strike, he was asked to report upon his methods to the Special Committee of the House of Representatives. There he said:

> Both sides [management and workers] must recognise as essential the substitution of exact scientific investigation and knowledge for the old individual judgement or opinion, either of the workman or the boss, in all matters relating to the work done in the establishment. And this applies both as to the methods to be employed in doing the work and the time in which each job should be done.

Decisions about how work should be done had previously been left to the workers. Taylor believed that these decisions should be taken by management so that some order and precision could be given to the organisation of the factory or office – but separating the 'doing' part of the job from the 'thinking' part made jobs less interesting to do for the workers. When workers have no say in how the work is done and have a repetitive task to perform, they may feel a lack of involvement, both with the job and the organisation as a whole. These feelings of alienation can result in low motivation, absenteeism, lateness and high staff turnover.

Despite these problems with Taylor's 'Scientific Management', his ideas are still widely used today. The main principles of 'Scientific Management' are:

1 The development of a true science of work

Decisions should be taken by managers as to exactly what the workers should do during 'a day's work'. The work needs to be investigated scientifically, observed and measured by managers so that the workers know what is expected of them. They should be paid a higher than average wage, according to the amount of work done.

2 The scientific selection and progressive development of the worker

The best person for the job should be chosen. They should be trained to be a 'first class worker' and not just have to follow the person they happen to work near. Taylor considered it the responsibility of management to offer workers further opportunities for training and promotion, depending upon the worker's skills and abilities. Workers should to be able to do 'the highest, most interesting and most profitable class of work' for which they could become 'first class'.

3 The bringing together of the science of work and the scientifically selected and trained workers

Taylor felt that a 'mental revolution' was needed so that 'Scientific Management' could work properly. He maintained that managers' and workers' attitudes needed to change to enable them to work together successfully. He believed that the main source of resistance was management and that workers are willing to co-operate in learning to do a good job for a high rate of pay.

4 The constant and intimate co-operation of management and workers

Management and workers should divide the work between them, so that everyone does the job to which they are best suited. Managers should specify how the work is to be done, how long it should take, set the wages and quality standards, and supervise and control the workers doing the job. Taylor's idea of dividing up the work was that managers should organise the work and the workers should do the job, as laid down by the manager.

All these ideas were new and mostly had a very good effect on the industries which implemented them. However, there were drawbacks:

- Many jobs do not have one 'best way' and can be altered to suit individuals.
- People often work for reasons in addition to money – such as companionship. Taylor believed that people should concentrate on the task in hand and be kept apart. They should not be allowed to speak to one another so that work is not interrupted.
- Giving all the decision-making aspects of work to management makes the work less interesting, as does breaking the work down into specialised parts so that people perform one small task all day, every day.

Frederick W Taylor takes a lot of the blame for the modern work organisation problems of assembly line boredom and alienation. Taylor did recommend organising work into small and separate tasks, but his plan was not to make things difficult for workers. Since the sixteenth century, workers had been ill-treated, exploited and underpaid by their employers and Taylor intended to put this right. Managers did not organise the work, leaving decisions about how the work should be done to their employees, and as a consequence all workers did things as they saw fit. Managers did not know how much output to expect from their workers and gave very little thought to the design of jobs. Taylor was implementing his ideas in 1911 with the intention of increasing production *and* workers' wages. F W Taylor's 'Scientific Management' aimed to improve the workers' situation and make work organisation more efficient.

The Ford Motor Company

Henry Ford originated the idea of the moving production line for the mass production of cars.

In the early part of the twentieth century, when cars were first introduced, they were a symbol of status and wealth. Ford intended to change the fact that cars were only for the rich. The Model T was to be for the masses – a car almost everyone could afford. To make a cheaper car, Ford introduced various efficiency measures. He mechanised wherever possible and broke down tasks into their smallest parts. One worker would perform the same task over and over again, producing just one very small component of the whole operation.

The work was not enjoyable and by 1913, employees of the Ford Motor Company were leaving the company at such a rate that Ford had to hire ten times more workers than they needed just to keep the line moving. Ford decided to double wages in order to get the best people and motivate them to work hard.

Henry Ford wanted to use the most up to date ideas about production, particularly those of F W Taylor.

Charles Sorensen, one of Ford's top production people, started an assembly line by pulling a Model T chassis slowly by windlass across 250 feet of factory floor, timing the process. Behind him walked six workers, picking up parts from carefully spaced piles on the floor and fitting them to the chassis. By installing an automatic conveyor belt, a whole car was eventually assembled in 93 minutes.

Many firms have since followed the lead of the Ford Motor Company and have used their production line methods to cut costs and increase efficiency.

Manufacturing pottery

The factory used in this case study employs 150 people and manufactures mugs and tableware. The business is successful. 'We've gone through three recessions in the 25 years we've been in business,' commented a spokesperson for the company.

The factory uses similar production methods to the larger manufacturers such as Wedgwood and Royal Doulton. The differences are that this smaller factory is a much leaner organisation, production costs are lower, and staffing is very cost effective.

Everyone in the factory is on a bonus depending upon the amount they produce. They have to achieve a target before bonus payments begin and then they may be able to take home an extra £20 to £50 each week, depending upon their output. When the bonus system was implemented several years ago, production increased dramatically. 'All the time wasting that went on disappeared.'

Visitors to the factory have commented that it's 'like a beehive', with everyone working extremely hard. In addition to the bonus, there is an incentive to keep working in that if any one person stops, it will stop those next along the line and so on. It affects everyone's bonus if one person does not work. 'If a machine goes down they start shouting and the language is blue.' The fitters who mend the machines have to be quick as everyone is waiting for the machines to be repaired so that they can return to earning their bonus. Their manager believes that once people earn a bonus regularly, it becomes a part of the income they expect and need.

The workforce are all keen not to waste any time. One of the drawbacks of mass production can be carelessness and therefore quality control becomes very important.

'It's important that they don't deviate from what you've set out. If there's anywhere they can go wrong, they will. You want people to do the job they are supposed to do.'

'The difficulty with trying to be democratic in this industry is that a lot of skills have gone and machinery has replaced a skilled workforce. The workers are tied to the machine – the machine does the job. There aren't the skills there were years ago.'

Each employee specialises in a particular job and does the same job each day in the same part of the factory. Tasks such as putting handles on mugs, taking the mugs to the kiln, or sticking transfers with the company name on the bottom of mugs, are all separate jobs which individual employees specialise in.

The company exports to many countries throughout the world. 'We've always kept very busy,' says the spokesman. 'We've never made anyone redundant through lack of work.'

QUESTIONS

1 In which ways is the pottery factory run along Taylor or Fordism principles?

2 Why do you think this system of management is so successful in this factory?

3 Why are people happy to work for this company?

The Hawthorne Studies

The Hawthorne Studies were conducted at the Western Electric Company, Hawthorne, Chicago from 1924–1933. The company made telephone equipment.

The first experiments within the company concerned the effects of changes in the lighting on the workers' productivity. Two groups of workers were isolated and the lighting conditions for one group were unchanged, while for the other group the lighting was made brighter and dimmer. No differences in output were found between the two groups and, in fact, production rose in both groups. This was named 'The Hawthorne Effect' – the fact that people tend to be self-conscious and behave differently when they think they are being watched. Both groups worked harder, because they were being observed and not because of their working conditions.

After these first experiments, an Industrial Research team directed by Elton Mayo took over. Elton Mayo was an Australian who spent most of his working life at Harvard University in America supervising research. Mayo was interested in such things as worker tiredness, accidents and turnover, and the effect on these of giving workers more rest breaks and changing the working conditions. Mayo's first experiment was known as 'The Relay Assembly Test Room' experiment.

The Relay Assembly Test Room

In April 1927, six girls were selected from a large department of the Hawthorne Works. They were chosen as average workers and their work involved assembling telephone relays. The idea of Mayo and his team was to study the girls' output while varying the working conditions in order to identify the best conditions for maximum production.

The girls were interviewed by the superintendent of the inspection branch of the company who explained the experiment to them. They received a lot of attention, including regular medical examinations every six weeks. An observer stayed with them throughout the working day and questioned them each morning about what food they had eaten and how well they had slept, which was noted down in a log. Whenever changes were made in the conditions of the experiment, the girls were consulted and suggestions which did not meet with their approval were abandoned. The experiment lasted for five years.

Changes made to the girls' working conditions were varied:

- no change for the first five weeks
- a group payment according to the output of the six girls in the room
- increasing the amount of rest breaks
- introduction of meal breaks with lunches provided by the company

- work stopped earlier each day and then reverted to the original time
- work on only five days instead of the standard six
- no rest breaks, no special meals, original working times and days

The output of the group kept rising until it reached a high point from which it did not alter. The notion that working conditions and production were related had to be abandoned. The group's output had continued to rise regardless of the working conditions. As the researchers could not find any scientific reason as to why output kept rising, they asked the group why they worked so well together.

Reasons for the increased production:

- The girls felt very special, because the company and their observer took a great interest in them.
- They were not supervised by their old factory supervisor, but by the observer, and so they did not feel as pressured.
- They were consulted on the changes made and participated in decisions as to any changes which were to be implemented.
- The six girls became good friends – they gave one another birthday presents, met socially after work and were allowed to talk freely together during work.

It became obvious that people would produce a greater output if they enjoyed their job and had friends at work, rather than just a piece rate system to motivate them through money. This was the start of the 'Human Relations Movement', which saw workers as people with social needs rather than as money-making machines.

The Bank Wiring Observation Room study

The Bank Wiring Observation Room study consisted of fourteen men organised into three subgroups, each of which had three wirers and one supervisor. Unlike the Relay Assembly Test Room, the supervisors were the department's usual supervisors, their main function being to maintain order and control. The observers noticed that there were two informal groups with their own leaders who had not been designated by management but had emerged from the original group of fourteen.

These informal groups had their own rules of behaviour or 'norms'. The men's output was far less than it could have been, because they were purposely restricting output. Group members gave incorrect reports to management on the amount of production so it appeared that output was steady. The weekly total was correct and tallied with the actual production, but daily variations were hidden from management. Group members were not earning as much as they could have done if they had worked harder.

The rules of behaviour in the informal groups were:

- not to do too much work. People who worked hard were 'ratebusters' and risked getting the amount of money paid for each unit of output reduced for the whole group.
- not to do too little work. This might also cause management to investigate the work being done. People who did too little work were 'chiselers'.
- not to tell the supervisor anything bad about other workers. Anyone who did was a 'squealer'.
- supervisors and inspectors were expected to act as one of the men and not as a superior. While they were present the men behaved conscientiously but when they were absent the men relaxed and joked.

If anyone disobeyed these rules, they would be made fun of or ignored, or there would be a physical fight.

Although the men could have earned more money if they worked harder, they were afraid that consistently high outputs would cause management to change the rate of pay. They were also afraid of being laid off if they produced more work, as less workers would be needed.

The Relay Assembly Test Room and the Bank Wiring Observation Room experiments had opposite results in that one group of workers produced greater output while the other restricted output. In spite of these findings, both experiments demonstrated the impact of informal groups and peer pressure (influence from friends or colleagues) as a motivating force.

Conclusions from the Hawthorne Studies

1 People are motivated by things other than money.

2 People need recognition and to have a sense of belonging at their workplace.

3 A person's attitude to work is strongly affected by the group to which they belong in the organisation.

4 The informal group has a powerful effect on motivating individual members, and this is not always in the interests of the organisation.

The experiments showed that people care more about what their fellow workers think of them than an incentive pay system imposed by management. People would rather earn less and be well thought of within their group. The 'human factor' became important in the management of workers.

Teamworking at Rolls-Royce

*John Spragg (right) and his team in the Connecting Rod Shop at
Rolls-Royce*

What does 'Rolls-Royce' conjure up in your mind? The best car in the world – craft-
manship, fine engineering and quality? Skilled men, having served a long apprenticeship, slaving lovingly at their craft for years on end? This was all perfectly
correct until 1991 when the people element changed. Due to a loss-making situation in the Vickers Group of £60 million, to which Rolls-Royce made a substantial
contribution, redundancies were made. In 1990 Rolls-Royce employed 4,600 at
their main factory in Crewe; by 1994 only 2,300 worked there.

In 1991, drastic changes were made to the organisation of work at Rolls-Royce
and teamwork was introduced. They had never dealt with mass production to the
same extent as other car manufacturers. Despite this, John Spragg, a team leader
says, 'People were compartmentalised, they left their brains at the gate and twid-
dled the same handle every day.' Peter Griffiths, their training adviser agrees;
'People were introspective and concerned only with their immediate area of work.'
There were some specialist departments and experimental areas involved in proto-
type or specialist work, whose members had the opportunity to use a greater variety
of skills and had a wider range of work, but those departments have now disappeared. Peter Griffiths explains: 'Manufacturers are now more involved in working
on prototypes. There's far more trust now than there ever was in the past. More
detailed information is given out to people and they are trusted not to tell the newspapers. The last person to find out about new products used to be the guy on the
production line. Now attitudes are changing towards sharing knowledge of jobs and
skills and that's due to the introduction of teams. People feel more comfortable and
less threatened; it has removed competition between individuals.'

Particular jobs used to be owned by a particular trade. Filling up the water bottle
for the windscreen washers was owned by the auto electricians and no one else
could do it. 'People often accuse the unions of fostering these demarcation situations,' says Peter Griffiths, 'but the unions are just representing the people who do

the job.' People used to hold on to the knowledge they had about how to do their job because it gave them power, status and a feeling of security, and meant that others had little opportunity to broaden their skills. (Demarcation means that particular tasks in a job may only be done by members of a particular union.)

John Spragg remembers the class system when he first started at Rolls-Royce fourteen years ago. People whom he considered talented in their private lives were nothing more than 'button pushers' at work. At home they did bell-ringing, scuba-diving and made furniture to craftsmanship standards. John himself tried giving his immediate boss, a setter (a skilled occupation), an idea for improvements to the work process. 'He threw it across the shop and shouted, "Who do you think you are?"' remembers John. Some time later, when a suggestion scheme was implemented, John earned thousands of pounds for his ideas. The suggestion scheme is no longer in existence as it would be too encouraging of secrecy to fit in with the new era of teamwork. Suggestions are now freely given and new ideas worked upon within the team. All the innovations made by the team are listed and displayed on a board in their zone, to recognise their achievements. The hundreds of pounds saved by the company from each change is noted at the side.

John Spragg's team finished the connecting rods which connect the piston to the crankshaft inside the engine. Their first achievement was to change the coolant in a multi-drilling machine. It had previously used oil for the cooling process, which the team could see was rather a waste. Now it uses only 5 per cent oil and the rest of the coolant is water, giving a 95 per cent saving on the cost of the oil. 'There's not a job we've not tackled and improved,' says John proudly.

There are 22 different jobs in the connecting rod section and all six members of the team can either do them or are learning to do them. The situation as to who has which skills in the team is displayed on the team's board, along with photographs of each team member, production targets, scrap levels and defects (mistakes). Their achievements of always reaching their targets, having decreasing scrap levels and almost zero defects are clear for any passer-by to see.

'We have solved problems and gone through all the jobs on the department to improve everything. Any machine can be run by anyone. Everyone knows all 22 jobs, as well as setting-up and inspecting,' comments John.

Targets are given in the morning. It's now everyone's business to hit the target. Targets are driven by sales. Manning levels are appropriate to different targets – sometimes overtime is needed.

As a result of massive redundancies over recent years, the workforce is generally younger than it was. When teamworking was first implemented, people were not used to having to think for themselves. 'They sat around moaning,' says John Spragg, 'but now they think, "What are WE going to do to put it right?" and they take responsibility for the problems themselves.' The workers were so used to feeling powerless and having people above them to blame, that it took them a while to adjust to the new thinking. Engineers used to be a class apart and could only be reached by going through the foreman. Now there is an engineer attached to the machine shop and when the team are stuck with a problem, they can call in the engineer immediately. 'There are no doors shut to us now,' says John.

There used to be a culture among the workers of, 'We've done our bit now – it's over to you.' There were long lines of communication and decision making was a long process. A minor engineering modification needed hierarchical [managers/supervisors] and cross-functional [other departments/areas] permission. Now changes can be made within hours and authorised at the point of the problem.

Production targets are arrived at through discussion. Rolls-Royce as a company is more focused on market needs. 'We're better at changing our plans in a short time scale,' says Peter Griffiths.

To help the teams understand the business side of their daily work, team leaders are briefed periodically by the manufacturing director. He gives information on new developments and the situation the company is in. He answers any questions the team leaders wish to ask. 'People then feel more secure,' says John Spragg. 'We know whether we can go out and buy a new washing machine.'

'Everything used to be very functional,' continues Peter. 'There are now cross-functional teams established to look at a number of issues. People who have an interest in an issue are brought together.' Peter leads a team looking at the personnel function and procedures. His team consists of a security guard, a nurse, a trainer, a secretary and a quality assurance technician. At present they are looking at how shop floor accidents are handled and how everyone concerned works together on the process.

'The whole idea of teamworking is to help one another,' John Spragg points out. People on the shop floor are training the staff in order to break down the barriers. The staff in the offices will know about what actually goes into making the car.

Peter Griffiths concludes: 'There isn't any monetary reward. The greatest motivation is to see the company succeed and continue and survive. We all need to be able to pay the rent or mortgage.'

QUESTIONS

1 How has the organisation of work changed at Rolls-Royce over the past few years?

2 What benefits are Rolls-Royce gaining from the new organisation?

3 What benefits to employees are there from teamworking?

Attitudes and work organisation

One of the factors which may shape people's attitudes towards their work is the way the work is organised. Some people enjoy being consulted and want to help to solve problems at work. If the work is organised so that they have some power over what happens at work (otherwise known as empowerment), then those people will gain greater job satisfaction.

If the employer knows that certain jobs are repetitive and tedious, he or she may feel that the workers cannot be motivated through promises of job satisfaction and promotion. The employer may be obliged to offer a 'piece rate' system, and pay employees according to their output. This may have the effect that the workers themselves then become preoccupied with exactly how much they earn and ways of taking home more pay. The nature of the work shapes the workers' attitudes towards it.

ROLE-PLAYING ACTIVITY

Machine worker and participative worker

Objectives

1 To demonstrate the effect of organising the workforce in different ways on individual attitudes and productivity.

2 For each group to build a structure with handmade paper straws and sellotape which is not only strong, but also pleasing to the eye.

Materials: Scrap paper – either A4 or A5 size
Sellotape

Instructions

1 Divide into groups of six to eight people (groups must be of equal size; those left over should act as observers).

2 Half the groups will role play 'machine worker' and be organised along specialisation and division of labour lines. They will elect two people to act as managers who will do the actual building of the structure and organise the workforce. The workforce will only manufacture the straws by rolling and sellotaping the paper. They will not be involved in decision-making about the structure.

3 The other half will role play 'participative worker' and the whole group will work together as equals to produce the structure of paper straws.

4 Fifteen minutes are allowed for the manufacturing of straws and the building of the structure. The observers will make notes on the behaviours exhibited during the process.

5 Structures are to be displayed and a vote taken as to which one is the strongest and most beautiful. Observers will vote as well as group members.

6 Observers report on the reactions of the workers and management to different working styles.

7 Individual team members give their opinions as to their preferred work organisation method and the effect on production and attitude to work.

8 The facilitator sums up as to which method of organising the workforce proved to be most effective and what problems and advantages appear to be involved in each method.

Nigel

Nigel was a skilled aircraft fitter in a factory for over 16 years. In October 1992, he was made redundant.

'I was a skilled man. They'd had several lots of redundancies during the time I worked there, reducing the labour force from 2,000 to 600. I had always been worried about being made redundant, but I never thought it would happen to me. When they announced they were getting rid of another 190, I was blasé about it. I thought, "It's no good worrying, it will either happen or it won't." You get shell-shocked and fed up of worrying because they were a very threatening management – always saying they would shut the factory.

Nigel – former aircraft fitter, now unemployed

'On the day they announced the redundancies, my manager called me into the office at 10.30 in the morning and said he'd done a skills assessment on me. Foremen and junior management had been receiving training on doing skills assessments. He said, 'You're all right, you're not perfect, and we're making you redundant.' I was surprised. He asked if I understood, I said "Yes" and he said, "You can go now".

'I went out and started packing my tools away. I had been doing a difficult job and they gave it to a young man who had just finished his apprenticeship. He asked me to show him what to do, and I did, but very quickly. I had nothing against him, but it wasn't my job to teach him and I knew he would have trouble coping with it.

'I packed my tools and said goodbye to a few people. If I wanted any help or information on how to sign on or what to do next, there was nobody there to answer any questions. I put my tools in the car and went home. When I got home, it really hit me. It was a quiet weekday afternoon, there was nothing happening and I didn't know what to do. I felt at a loss.

'I went back to work the next day to collect the rest of my things. I didn't know how much redundancy money I would get or when I would have it. There weren't many people about; it was as if senior management were hiding.

'The firm had arranged to have career consultants in to give us advice. It did help to fill the time a bit – a couple of hours twice a week. It helped to keep me occupied. I felt I couldn't just do nothing. I tried to enrol on a university course, but as it was the end of October, it was just too late. I had no counselling about what course to go on so I was in the dark.

'I started getting nervous illnesses. I felt that I had nothing useful to contribute to the world. I wasn't wanted any more and felt rejected. I felt that I'd got valuable skills and they weren't wanted.

'The police stopped me one evening as I was driving along, and they asked me what my job was. I was too embarrassed to say that I was unemployed, so I just said that I did my old job.

'Jobs on offer were pathetic. Firms said that they wanted skilled fitters but they were actually labouring jobs. The pay was pitiful. If I'd been married with children, I would have been under greater pressure to take a job. The dole cheques only pay the mortgage, they don't cover food. I have to use my savings for that.

'After some months pass by, you gradually find things to occupy your time. It's not so bad then. One of the leaflets from the Job Centre said not to throw yourself into DIY activities because looking for a job is a full-time activity. But looking in the paper and going to the Job Centre doesn't take all week. I do feel lonely at home and go out in the evenings for companionship. At work there was always a lot of good humour and cheerfulness.

'Good jobs need high level qualifications. The only job interview I've had was through an employment agency who got in touch with me. When I went for the job it wasn't skilled. I realised that the Job Centre wasn't going to find me a job, so I decided to get myself better qualified. I have been accepted on a university course. The future is still uncertain. I'm hoping that I'll have the ability to do the course and that we have an economic upturn by the time the course is finished, so that I can find employment.'

Attitudes and the hierarchy of needs

In the above case, Nigel was made redundant from a job he did for over 16 years. When people go to the same place of work every day for a period of time, it can become like a second home to them, a place where they are expected, welcomed and needed. They have friends and colleagues there, and they belong to a group or department. They have an identity and status in the organisation. They have a valued skill which is recognised as being essential to the organisation. These things help to give people confidence and self-esteem. Very importantly, a job provides money to allow a person to achieve a given standard of living. People are faced with the prospect of poverty when they lose a job.

Redundancy is like a bereavement in that there is a sense of loss and a period of grief. A person's whole way of life is changed. The familiar buildings in which they spent their days are now closed to them. Contact with previous colleagues is cut off and they are faced with long, silent days with nothing to do. Work meets many different needs and is an important way of life in our society.

Work is also often interesting and challenging, and allows people to do things they might not otherwise get the chance to do. Pilots probably could not afford to buy their own jets to fly; lawyers wouldn't have so many opportunities to construct and argue a case; social workers would not naturally come into contact with people they would like to help. Work gives people the opportunity to have a go at something they really want to do.

Therefore, work often meets people's needs. People need money, the security of knowing they can pay next week's rent, other people to talk to, and to feel worth while and needed in society. Work can meet these needs in different ways. Why would someone:

- eat a meal?
- padlock their bicycle to some railings?
- sit with others at lunchtime?
- do a really good job on a special project their boss had assigned to them?

The answer could be the same for every question – *because they needed to.* Yet different needs surface in each circumstance – basic physiological needs to relieve hunger or thirst, the need to feel safe and secure, social needs for companionship, or the need for praise and recognition to make them feel good about themselves.

We cannot progress from one need to another until the first need is partially met. For example, those who are ill, hungry or tired have difficulty concentrating on other things. A person feeling unwell would probably prefer to go to bed than do anything else, and someone feeling hungry would rather tuck into a hot meal than answer telephone calls at work or serve hamburgers to others. This idea, that we cannot meet higher needs before basic needs are satisfied, was first put forward by **Abraham Maslow**.

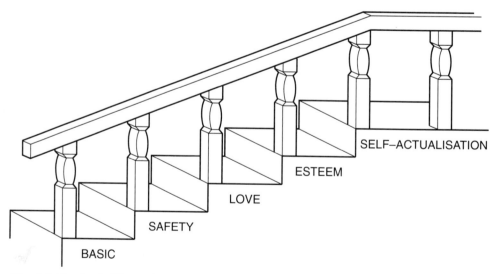

Fig. 1.3 Maslow's Hierarchy of Needs

Maslow's Hierarchy of Needs

Abraham Maslow wrote an article entitled 'A Theory of Human Motivation' in a magazine called *Psychological Review* in 1935. He put forward the idea that all human needs could be grouped into five categories. These are arranged in a hierarchy of importance so that the lower level needs must be partly satisfied before higher level needs become active.

We must satisfy each need to a certain extent before we can move onto the next. A lonely person will perhaps only feel the need for social contact when he or she has had sufficient sleep and something to eat. Great hunger or tiredness (basic needs) may prevent a person from thinking about a need for love.

Only those needs which have not been met will motivate a person. You will not be motivated to try to get to sleep when you have just slept all night long. You are not motivated to defend yourself if you are sure that you are free from attack.

Although needs are a personal matter and are with us all day, all of our lives, an employer can help employees to meet their needs so that they can concentrate on their work and derive satisfaction from it.

Needs and the workplace

Examples of needs and how employers can help their employees to meet them:

Need	Example	Meeting the need at work
Basic/ physiological	Air to breathe, a comfortable temperature, food and drink, sufficient sleep, shelter, clothing.	Heating/air conditioning systems, ventilation, canteen, drinks machines, money.
Safety and security	Relief from pain and illness. Freedom from accidents and other threats to physical and mental well-being.	Medical Centre, first aid facilities, Health & Safety at Work officer, safety equipment, e.g. guards on machinery or bulletproof glass in places such as banks. Pension schemes.
Love/ social	Companionship and friendship. A sense of belonging	Organising the work in groups. Rest rooms/staff rooms for employees to meet at break times. Social events, sporting events. Newsletters.

Need	Example	Meeting the need at work
Esteem	Self-respect and self-esteem.	Praise, recognition for good work, appreciation, awards, fringe benefits, above-average pay.
Self-actualisation	Doing what we are suited for. Being everything we are capable of being.	Letting people use their talents and abilities. Allowing people to choose what they like to do in their job.

People who are cold in their workplace because there is no heating on in winter will have difficulty concentrating on higher needs. Therefore, it is up the employer to meet some of the basic needs. Other needs, such as the basic need for sleep, are not the responsibility of the employer.

Meeting the lower order needs: physiological

Meeting the lower order needs: safety and security

As the needs are met, the higher order needs become more individual and therefore slightly more difficult to meet. Within a given band of temperatures, people are comfortable to work and will have their basic need for reasonable heating met. But when an employer is attempting to meet esteem needs and increase people's self-esteem, he or she may inadvertently lower the self-esteem of others. Giving managers luxury cars or their own car parking space may have a good effect on the managers concerned, but the other workers will feel that they are of a lower value to the organisation than the managers. Many firms are now moving towards 'single status', and allowing everyone to use the same car park, canteen, pension scheme and uniform. This helps to give the employees the feeling that everyone is working together for the organisation and not that the organisation is there purely for the benefit of management.

Self-actualisation needs are also difficult for employers to meet. If the accountant in the organisation can play the piano, it is not the responsibility of the employer to provide the accountant with a piano upon which to practice, even though it would contribute towards self-actualisation. Many people do not achieve all that they are capable of; it is sufficient if the organisation is providing them with a job they enjoy doing. This helps them to achieve doing something they are suited for.

Money is relevant to every category of needs:

BASIC Wages and salaries give people the ability to provide themselves with food, clothing and shelter.

SAFETY People need money to provide themselves with door locks, burglar alarms, garden fences, etc.

LOVE Pubs, discos, concerts, parties all cost money. The higher the salary the more socialising can be done.

ESTEEM People on above-average salaries feel valued by their organisation.

SELF-ACTUALISATION A good salary can provide people with the ability to pursue their hobbies and interests.

Higher order needs differ from lower order needs because they cannot be met fully. We may feel full to bursting after a meal and that we couldn't eat another thing. But when someone gives us praise and says what a good job we've done, we want more praise. We cannot get enough of it.

The order in which the needs are fulfilled is not rigid. Most people may meet their needs in the order according to the hierarchy of needs. Others may omit certain needs and go straight on to higher order needs The artist may be concentrating on painting in his or her studio and forget that he or she has not eaten all day or that there is no heating on. The artist has gone straight to self-actualisation and missed out all the other needs. For some people, self-esteem is more important than love or social needs. A person may be ambitious and prefer to work late and at weekends rather than spend time socialising or with his or her family. Others may not go beyond meeting their basic needs. Someone unemployed for a long period may value the money gained from a tedious job so much that he or she is unconcerned with self-actualisation and self-esteem.

Individual attitudes and the hierarchy of needs

Every person is different, with slightly different needs. Some people need nine hours' sleep each night while others only need six hours. Some people enjoy working alone on a creative project and get totally immersed in it, while others go to work purely for the companionship it provides of working within a team.

The nature of an individual's needs will shape his or her attitude to work. People go to work to meet their basic needs of providing themselves with food and clothing in order to live but some people may have alternative incomes and go out to work to keep themselves occupied. Money affects every need and therefore matters to everyone. Those on low incomes who are short of money may feel that money is more important than anything else. They will be interested in any scheme their employer has which will allow them to earn more money.

Those people who feel comfortable on their salary will count needs other than money as the most important, although such needs as having greater responsibility at work or more promotion will often involve salary increases.

People will have a more positive attitude to those jobs which help them meet their needs. They will be more committed and loyal to the organisation, derive greater job satisfaction and have an enhanced self-image than if their job did not meet their needs.

TASK

What are you doing to meet your needs?

Answer the following questions individually, then discuss your answers within a group.

1 Make a list of the things you have done today to meet your needs.

2 Do you meet different needs on different days of the week? (For example, weekdays and weekends.)

3 Why are you reading this book? Does it meet a need?

4 Why are you attending college/studying?

5 What are your goals for your future? Will they meet your self-actualisation needs?

6 How have your self-actualisation needs changed over the past five years?

Employee benefits at Hallmark Cards

Hallmark was started by Nebraska teenager Joyce Hall when he started selling postcards in 1910. Hallmark now has sales of over $2.7 billion per annum and is the leader of the greeting card industry.

Hallmark exports to over 100 different countries, makes cards in 20 different languages and employs over 30,000 people worldwide.

Hallmark have always been very forward-looking. They were the first company to adopt self-serve greeting card fixtures instead of keeping cards in drawers, as was done previously. They started the card shop concept, computerised re-ordering and wide-scale advertising in the card industry.

Mark Rivers – human resources manager, Liberty distribution centre, Hallmark Cards, USA

Liberty Distribution Centre is a 44 acre building designed to warehouse and ship more than one million wholesale packages to Hallmark customers daily. There are 1,200 people employed on three shifts at Liberty, Missouri. On average, therefore, there are only 400 people in a 44 acre building at any one time. It is largely automated, with conveyor belts being pre-programmed to tip off cardboard cartons at the appropriate spot and trucks running along tram lines seemingly by themselves.

Outside, hills have been carefully landscaped to hide the vast windowless building from passers-by. The company prides itself on its many community care programmes and comprehensive employee benefits, and has a high employee-retention rate.

The human resource manager, Mark Rivers, explains, 'Joyce Hall said, "We want our folks to grow with us, to succeed with us and have part ownership of our business". The caretakers of the business have continued with that spirit. Our most valuable asset are our people, they should reap the benefits.'

Hallmark put great emphasis on quality. The standard of quality they have achieved in fulfilling orders is so high the retailers no longer check their orders. Hallmark staff are more accurate at packing the orders than the retailers are at checking them when they receive them. 'Our quality is so good that customers trust us,' says Mark. Customer orders are filled within two days of receiving the order at Liberty. Accuracy is 99.2 per cent.

'Our benefits are very good,' says Mark. 'We're not *the* top, but in about the top 20 per cent of all American companies. We want to be attractive to folks, for folks to have the best, but we don't want to give away the farm,' says Mark.

'We do surveys on a yearly basis to find out what's happening in the business community as far as pay and benefits go,' says Shelia Jenkins, the human resources representative. 'We say that we want to be near the top.'

Hallmark are near the top of the league with salaries as well as employee benefits. Hallmark estimate that they spend over $15,000 on average, in addition to salaries, on each employee in career rewards benefits. Some of these benefits are as follows:

- Employee Profit Sharing and Ownership Plan.
- Thrift savings plan – Hallmark adds 20 per cent to the amount contributed by the employee. Employees can save 2, 3, 4 or 5 per cent of their salary and choose between a range of options as to how the money is invested.
- Health care expenses. Hallmark pay approximately 80 per cent of hospital and dental expenses for the employee and their family, up to a given amount.
- The Vision Care Plan allows employees and their dependants to have an eye test, one set of lenses and new frames every 12 months, or an allowance towards contact lenses.
- Disability benefits for those who cannot work because of illness or accident, for up to six months.
- Retirement benefits. A regular monthly sum is paid by Hallmark to previous employees, the amount depending upon length of service. They also contribute to medical, dental and life insurance expenses for past employees with 10 years of service or more.
- Survivors' benefits. Life insurance is paid to the spouse of employees who die whilst in the employ of the company. Dependents are also insured by the company.
- Holidays. Employees get 80 hours of holiday time after their first year with the company. This increases to six weeks' holiday after 30 years of service.
- Discounts on Hallmark products. In the card shop, Hallmark products are half price and there is a 20 per cent discount on all allied products.
- Subsidised meals in the cafeteria. At Liberty Distribution Centre, drinks are free from the drinks machine.
- Adoption assistance. Financial assistance is given to those employees who wish to adopt a child, up to $5,000.
- Educational loans. Loans are available to those employees who have sons or daughters at college.
- Educational assistance. Those employees who wish to take part-time courses will have their fees paid to a maximum of $2,500 by Hallmark.

Certain benefits, such as the discount on Hallmark products, are available immediately to new employees, but most come into effect after 91 days' service and there are a few increases in benefits according to years served.

'The intention is to retain people, make them feel good about where they work, get them to contribute and participate,' says Mark. 'We guarantee employment.

We've never had to practice our layoff policy, but we do have one. If our backs were up against the wall, we'd have to use it,' says Mark. In the past, when business has not been going well, Hallmark have put people on different assignments within the company or loaned them out to the community to work, with no change in pay.

Does fame and fortune equal self-actualisation?

For 2 Unlimited, purveyors of Euro techno-pop, it's business as usual; flights to exotic destinations, endless interviews and their 'nth' appearance on Top of the Pops.

Ray S Lijngaard, the Euro pop star, is stomping around the stage at Top Of The Pops in pursuit of an invisible punch bag. Now and then he bashes uninterestedly at a space age piano. Ray is wearing a chainmail trouser suit and he's not happy about it.

'Feel this, man,' he suggests, offering the nape of his chainmail jacket for inspection. 'Great for TV, but it's too hot, man, too hot for playing live.'

2 Unlimited are not noted, of course, for their reputation as Mega City van-hogs. They have never spent 28 nights locked in a Transit with the intention of scrawling their name in black marker pen on the walls of every toilet in Great Britain. They are much too smart for that. Instead they zoom around the world on press tours conducting automatic-pilot interviews for the 'popular' press.

They're as perfect at their job as the Pet Shop Boys are at theirs: ambassadors of techno-trash and masters of Woolworth culture at the same time. Your eight-year-old sister probably loves them, but the point is, *you should too.*

'When we go on TV I get them to show me how to play the keyboard parts, y'know, because it's better than just going blah blah blah ...' (Ray mimes bashing uninterestedly at the piano).

They have no idea how their records sound the way they do. The point is, however, that they take a form casually derided for years (unstoppable hit machine) and instil it with a wit and direction that should be applauded from a great height.

Get ready for this: 2 Unlimited have appeared on Top Of The Pops eleven times. They have had Number One hits around the globe ('No Limits' was Number One in nine countries and won gold discs in territories as diverse as Australia, Latin America and the Far East). It must all be a far cry from Ray's former life as a chef.

'I was a cook at Amsterdam Airport. It was Business Class, though, so I used to see all these successful people coming in, and all these planes taking off everywhere. That kept me going.

'The thing with fame is you always expect more and more from it, to prove yourself. People are never happy man, they're spoilt.'

2 Unlimited's schedule permits us half an hour in their company. After that they are due for another TOTP rehearsal, a final run-through and a flight leaving tomorrow morning, headed for India. They will be there for six hours before flying on to

Hong Kong. They are massively successful in both places. Is their lifestyle all it's cracked up to be?

Anita: 'It's not how you imagine it as a child. When you're a child you think that when you're famous you're rich, you're beautiful, you're wanted, that you've got loads of friends … you think you're always happy and can do whatever you like, but it's not true. We're working harder than ever before.'

Anita used to work in a police station. Is this job better than that? She pauses.

'Um … yeah. I like my job more, but sometimes I just want to get out.'

It's time for another rehearsal. She sighs.

'I still can't get any dinner.'

2 Unlimited are a travelling press circus. Their input on their own records is minimal (Ray is ever-willing to announce that he considers himself 'a rapper', presumably on loan to the band).

They leave the TOTP studios for a meal seconds after completing their fourth rehearsal of the day. There is only time for a brief goodbye. Michel's (their manager) portable phone bursts back into life. Then the three of them disappear.

Adapted from: 'Maastricht Bleepy' by Paul Moody.

Source: New Musical Express, 18 September 1993, page 23. Reprinted by kind permission of Paul Moody.

QUESTIONS

1 How are the needs of employees at Hallmark Cards met?

2 Which needs are unfulfilled for 2 Unlimited's Ray and Anita?

3 Which job (working for Hallmark or being a member of 2 Unlimited) is best for meeting people's needs?

4 Why does Ray say that famous people are spoilt?

5 Why does Anita feel like getting out of the group sometimes?

6 Could Hallmark improve the way in which it meets its employees' needs?

Factors affecting individual work attitudes

Organisational culture

The American woman staying in an English home was shocked that dinner napkins were not used at every meal. The British businessman was dismayed that in meetings with French company managers they did not say what they thought during the meetings but had many breaks where they discussed private deals and liaisons. The Japanese businessman was unhappy to discover that in a British organisation, the managers saw themselves as individuals competing with one another rather than as part of a team who all work together. Seven-year-old Tom from Lancashire was surprised to find that when he went to tea with his friend George, who lived across the road, the television was switched off during meals. Tom assumed that everyone had the television on all the time at home, as they did at his house.

Norms

The way things are done in our home, town or country is our culture. It is a set of assumptions and it governs the way people see, think and feel about things. The way we normally do things are our 'norms'. Things done differently are against the norm and appear to us as strange or unacceptable behaviour.

A British student, staying with a French family on an exchange visit, was unpleasantly surprised to find the fresh strawberries she had been looking forward to for dessert, plonked onto her dinner plate which was covered in sauce from the chicken they had had for the previous course.

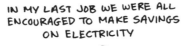

IN MY LAST JOB WE WERE ALL
ENCOURAGED TO MAKE SAVINGS
ON ELECTRICITY

PERSONNEL

She had assumed that she would be getting a clean plate for dessert. The french family mopped up their sauce with bread, assuming that they would use the same plate for dessert.

TASK

In groups, discuss the following questions:

1 Have you been abroad on holiday? If so, did you notice that anything was done differently than it is in Britain?

2 Have you visited different parts of Britain where you noticed that small things were done differently to the way they are in your home town?

3 Have you visited friends or relatives who do things differently to your family when they are at home?

4 In what ways might it be difficult for people from different cultures to live and work together?

Organisational culture is a set of shared values and beliefs that organisation members have about how things should be done in their organisation. The type of culture an organisation has can be distinguished by studying the traditions, history, status symbols, communication methods, behaviour of members and the environment in which it operates.

Types of organisational culture

Power

The leader is the source of power. The leader controls everything that happens in the organisation. Information is fed to the leader from all departments or functions of the organisation as workers wish to gain favour with the leader and influence the leader's decisions in their favour. The only person who knows everything that is happening in the organisation is the

leader. A leader may allow free access, which means that he or she is constantly bombarded by employees wanting to ask or tell things. Another leader may restrict contact to a senior team. Everyone else uses the grapevine as an information source to try and find out what is going on.

In-fighting, especially at the top, can be fierce. Decisions made on all kinds of things, from pay rises to who leads the new product launch, are the result of power struggles rather than reasons other cultures might forward, such as seniority or fairness.

Those holding power value their own success most. They often have personal charisma and charm. They have many sources of information and connections with useful people. They often work on intuition and take risks.

The successful leader will be well respected and considered to be unique and inspiring. Yet other cultures might see him or her as untrustworthy and as a 'wheeler dealer' type.

Status

Status is the position of one employee in relation to others. An individual's status is determined not only by his or her job title but by other qualities he or she brings to their group or  department. Determinants of status are job title, salary and the nature of the work. Other factors affecting status are education level, qualifications, age and sex. Those with power in the organisation have status symbols such as luxurious offices, cars, and their own parking space.

People working in status cultures will be constantly striving to attain status symbols, promotion and the prestige areas of work. The emphasis is on individualism, and not teamwork. Workers compete with one another for the best jobs and the most prized status symbols. Someone who has fallen from favour may arrive at work to find that his or her belongings have been moved out of his or her office to some lowly spot. He or she will be forced to resign or else live with the embarrassment and disgrace of losing status symbols.

The status culture has more employees without status symbols than it has with, so it can create a 'them and us' situation where the workers lower down in the organisation feel alienated.

Many UK organisations are moving away from the status culture by having open plan factories and offices, uniforms for all and shared canteens and car parks.

Task

The task culture often consists of people who like to solve problems in teams or groups. Each person has their own area of expertise and he or she shares this with the team for the benefit of the project on which they are working. People are respected for their technical expertise.

Individuals' attitudes are often more positive towards their own group than to the organisation as a whole. People's status in the organisation and their job title is of little importance compared to their knowledge, working relationships and their respect for the competence of the other team members.

Controlling the workforce is difficult in task cultures. Control is achieved by senior management allocating projects, people and resources. The actual control of projects is left to project or team leaders. Team members' attitudes could become negative in task cultures if there is a lack of growth in the organisation or in their project area. Resources may be cut or diverted to other areas where there is growth. Morale and job satisfaction will fall and the team will lose interest in their project.

Task cultures are suitable for organisations going through constant change as they are good at planning and problem solving. As most work in organisations is routine, task cultures are not usually appropriate.

Person-orientated

The person-orientated culture serves the individuals in the organisation. Procedures and roles are there to meet the needs of individuals and they are subject to change, according to the wishes of the individuals presently in the organisation. Very small professional businesses may have this type of culture. It is the most unusual organisational culture. Specialists in larger organisations, such as hospital consultants and

computer analysts, may have this type of culture between themselves. They may feel more loyalty to one another than they do to the larger organisation. They often support each other and form an elite friendship group in the organisation. Although they are difficult for senior management to control, the culture may easily change if members leave.

Role

The role culture is a bureaucracy. Rules, procedures and job titles are all of great importance. All the functions work according to the overall plan, so senior management merely have to co-ordinate departments to make sure they are meeting the plan. Individuals are selected to do certain tasks. These tasks should be completed exactly to a specification and no more or less. Anyone

doing more than the specified amount of work is considered a threat. Colleagues and superiors would be suspicious of their motives for doing extra work.

Power is determined by rules and procedures and the allocation of work. A role culture can only operate properly in a stable environment. There has to be an unchanging external environment or the firm must have a monopoly position in the product market. Banks and the civil service are examples of role cultures though these are now beginning to change.

Role cultures cannot cope with a changing environment – some organisations go through constant crises and product innovations, entering new markets with new customers – these would not suit the role culture.

Creative and innovative people would be frustrated by working in a role culture. Role cultures are the most common type of organisational culture. When firms grow, they may have an area that remains task or power culture dominated, but the rest of the organisation will usually change to being a role culture. Managing large numbers of employees does require job titles and specifications, defined areas of responsibility and procedures to follow.

Individual work attitudes and organisational culture

Generally, people will tend to have positive attitudes towards work if they are in an organisational culture which suits them. Communication methods, ways of working, and ways of promoting people will all seem quite natural to them. Those in the wrong culture will feel lost and alienated. A person who prefers the role culture will want to know what forms to fill in and what the normal procedure is for doings things. This will not be appropriate in the power culture. In the power culture, communication is done on an informal face-to-face or telephone basis. Deals and agreements are made quickly. Opportunities are reacted to immediately. The person who likes the certainty of the role culture would be totally confused by what he or she would consider to be 'underhand' dealings.

Similarly, the person who prefers a power culture would be frustrated and amazed at the insistence on following the correct rules for everything from getting new paperclips to the way people are spoken to on the telephone. A person finding him or herself in the wrong organisational culture may well develop negative attitudes towards work, because his or her efforts will be ignored or even punished. Responsibility and promotion will not be given because others see him or her as incompetent, odd or immoral.

Most organisations are a mixture of different cultures. It is quite possible to work for a role culture, but be in a section of a department where a task culture dominates, due to the need for planning or project work. People who have a preference for one type of culture may be happy in an organisation with a different culture predominating, as long as they are in a department with a culture which suits them.

QUIZ

Which type of organisational culture are you best suited to work in?

Make a note of your answers to the following questions:

1 When you're going out for the evening, do you prefer to:
   (a) Go out with a group and discuss what to do together?
   (b) Be with the in-crowd?
   (c) Go somewhere expensive and fashionable?
   (d) Go with one or two close friends?
   (e) Go on an organised trip out?

2 What sort of boss would you prefer to work for?
   (a) None, they're not needed when people are motivated to work together.
   (b) One who listens to you and gives you helpful information.
   (c) One who'll recognise your good work and promote you to a better paid job.

   (d) One who respects your knowledge and treats you more as a colleague than a subordinate.

   (e) Someone polite who does their job and lets you do yours.

3 Where should an individual's responsibilities lie at work?

   (a) To their team or group.

   (b) To themselves.

   (c) To the boss.

   (d) To colleagues.

   (e) To the organisation.

4 What do you think is the best form of communication at work?

   (a) Group discussion.

   (b) Meetings, telephone, faxes – anything to contact the right people.

   (c) Car telephone.

   (d) Face to face.

   (e) Memo or letter.

5 What sort of office would you like at work?

   (a) Open-plan, shared.

   (b) Next door to the boss.

   (c) The biggest and the best possible.

   (d) Something comfortable, near to colleagues.

   (e) The one that goes with the job.

6 What is your view of someone getting a job in your organisation because he or she is a friend of the boss?

   (a) It depends on whether he or she is any good at the job.

   (b) I just accept that that's the way things are.

   (c) Not OK if it was a job I was going to apply for.

   (d) OK if I get on well with him or her.

   (e) Scandalous and unacceptable.

7 A person who works hard at their job until late every night is:

   (a) A good worker.

   (b) A fool.

   (c) Looking for promotion.

   (d) In need of help and assistance.

   (e) Doing far more than is required.

8 New recruits to the organisation should be:

   (a) Good at working with others.

   (b) Useful to the organisation.

   (c) Made to start at the bottom.

   (d) Easy to get along with.

   (e) Selected as being competent to do a particular job.

Now give yourself a score:

Mostly (a)s?
You prefer to work in a task in a task culture. You like group work, solving problems together and planning for new ventures. You prefer to be appreciated for your knowledge and talents rather than long service or status in the organisation.

Mostly (b)s?
You like to work in a power culture. You enjoy the political life of using your influence, charm and contacts at work. The lack of rules and flexibility of the organisation suit your desire for change and constant improvement.

Mostly (c)s?
You prefer a status culture. You would like to have a big office, expensive car, your own secretary and expense account. You feel that they are worth working for and that organisations are class systems that employees can make their way up in.

Mostly (d)s?
You prefer to work in a person culture. You like to be valued for your skills and abilities and have true friends to work with. You want to be among a select group who help one another.

Mostly (e)s?
You like to work in a role culture. This is handy because there are a lot of them around. You prefer to know exactly what to do and what everyone else should be doing. You like a clear cut situation where creeping to the boss doesn't get you anywhere. You feel that if everyone obeys the rules and follows the procedures, there will be no problems and hassles.

Kaizen – the art of continual improvement

European Components Ltd manufactures components for the car industry and is located on two sites in the city of Belfast. The company's Japanese owner, the Takata Corporation, is the world leader in safety systems.

While the management of the company has been left largely to a local management team led by a local managing director, the Japanese influence was an important factor in the company deciding to use *kaizen* as the means of implementing necessary changes.

Kaizen is a philosophy originating in Japan and is considered to be fundamental to that country's competitive success in the world market. The word comes from two Japanese words: kai, meaning 'change', and zen, meaning 'good (for the better)'. So kaizen means 'continual improvement', and, as applied to companies, it means a system of taking small steps to improve the workplace.

The underlying principles are that the system should be driven by internal and external customers and involve everyone through systematic and open communication. Focus on the customer is important to kaizen. Everyone must understand customer requirements and deliver quality and service.

The system starts with the premise that people are an organisation's most important asset. This is put into practice through teamwork and active involvement with open and shared information. In kaizen, the process is as important as results: attention is paid to detail, and the process is seen as a learning opportunity. The techniques include:

- customer satisfaction
- total quality (zero defects)
- just in time
- cross-functional management
- policy deployment
- total productive maintenance
- Five-S (good housekeeping)
- Muda (eliminating waste)
- PDCA (plan-do-check-act) cycle
- visual management
- quality circles

One of the most significant techniques used is 'policy deployment'. The first step in the process was determining the company's goal, which was to be the leading seat-belt supplier in Europe.

A number of five-year targets were then set in order to attain this goal. They were to achieve a 30 per cent market share, zero defects in all activities, factory costs equivalent to 75 per cent of sales and improved internal/external communications.

Each department's responsibilities were then examined in the light of these five-year targets. For example, the personnel department's contribution to achieving the target of factory costs to be 75 per cent of sales included tying in elements of the training plan to save costs; flattening the organisational structure by taking out layers of management; and reducing monthly costs in canteens, absence levels, company sickness payments, department budgets, overtime, and the company magazine.

Detailed improvements are specified on monthly assessment forms for each item. For example, if a department is planning to reduce scrap, the problem is analysed and training needs to assist the improvement are identified. These are then built into the training plan.

Muda is the Japanese word for waste and is described as anything that does not add value. This is a difficult concept to grasp, as the Japanese do not tolerate overheads and indirect costs in the way Western companies do. Anything that does not directly contribute to a company's product does not add value. Indirect costs such as moving materials from stores or inside a department do not add value. Value is that part of the job which customers pay for.

The most important type of muda is over-production. Keeping a high inventory level – whether it be parts in production or hospital beds – means problems are hidden. Once the stock level drops, these problems are highlighted and the kaizen process ensures each of these obstacles or problems is clearly identified, analysed and solved, avoiding the 'I told you it wouldn't work' syndrome.

One of the most powerful techniques for solving problems is the PDCA cycle. This is an endless improvement cycle in which one has to:

PLAN – survey/understand/identify
DO – adequate actions
CHECK – verify effects/evaluate
ACT – feedback to upstream sources

Another fundamental component of kaizen activity at European Components is the 'Five S' or good housekeeping campaign. This was undertaken for two reasons: first, to ensure a safe, pleasant and efficient working environment, and secondly, to ensure a good first impression of the plant by visitors, particularly potential new customers, on the grounds that a company never gets a second chance to make a first impression. The five stages of this programme are:

SEIRI – separate out all that is unnecessary and eliminate it
SEITON – put necessary things in order for use when needed
SEISO – keep workplace and equipment clean
SEIKSETSU – make cleaning and checking routine
SHITSUKE – standardise and continue

The Five-S campaign does not mean that everything is thrown out which is not currently being used. Some equipment may be required infrequently – these items should be stored separately from everyday use items.

Kaizen can achieve significant results. It gives, when properly led by the chief executive, an important focus to an organisation's activity.

Kaizen is not a quick fix. It is hundreds and thousands of small changes – not big changes. Perhaps this is where we fall down – we expect too much too quickly and lose heart if we do not get it. Kaizen does not have to be expensive, but it does require involvement, commitment and openness. It starts with a system of policy deployment – taking the business goals, breaking these down into targets and then brainstorming how each department can reach the targets and ultimately help meet the goals.

By Vivienne Walker

Source: Personnel Management, pp. 36–8, August 1993. Produced by kind permission of Vivienne Walker.

QUESTIONS

1 What does 'kaizen' mean?

2 How has it been implemented at European Components?

3 To what extent is European Components a role and a task culture?

4 The case study states that European Components have 'flattened the organisational structure' by taking out layers of management. What type of people might this upset, depending upon their cultural preference?

5 'Muda' is the Japanese word for waste and it entails getting rid of anything in the organisation which does not add value to the product. Why might this concept be disliked by someone who prefers to work in a status culture?

6 How can you tell that European Components does not have a power culture as the dominant organisational culture?

7 What steps would you take to implement kaizen in your own home or bedroom?

The relationship within the organisation between functions and departments

Functional organisation is the most common way for departments to specialise in a firm. Functions such as accounts, servicing and manufacturing are organised into departments. Each department handles a separate area of the delivery of the product or service to the customer. An organisation chart (*see* Fig. 1.4.) shows what people do in the organisation, who they are responsible to and how many functions or departments there are in the firm.

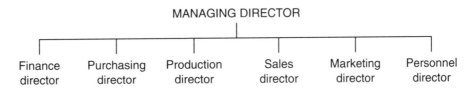

Fig. 1.4 Organisation chart

Functions and departments make efficient use of specialised resources. This type of organisation is easy to control and each manager needs only one specialist range of skills – they do not have to be experts in all parts of the organisation.

As organisations grow, the functional organisation becomes less popular.

Difficulties with the functional organisation

Multiple products

Many firms grow through diversification into different product areas or by acquiring companies which have different product lines to themselves. The chocolate factory may merge with a soft drinks company, as in the case of Cadbury Schweppes. This makes it difficult to keep production, sales and the other functions together for all the products. Many companies form a different organisational structure based on product as they grow.

Decision making

Also, as firms grow with the functional structure, communication and decision making are slower as department heads have to contact head office for instructions. The functional structure makes it difficult to see clearly how well departments perform. There is no profit or output for each department upon which to judge performance. It is difficult to determine which function is responsible for errors or successes. If a new product fails it is very difficult to know who is to blame.

Conflict between functions

Senior managers may have problems co-ordinating all the functions as the organisation grows. Members of different departments may feel isolated from other departments. People working in the sales department may identify solely with that department and come into conflict with other functions.

Different objectives

The sales department are rewarded for selling as many of the product as possible and they expect the production department to have the goods ready for delivery immediately. The production department do not want to have huge peaks in demand as this means they have very quiet times and then hectic periods – they prefer steady demand. It is a nuisance for them if the sales department keep making sudden demands for different sizes of orders with early delivery dates.

Similarly, the purchasing department wish to take advantage of special offers and bulk buys. The finance department does not appreciate vast outflows of money for purchasing more stocks of raw materials than is necessary.

Resource allocation

Departments can also easily come into conflict on the subject of resources. If one area has new offices or computers or more staff, the other departments will feel neglected and demotivated. They will feel that they do not matter to the organisation as much as the department which has been allocated the resources.

Employee attitudes

Employees can easily forget the overall goals of the organisation and become embroiled in inter-departmental conflicts. This is damaging to the organisation as a whole. Attitudes towards other functions and departments can very easily become negative if senior management are not constantly vigilant to ensure good communication in the organisation.

QUESTIONS

1 How can management improve attitudes between different functions in an organisation?

2 If you had your own small company, how would you organise the allocation of work?

3 Have you worked anywhere where there was conflict between departments?

Re-engineering

Management consultants are making millions of dollars out of re-engineering in America. It is the latest fad in a long line of new cures for business ills. But what is it?

Businesses produce a service or product for their customers. They all manage to do this, otherwise they would not stay in business. It is *how* this is done that re-engineering looks at. Some businesses may have grown in a haphazard way over many years. Other businesses may have planned their growth carefully and are now wondering whether they were going in the right direction. Many businesses are looking for improvements in how they do things, so that costs can be saved and profits increased. Management consultants implementing re-engineering plans (also called 'core process redesign') attempt to identify exactly what processes are taking place in the business to produce the product or service.

Questions such as 'What does the company want to achieve?' and 'What is it doing to achieve it?' need to be asked. The answers to those questions provide the starting point to the re-engineering process. It may be that they are not doing the things they need to do to achieve their objectives, or that they could be doing them more effectively.

Traditionally, if businesses wanted to improve their processes, they would ask heads of departments to review the performance of their section. The finance director or purchasing manager would write a report on what their department did and how it could be improved. Recommendations would normally be about specific tasks and would often show small improvements.

Re-engineering looks at the *whole business:*

- The strategy it uses to achieve its objectives.
- The processes going on in the business to make the product or service.
- The technology used in the business, especially the information systems.
- The people who work in the business.

Re-engineering is concerned with major improvements and not with fine details. The production manager of an area which produced small parts for the rest of the factory, reporting on small improvements to be made in their department in the past, would never recommend that the whole department be closed and the work be subcontracted out. Re-engineering takes a look at the entire organisation. The idea of process and work study can be traced back to F W Taylor. Re-engineering can be thought of as being similarly authoritarian. The workers are informed of changes to be made after the decisions have been taken.

In the UK, re-engineering has only been taken up by the financial services sector. The National and Provincial Building Society's 're-design programme' was started in 1990. They plan to reduce eight levels of management to three levels and more than 20 grades of jobs to four grades. The changes are going ahead very slowly because managers may feel threatened by the loss of power. The board of directors is now the 'direction management team' and directors are no longer responsible for functions such as finance and marketing; they are directors of 'customer engagement' and 'customer requirements'. There is a dual system of competency assessment and performance-related pay. The building society hopes to reduce the average time it takes to process a mortgage from 27 days to as little as one day.

Re-engineering is not a 'quick fix': it does take years to implement. In America, it is still a growing trend. By the time it takes off in the UK, the Americans will probably have moved on to something else.

Shocking to the core

Re-engineering is all to do with radically reviewing how a business works in order to achieve dramatic improvement. Michael Hammer, the business consultant who coined the term 're-engineering', says those who seriously adopt re-engineering techniques find that they can do the same work with 40–80 per cent fewer employees. One survey respondent admitted the greatest barrier to business process re-engineering (BPR) in his company was 'getting the turkeys to vote for Christmas'.

'Don't underestimate BPR,' says Rohit Talwar, head of business re-engineering at BMS Bossard and chairman of the Strategic Planning Society's BPR special interest group. 'There are obscene levels of hype and false expectations being generated. As a result, some firms are being seduced into expensive and disastrous initiatives. Radical, step-change improvements in service, efficiency and quality can be achieved – but you have to be prepared for a great deal of pain to get them. Why? Because re-engineering means fundamentally changing the "way we do things" and that means changing the culture.'

Re-engineering may not be rocket science but it does require a clear sense of strategic direction and priorities, genuine chief executive and top management commitment and a massive investment in training. Turkeys often drag their feet, but without their vote any BPR effort is doomed. The scale of a purist's re-engineering effort is so vast that many organisations opt for a watered-down version. Re-engineering should not then be blamed if they are disappointed with the results, argues Chris Skinner of Highams Systems, who draws a distinction between BPR (directed at individual processes in an *ad hoc* fashion) and business re-engineering (BR, a total big-bang business rethink).

'Many firms jump in at the pragmatic level of BPR and change some of their simple, low level processes without doing anything fundamental to the business. It's like improving the design of your car's hub cap or door. They are components of the car but not the whole car. Business re-engineering means rethinking the entire business. It means starting with a vision of a whole car.'

Sun Life's new policy

Sun Life Assurance Society started re-engineering three years ago. Now the Bristol-based organisation exudes energy, enthusiasm and excitement about its re-engineering experience.

Managing director, John Reeve, is the source of Sun Life's missionary zeal. At the end of the 1980s, recognising that tough times (more competitors, more regulation, more new products, more recession) were ahead, he ordered a radical business review. The findings were only partially encouraging.

'Industry surveys showed quality of service to be increasingly important to brokers, Our reputation was better than most, but our service levels were still only perceived to be fairly average. We were satisfying but certainly not delighting our customers,' says Michael Baker, project manager of customer service review.

Sun Life plunged into turbulent re-engineering waters in its quest for the delighted customer. In came consultants McKinsey and Hay to plumb the corporate soul. 'Where are we going?' 'Where is the industry going?' Next, they reviewed the core processes. The findings were disturbing. Issuing a new life assurance policy was a typical core process involving administrative steps carried out in different departments. No one, it seemed, was in charge of a process from beginning to end; each step was hampered by bottlenecks, ambiguity, delays and errors. A process which should have taken 15 days limped along for 46 days. Once a department had done its bit, the paperwork fell into 'black holes' of inactivity.

In June 1991, Sun Life began re-engineering its core processes in a two-year, three-wave programme. All processes were put through a six-stage wringer of documentation; analysis; brainstorming ideas; evaluating solutions; detailed redesign; and implementation. The objective was to be a pace-setter – to reshape the organisation into a more efficient and effective one but, vitally, one which has a predominant customer focus. Sun Life's metamorphosis from an organisation based on functional specialists to one based on multi-skilled employees required massive restructuring.

For Sun Life's brave new world, redesigned, streamlined processes were organised around multi-skilled teams to ensure that responsibility for a complete, end-to-end process was handled in one place. Massive investment in training and communication programmes would broaden and enhance employee roles, responsibilities, skills and competencies. Sun Life's historic hierarchical seven-layer management structure was transformed. A pilot experiment in the 1,200-strong customer service department slashed the multiple level hierarchy to customer service managers, team leaders and teams supported by two other roles: a dedicated trainer and a technical expert. Team members, formerly skilled in about one-quarter of a process, familiarised themselves with the other 75 per cent. New reward structures based on pay for competencies and customer-related performance measures were introduced.

Baker is confident of a two or three year payback period. Already Sun Life boasts 40–90 per cent improvements in process turnaround times; 10 per cent reduction in the unit costs of some processes; and 50–80 per cent quality improvements (work performed right first time). Sun Life confidently predicts a significant increase in job satisfaction among employees and greater customer satisfaction leading to increased business.

Baker reports that the 'black holes' in one process, the Life New Business, have been filled – the process gallops along in 21 days rather than 46. Faults in the company's communication lines are being filled. Employees had a first annual general meeting this year. Peter Sissons has chaired an 'open house' no-holds-barred Question Time, and videos, focus groups, attitude surveys and training seminars keep momentum high.

'We have an open style of management that was inconceivable three years ago,' says Baker.

Sun Life Assurance's road to re-engineering enlightenment sounds untroubled. It wasn't. Nor is the journey yet complete. 'Anyone who underestimates the size or difficulty of the task of making the organisation transformation will certainly fail,' says Owen. No pain, no gain.

Adapted from 'Shocking to the Core' by Judith Oliver.

Source: Management Today, August 1993

QUESTIONS

1 Why can re-engineering be considered to be authoritarian?

2 Why do managers feel threatened by changes at the National and Provincial Building Society?

3 What improvements have Sun Life Assurance made to their business?

4 What changes did Sun Life make which would affect their office workers?

5 What effect on workers' attitudes might 're-engineering' changes have in any organisation?

6 How might re-engineering or other major re-organisations of firms, affect the relationship between functions or departments in an organisation?

7 Is organisational culture affected by major reorganisations of the way companies do things?

Performance Criterion 2
Factors affecting motivation at work

The personal needs, drives and aspirations which determine behaviour

Human behaviour is based on needs, drives and aspirations. Behaviour is caused by, and causes, needs, drives and aspirations. People do things because they need to, they feel driven towards them or they aspire to have them. Behaviour in turn causes needs, drives and aspirations. When a person has been running to catch the bus, he or she needs rest. When someone has been blowing up a balloon, he or she may feel the need for air or water.

The dictionary defines these words as:

NEED – necessity
DRIVE – urge, push in a direction
ASPIRATION – desire

They are all concerned with motivation. People are motivated to do things because they are seeking a necessity they require – food or water, or they want something sufficiently for it to become a necessity to them – responsibility at work, job satisfaction, the knowledge that they will have a good pension when they retire.

People who need job satisfaction will leave their job if they feel that the job is not worth while. They may stay on temporarily until a job comes up that appears to be more satisfying, but they will not be motivated to do their present job for the satisfaction it gives them.

Needs, aspirations and drives do not have to be met at work. People can satisfy their needs, drives and aspirations in different ways. An individual's needs for companionship and status may be, for example, met by joining a local club, political party, or an amateur dramatic society. This will provide social contact and someone to talk to as well as giving status if the person is prepared to work hard to become one of the 'leading lights' of the organisation. Those who aspire to leadership positions and cannot attain them at work often turn to social or union activities in which they can be the leader, or one of the leaders.

Theories of motivation

Physiological

Physiological or content theories of motivation are explanations of motivation that emphasise internal characteristics of people. They look at what is happening inside people that makes them want to do things.

These theories include:

- Maslow's Hierarchy of Needs (see page 29)
- Alderfer's ERG Theory
- McClelland's Needs Theory

Social

Social or process theories of motivation are explanations of motivation that emphasise how individuals are motivated by forces outside themselves. They look at the steps that occur when an individual is motivated.

These theories include:

- Vroom's Expectancy Theory
- Equity Theory

Alderfer's ERG Theory

Psychologist Clayton Alderfer's ERG Theory is very similar to Maslow's theory on the Hierarchy of Needs. Both theories see needs as the motivating force behind behaviour. People are motivated to do things by different needs. Alderfer identified three different needs, the first letters of which make 'ERG':

1 **Existence needs** – those which give us physical well-being
2 **Relatedness needs** – the need for social relationships
3 **Growth needs** – the need for personal growth and development

The ERG needs are fewer than Maslow's Hierarchy of Needs which has five. The second difference between Maslow and Alderfer is that Alderfer considered that people could move around the hierarchy meeting their needs. People do not start at the bottom and work their way up. People might be meeting their relatedness or social needs whilst tired or hungry. They might meet their need for personal growth by studying alone, even though they feel lonely.

Alderfer also argued that people can go backwards in meeting needs. If people are frustrated in meeting their higher order needs – no job satisfaction, no recognition of their work – they may start meeting lower order needs even though they are already satisfied. People may eat too much, drink too much, concentrate on making money, etc., to compensate themselves for not achieving the higher order need.

McClelland's Needs Theory

David McClelland formulated a theory based on needs as motivators. People learn in early childhood that certain ways of behaving lead to good things happening to them. The child who tries hard at school may get praise from his or her parents. The child who is aggressive and a bully can make other children do what he or she wants. The child who is sociable and interested in others has plenty of friends. According to McClelland, being rewarded for certain behaviours causes people to develop a need for these rewards.

McClelland argues that there are three basic needs, which he abbreviated to N-Ach, N-Aff and N-Power:

1 ACHIEVEMENT (N-Ach) People who have a need for achievement want to 'get the job done'. They are task orientated.

2 AFFILIATION (N-Aff) People who have a need for affiliation want approval from other people. They are people orientated.

3 POWER (N-Power) People who have a need for power want influence and control over others. They are self orientated.

1 The need for achievement

People with a need for achievement prefer to work on their own and like to have quick feedback on whether their efforts have been successful. They do not depend on others for approval, they set their own targets for themselves and are happy to strive for them alone. They are the 'doers', the action people in the organisation, and they like to get things done. They cannot understand people who enjoy chatting all day or who hesitate in making decisions.

2 The need for affiliation

People with a need for affiliation are sensitive to the needs of others. They seek approval, both from superiors and subordinates. They prefer to get work done with others, or by liaising with other people. Some people have such strong N-Aff needs that they do not manage to get much work done. Other people also have N-Aff needs, but not at the expense of doing their jobs. They are interested in the feelings of others which may well make them the best sort of leaders or managers.

3 The need for power

There are two different ways of gaining power: through bullying or aggressive behaviour, or through personal influence and communication.

People with a need for power will apply for promotions and take on responsibilities at work. They like competition situations and having the power to make decisions. They are not necessarily 'the bad guys' as someone has to lead and all three needs are required for an organisation to function effectively.

Managers and McClelland's Needs Theory

Many people who start or run their own businesses have a high N-Ach. McClelland therefore considered them essential for a strong economy. They create jobs and wealth in the country. They need to feel they have achieved something, therefore managers high in N-Ach will set targets for themselves and others which are important to them to reach. People with low N-Ach avoid challenges, responsibilities and risk and are therefore probably unsuitable for management positions.

A manager with a high N-Aff may have a co-operative, team-centred style of management, but this is not necessarily the case. He or she could be autocratic, but adopt a caring and interested attitude towards his or her employees. A manager will usually want friendships at work and therefore likes to have a 'second in command' or a management team with whom he or she can share feelings and gain support.

Managers with a high N-Power may be constantly wishing to increase their staff or move on to higher positions, or they may be content with their present position as long as they reassure themselves that they have influence over their subordinates. They are usually good communicators and care what their subordinates do and say.

What drives and urges have you got?

Answer the following questions, then add up the number of (a)s, (b)s and (c)s you've got at the end.

1 A friend phones you at work during a busy period. She is heartbroken because her boyfriend has dumped her. Do you:
(a) Say you've got to get back to work and that you'll ring her tonight?
(b) Listen to the whole story and keep talking to her until she feels better?
(c) Talk to her just long enough to cheer her up a bit and say you'll see her later?

2 A person you didn't like at school starts work in your office. Do you:
(a) Ignore him or her?
(b) Be prepared to see him or her in a new light and become friends?
(c) Pretend that all is forgiven, but continue to dislike the person?

3 You are the most junior person in your office. Do you dream of:
(a) Having your excellent work publicly recognised?
(b) A really good office party?
(c) Promotion?

4 People you work with often waste time messing about. Do you see them as:
(a) A burden to the organisation, and no help to you when you're trying to get work done?
(b) People to be on friendly terms with, but not to be seen with when the boss is anywhere around?
(c) Good fun?

5 You promised to ring a customer and it's now home time for you. Do you:
(a) Ring the customer straight away and stay at work until the business is completed?
(b) Go home and leave the call until tomorrow?
(c) Ring the customer if there's nothing more important to do and make it clear, in the nicest possible way, that you're giving a very good service?

6 If you were thinking of starting your own small business, would you:
(a) Set up on your own and run it as you want to?
(b) Start a partnership or small company with friends?
(c) Employ people to work for you from the beginning?

7 What sort of exercise would you prefer:
(a) Jogging/running?
(b) Anything that's a good laugh?
(c) Team games, with the objective of becoming captain?

8 You are a student. Friends invite you out for the evening when you should be working on a college assignment. Do you:

(a) Stay at home and work?

(b) Go out and leave the assignment unfinished?

(c) Go out, but leave fairly early and stay up until you finish the assignment as you don't want to get into your lecturer's bad books?

Scores

Mostly (a)s?

You have a need for achievement (N-Ach). You are a doer, interested in getting the job done. You don't need other people to give their approval or set targets for you. You know what you want to do and you go for it. Perhaps considering and listening to other people occasionally might show you that life is going on outside work.

Mostly (b)s?

You have a need for affiliation (N-Aff). You prefer to be with people than working alone. Your consideration for others may be detrimental to your career – the job needs doing sometime. Don't leave it all to someone else to do the work.

Mostly (c)s?

You have a need for power (N-Power). You want to influence and control other people. You can see that everyone may be useful to you at some time and therefore you are careful not to have disagreements with people or upset people. Your main aim is to be promoted and manage your organisation. You may also be able to take on a leadership position through your outside interests.

A mixture of all three?

You are a rounded personality, not too extreme on any one need. You can see that the job needs doing without neglecting people's feelings. You would make a good boss, especially if you have a few (c)s thrown in.

Social theories of motivation

Vroom expectancy theory

This theory is based on the idea that needs cause behaviour. Further important points which this theory makes are:

- Motivation comes in different strengths.
- Motivation strength is determined by the perceived value of the outcome or reward.
- Motivation strength is also determined by the perceived probability that the behaviour (e.g. working hard) will cause the outcome or reward to occur.

Fig. 1.5 Chris likes Alison. Will he ask her to go to the disco?

Chris's motivation depends upon:

1 How valuable is the reward or outcome? (An evening with Alison.)

2 Will she say yes? (What is the probability of the reward occurring?)

Vroom's expectancy theory of motivation as an equation

Motivation strength	=	Probability that the outcome will occur following the action	x	Value of the result or goal

Chris's motivation

Highly motivated to ask	=	He thinks it very likely that she will say yes	x	Likes her very much and wants her to be his girlfriend
Not motivated to ask	=	He thinks she will tell him to 'drop dead'	x	He quite likes her, among several other girls

Chris will not be motivated to ask (even if he likes Alison very much), if he thinks she will definitely say no. Both parts of the equation need to be positive to achieve motivation. The goal must be worth while and the person must expect to be able to reach that goal.

People will be less motivated to try for promotion if they feel it is not really worth while, or if they think they will not achieve it even if they work hard and apply for it.

Which part of Vroom's equation is the reason for the lack of motivation in these cases?

Case 1
Adam was told at his interview at Asco Supermarket that he could work his way up to be manager if he tried hard. He worked long and hard but every time a vacancy came up for an assistant manager's job, someone well qualified from outside the company got it. Adam stopped being motivated and stopped working so hard.

Case 2
Jill was also told at her interview at Asco Supermarket that she could become manager if she worked hard. She, like Adam, also worked long and hard. As time went by, Jill noticed that the managers had to work late, and they always seemed tense, worried and busy. She also discovered that their salary was not nearly as much as she had originally thought. Jill stopped being motivated and stopped working so hard.

Answer: Case 1 – Probability of achieving the goal
Case 2 – How worth while the goal is

Vroom's theory is very useful as it reminds managers that providing good employee benefits and incentives will not necessarily motivate employees to work hard. People will only value the benefits and incentives if they see them as worth while. They will only work hard towards the incentives if they think they can achieve them.

Many firms provide benefits such as private health care. Some individuals do not value this very highly, despite the fact that it is expensive for firms to provide it. Also, many organisations give bonuses if employees achieve their targets. If the targets are too difficult, people will feel that they are unachievable and will not be motivated to work for them.

Managers can check that employees value the benefits and incentives provided by consulting them or allowing them to choose which benefits they receive. Employees' confidence that they can achieve goals also needs to be boosted and care taken about setting achievable goals. Appraisal interviews are useful for talking to employees about their aspirations for the future and how they can reach them. New goals can be negotiated which the employee feels are achievable – then they should be motivated.

Equity theory

Equity theory is the work of J Stacy Adams. Behaviour and motivation are affected by whether individuals see the situation they are in as being fair or not. In an employment situation people like to feel they are getting a fair exchange – the amount they put into the job (inputs) for the amount they get out (outputs). This exchange involves many factors besides money.

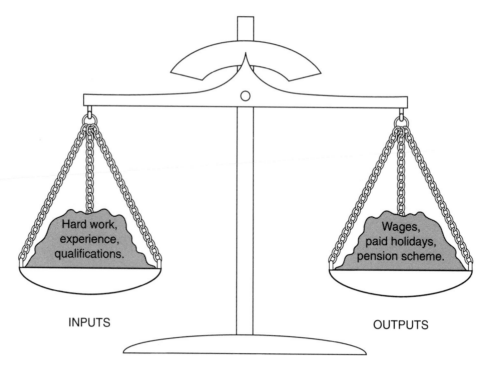

Fig. 1.6 The exchange of inputs for outputs

Good working conditions, convenient location, hours of work, etc., are all outputs which an employee may consider to be a plus factor in the employment exchange. A person with other responsibilities apart from work, such as young children, may want to work certain hours of the day and not have to travel away from home. A job which has these advantages may be accepted in spite of low pay. The hours and convenience are considered to make up for the low pay and bring the situation into one of a fair exchange.

Another person who is prepared to travel long distances, be away from home for long periods, work unsocial hours and has good qualifications and experience will expect to be compensated substantially for these inputs into the job.

Situations of inequity

When employees feel that they are not adequately rewarded for their inputs, or that other people are getting more money than they are for the same job, they will experience such things as dissatisfaction, anger and tension.

Individuals will try to bring the equity into balance by:

- asking for a pay rise
- doing less work
- moving some of the work load onto the better paid employees
- taking days off
- convincing themselves that they are not really doing the same work as better paid employees
- resigning

Individual motivation is strongly affected by feelings of equity or inequity. They will not wish to work hard if they feel they are being taken advantage of by the organisation. In order to be motivated to work, employees need to perceive the situation as equitable.

Choosing outputs

An American idea which is becoming more common in Britain is 'Cafeteria Benefits'. Employees can choose from a range of fringe benefits, rather like going to a self-service cafeteria with a tray to choose dinner. This means that if employees do not value holidays, extra pension or private health care, they need not accept them. Instead they can choose to have extra pay or other benefits.

This idea has the advantage that employees reach a state of equity much faster (and at a lower cost to the firm), than if they were given benefits they did not value. Employees have the advantage of gaining those outputs from the firm they really want, such as taking extra holidays or pay, and the firm saves money on those benefits their employees do not value.

I FIND IT SUCH A SATISFYING AND WORTHWHILE JOB THAT I DON'T NEED TO DRAW ANY SALARY!

QUESTIONS

1 Under what circumstances do employees often receive different rates of pay for the same work?

2 Which job would you least like to do? Is it a highly paid one?

3 Why might a manager give merit rises to some workers and not others? How could the manager believe the situation to be equitable?

4 Which benefits would you choose to have and not to have, if you worked for an organisation which had 'Cafeteria Benefits'?

5 Why are nurses not very highly paid yet work unsocial hours, such as during the night and weekends, and often have unpleasant tasks to perform?

6 Have you always felt well compensated for any work you've done in the past?

Satisfiers/dissatisfiers

Further factors affecting motivation are what Frederick Herzberg termed 'satisfiers' and 'dissatisfiers'.

SATISFIERS – motivating factors

DISSATISFIERS – maintenance (or hygiene) factors

Hertzberg concluded from his research that the satisfaction and dissatisfaction that employees feel at work are separate factors, caused by different things.
Satisfiers are concerned with the job itself. Dissatisfiers relate to the work environment.

Satisfiers	Dissatisfiers
The work itself	Company policy and administration
Promotion prospects	Relationship with supervisor
Achievement	Relationship with other workers
Responsibility	Working conditions
Recognition	Salary

Individuals will only gain satisfaction from the nature of the work itself; the feeling that they are working for promotion; feelings of achievement the work provides; or having responsibility or recognition at work.

Dissatisfaction will occur when the employee feels that company policy is wrong. If Tony wants to do a part-time GNVQ course and his manager will not let him have any time off work, he may consider this a bad policy and feel demotivated by it. Other causes of dissatisfaction may be poor relationships with supervisors or fellow workers, poor working conditions or low salary.

If the maintenance factors (dissatisfiers) are good, employees will not work harder. If people are given pay rises, new offices or factories, pleasant people to work with, they will not wish to leave the organisation, and will merely be 'maintained' in the job. The maintenance, or hygiene, factors provide loyalty to the organisation, but they do not improve worker performance.

Herzberg argued that some people are 'hygiene meeters' and are not concerned with the motivators. They merely want a good salary, pleasant surroundings and good relationships. If these people become managers, they will be difficult to work for, as they will not consider such things as making jobs more interesting, training courses and opportunities for promotion important for their subordinates. A neat and tidy office or factory is one of their top priorities at work.

TRUE OR FALSE QUIZ

Answer true or false to each of the following statements:

1 Maslow's theory is called the 'Hierarchy of Needs'.

2 Alderfer's and Maslow's theories are similar.

3 According to Alderfer, when people's higher order needs are frustrated, they start drinking too much.

4 Alderfer's needs differ from Maslow's in two important respects.

5 McClelland argues that people have three needs and that they are all equally strong.

6 People high in N-Ach are good at achieving targets.

7 People with need for power are aggressive and argumentative.

8 It was Alderfer who argued that motivation comes in different strengths.

9 Vroom said that people are motivated solely by rewards.

10 Both parts of Vroom's equation must be positive in order for a person to be motivated

11 Equity theory is about being paid enough money for the work completed.

12 People who consider that they are treated unfairly at work will attempt to get the input-output exchange back into balance.

13 Cafeteria benefits involve giving the workers a free choice about which outputs they take from an organisation.

14 If maintenance or hygiene factors are poor in an organisation, workers will be dissatisfied and want to leave the organisation.

15 Herzberg argued that motivators are recognition, company policies, feelings of achievement and an interesting job.

Answers:

1 True	6 True	11 False
2 True	7 False	12 True
3 False	8 False	13 True
4 True	9 False	14 True
5 False	10 True	15 False

CASE STUDY

Marks and Spencer PLC

Marks and Spencer, the High Street retailer, is well known for quality and excellence in their goods. They provide a superior service to both customers and staff.

Two hundred and twenty people are employed in their Hanley branch in Staffordshire, 66 of whom are full-time. There are also increasing numbers of temporary staff between October and Christmas.

Salaries are above average and after one year's service, staff receive a Christmas bonus of an extra four weeks' salary and supervisors get 10 per cent of their annual salary. Discounts of 20 per cent on stock are given to staff, up to £350 per annum for full-time staff and £150 per annum for part-time staff.

The staff dining-room has self-service hot and cold free drinks, self-service food machines plus a hot food cafeteria service. Staff can buy a three-course meal for the subsidised price of approximately £1. In the dining-room there is a lounge area with easy chairs and coffee tables, fitted carpets, troughs of plants and a pool table. In the cafeteria area, there are dining tables and chairs.

Marks and Spencer also provide health care facilities for their staff. A doctor visits the store once every two weeks to give free advice and her sessions are normally fully booked. A dentist also visits every six months to give advice to staff who require it.

Some services are now less common – Marks and Spencer used to employ chiropodists and hairdressers, for example.

Other health care services are:

- breast screening every 18 months for women over 40 years of age, or the wives of male employees
- cytology every three years

- health checks for employees over 30 years old which include blood pressure tests, cholesterol tests, height and weight checks and questionnaires on exercise and general well-being

Members of staff are all in the company pension scheme. This is non-contributory and they receive an annual statement telling them what their pension will be upon retirement.

There is also a profit sharing scheme. After two years' service, employees receive shares in the company. The number of shares allocated varies each year and is relative to the member of staff's annual salary.

The second type of share ownership is the Share Option Scheme. This takes the form of a savings scheme to begin with. Employees save money to purchase shares for five years, after which time a bonus is added. If the shares are left for a further two years, an additional bonus is added. At the end of the time period, staff can buy shares for the price the shares were selling at when they first started saving. Janet Gilford, the personnel supervisor, said, 'My shares were sold for £3.84 each, and I bought them for £1.82, which is the price they were when I took out the option.' There is a 55 per cent take-up on share options. If employees wish to take their savings out of the scheme before the end of the 5–7 years, they can do so.

In July 1992, Performance Awards were introduced to reward employees who work hard and take on extra responsibility. All staff go through an appraisal interview and supervisors decide which staff deserve a Performance Award. The award could be up to £5 per week on top of the salary.

'There's no restriction on how many Performance Awards someone can get,' says Janet Gilford. The store has a budget for Performance Awards. The budget is for 30 per cent of staff to receive awards, although it is possible to give a smaller sum of money to more than 30 per cent of staff. 'We can give half the amount to twice as many people, if we think they deserve it.'

The appraisal interviews are a useful two-way discussion, which include any areas of concern and the employees' perception of their training needs.

Marks and Spencer are a popular employer. On average, Janet's department receives ten letters every day from people wishing to work there. They do not often advertise for staff – any permanent positions are filled by temporary staff who have performed well while working in the store. They rarely need new permanent staff as so few people leave.

'We have just taken on 100 temporary staff for Christmas, and we could have filled each job three times over,' Janet points out. Temporary jobs are advertised through the job centre who do pre-screening and a first interview. The second interview takes place at Marks and Spencer. Students are employed from 13 December until Christmas to work in the food section.

Promotions to supervisor positions are normally in-store promotions. Managers are appointed by head office.

Zoe Coupe – Deputy Supervisor, Marks and Spencer PLC

Zoe has worked for Marks and Spencer for seven years. She started at the age of 16 on a two-year YTS scheme. After one year of the scheme, she was taken on permanently (although just part-time), and after six months was made full-time. She was promoted to deputy supervisor four years ago. She is responsible for the staff in her section, organisation, implementing moves of stock and the daily running of the section, which is ladies' fashions. She has worked in every department of the store, including the general office and the Customer Service Desk.

Zoe Coupe – deputy supervisor at Marks and Spencer

'The job itself is interesting, seasonal changes bring different emphasis in stock. I enjoy the contact with the customers. The technology and computers have meant that we can get information on what the top selling lines are, how much your department is taking. You can get more stock and generate more sales. We might be strong in certain areas and I can tell straight away whether it's available or on order. The closed circuit television helps to keep tabs on people so that security is increased.'

Zoe has responsibility in her job as Deputy Supervisor: 'It's satisfying, I felt good in myself that I'd proved myself when I got promotion. I hope to get some more promotion. For a job that doesn't require any qualifications, it's a good salary.'

Zoe does not feel that the job is quite as secure as it used to be. Several people have been made redundant from the store over the last two years – warehousemen, till controllers and catering staff.

Everyone gets on well together socially. 'Although it's a large store, everybody knows everybody. We're going out for a meal on Tuesday night as a group, although we don't do it too regularly.'

Zoe married last year and is working on her new house in her spare time. She also enjoys going to the cinema. 'I used to be in the Special Constabulary. I did this for three years. I haven't got time to do it now. Coming here to work straight from school, it gave me an insight into another job. It has made me more content in this job. I can see myself staying here until I retire.'

TASK

1 Which of the following are motivators and which are maintenance factors (satisfiers and dissatisfiers) at Marks & Spencer PLC?

	Motivators	Maintenance factors
(a) Part-time hours	☐	☐
(b) Christmas bonus	☐	☐
(c) Free drinks	☐	☐
(d) Subsidised meals	☐	☐
(e) Staff dining-room	☐	☐
(f) Health care services	☐	☐
(g) Pension scheme	☐	☐
(h) Profit sharing	☐	☐
(i) Share Option Scheme	☐	☐
(j) Performance Awards	☐	☐
(k) Appraisal interviews	☐	☐
(l) Staff training	☐	☐
(m) Promotion prospects	☐	☐
(n) Responsibility for a section	☐	☐
(o) The job itself	☐	☐
(p) Feelings of achievement	☐	☐
(q) Personal growth	☐	☐
(r) Recognition	☐	☐

2 Give examples from the case study of the motivators you have ticked, i.e. if you have ticked 'Recognition', say what forms of recognition for good work Marks and Spencer provide.

QUESTIONS

1 Which of Maslow's needs are being met at Marks and Spencer, and how are they being met?

2 Are Zoe's drives, needs and aspirations being met through her work?

3 Why do Marks and Spencer employ so many part-time staff?

4 Why do so few people leave their employment with Marks and Spencer?

5 What effect do you think the Performance Awards have on staff?

6 Do you know of another organisation whose employee benefits are different from those of Marks and Spencer? If so, how do they differ?

Job design

An important factor affecting motivation is the design of jobs. Production line jobs have been simplified so that often the worker just performs one task all day, every day. This can make the jobs demotivating to do. A worker might take a machine part off a press and place it on a conveyor belt, or watch lines of cakes to see if the cherries are in the right place. The person has to behave as if he or she is part of a machine and his or her job is less interesting than when several different tasks are performed. The motivation for a person to go to work to do such a job is companionship and/or money. There is very little motivation in the interest of the job itself. However, jobs can be redesigned to make them more interesting.

Job enrichment

If motivators are incorporated into a job, the job will be enriched and more motivating for employees to perform. The motivators to incorporate are those highlighted by Herzberg's research:

- opportunity for achievement
- opportunity for recognition
- work itself
- responsibility
- opportunity for promotion

The worker's involvement in the organisation and the job is increased by incorporating one or more of these motivators. Employees can complete a whole job, or a much larger part of the job than they did previously. The job is often enriched to include tasks which were performed by the manager or supervisor. The job therefore involves increased decision making.

Enrichment of many factory jobs may lead to abandoning the conveyor belt and production line, which are efficient methods of production. Costs may rise as a result of job changes. Firms may lose business as a result of changing job design.

Reorganisation of firms' structures, through re-engineering or continuous improvement schemes, may alter office as well as factory jobs. Managerial and other workers' responsibilities may be increased as a result of such measures as reducing the number of layers of management in an organisation. People may feel demotivated if they consider that they have been given a lot of extra work for no extra rewards. But if people feel they are achieving more and receiving recognition for their work, they will be motivated and have positive attitudes towards work.

Job rotation

Employees' motivation can be improved by their movement from one job to another. Job rotation may be organised by managers or the workers involved. In the packing department of a sweet factory, workers could change between:

- taking the packets of sweets off the conveyor belts and packing them into cartons
- labelling and wrapping the cartons
- lifting and stacking the cartons

This change could occur weekly, daily, half-hourly – whatever the workers or management consider is most desirable. Job rotation provides variety and helps people avoid the strain of repeating the same physical movements all day, every day.

This form of job redesign can often be done at no extra cost to the organisation as no new machinery or equipment is needed. It increases the flexibility of the workforce as employees can perform one another's jobs. This is useful during periods of sickness and at holiday time.

Job rotation can have disadvantages in that:

- mistakes are difficult to trace, or workers feel blamed for the errors of another person
- more training is needed for all the workforce if tasks are complex, and this is more costly for the organisation
- bad feeling may arise at changeover time if workers inherit untidy areas, half-finished tasks or work shoddily done
- the amount of variety within one job is still limited

Factors affecting job redesign

There is a limit to the way jobs can be redesigned in order to motivate the workforce. These factors are:

- technology – the equipment used in the performance of jobs often dictates how those jobs are done.
- level of mechanisation – highly mechanised jobs have less leeway in them for change than unmechanised jobs.
- cost of equipment – redesigns such as everyone building a total product at their workstation would require multiple sets of tools for the job.
- employee attitudes – some jobs may be more prestigious than others. Those job-holders may be reluctant to let them go and do the same as everyone else.
- management style – job redesigns often call for a change in the way supervision is carried out. If the workers organise the job rotation themselves, they may not need much supervision and therefore managers have to change their style.

Performance Criterion 3
Impact of monitoring factors on performance

Monitoring performance

Monitoring factors of performance encourages workers to co-operate with management in their organisation. Motivation, feedback to workers and commitment to the organisation can all be improved through monitoring workers' performance.

Until recently, there was an emphasis on the workers as a collective body, all receiving the same rate of pay for the same job. Trade unions, collective bargaining (when trade unions negotiate with employers on behalf of their members for improved pay and working conditions) and the idea of a 'going-rate' for a job are fading and pay has become more individual. Workers are encouraged to see themselves as separate from other workers and are rewarded for their work as individuals. Rewards are often linked to company performance, through profit sharing, as well as to individual performance.

There are various ways of monitoring people's performance at work. For those who work in manufacturing, it may be possible to monitor their performance very accurately. Someone making doughnuts in a bakery may produce 100 per hour, and so it is very easy to tell whether he or she is performing better or worse by measuring output.

For those who are not directly connected with production, such as maintenance engineers or people working in service industries such as nurses or shop assistants, performance is more difficult to measure.

Where performance is easy to measure, payment systems such as

- piece work
  OR
- measured day work

may be used.

In situations where performance is more difficult to monitor, the following systems can be implemented:

- performance appraisal
- performance-related pay

Piece work

Payment is made for the amount produced. For example, if 100 doughnuts are made in an hour and paid at 4p each, this gives an average wage of £4 per hour.

Measured day work

A basic wage is paid plus a bonus amount. If 100 doughnuts per hour is considered to be a reasonable amount for one person to make, then this could be set as a target. For any doughnuts made above 100 in an hour, the worker would receive a bonus.

Performance appraisal

A performance appraisal is normally a one-to-one interview between supervisor/manager and subordinate, carried out annually. The objectives are:

- to decide whether people are suitable for particular jobs
- to decide on the training, education and job experience needed by the individual
- to identify people suitable for promotion
- to give feedback on the individual's performance and provide an opportunity for the subordinate to discuss various aspects of his or her job
- to motivate employees and increase their commitment to the organisation

Many companies also use the appraisal interview to give pay awards. This can have a dramatic effect on the interview as people will be more interested in the pay award than the discussion about how they are doing at work.

The appraisal may consist of the supervisor informing the subordinate about written comments or gradings against specific job competencies. Ideally, if the subordinate has been making mistakes or doing badly generally, he or she should not hear about it for the first time during the appraisal interview. An employee should be informed on a day-to-day basis if his or her performance is unsatisfactory. The appraisal interview is then more likely to be positive and motivating rather than a 'telling off' session.

Many supervisors are reluctant to carry out appraisals as they find them embarrassing and time-consuming. There are benefits for everyone though:

Appraisees
(a) receive feedback on their performance
(b) learn what is expected of them
(c) can say what training they think they need

Appraisers
(a) have a monitoring mechanism to measure the performance of their staff
(b) have the opportunity to find out more about the aspirations and needs of each member of staff
(c) can motivate and encourage better performance from staff in order to improve their areas of responsibility

Appraisal interviews can improve communication in the organisation, improve employees' understanding of the organisation's goals, and assist with manpower planning by identifying staff suitable for particular promotions or shortages of staff suitable for more senior positions.

Performance-related pay

This is increasingly being introduced, both for white-collar and blue-collar employees. In those organisations operating systems of performance-related pay, the amount of a person's salary which is awarded for performance is normally around 5 per cent. It is therefore a very small proportion of a person's salary, but is generally considered by workers to be welcome, important and motivating.

Managers are given a budget by the organisation for performance-related pay. The budget may mean giving a proportion of workers a certain percentage rise. In Marks and Spencer PLC, the budget is for 30 per cent of the manager's subordinates to receive an award. The manager has the discretion to award more than 30 per cent of employees, as long as he or she stays within budget. If 60 per cent of employees are awarded the performance-related pay, then the manager could give them all half of the 5 per cent, or whatever the amount of the 30 per cent the figure may be.

Monitoring performance at First Chicago bank

There are around 15,000 banks in America, and First Chicago is the thirteenth largest of these. It employs 14,000 people and has branches overseas in London, Tokyo, Sydney and Hong Kong, as well as in Chicago, New York, Dallas and Los Angeles. The bank has three separate lines of business:

1 Commercial – banking for larger companies
2 Middle – banking for small businesses
3 Visa Card and personal banking

First Chicago is the USA's third largest issuer of Visa Card and Visa Card is its biggest earner.

The bank has performance appraisals and merit pay. The idea of performance appraisals, according to Nancy Seever, the vice-president of human resources at the bank, is to improve performance, give feedback and coach, both on strengths and weaknesses.

'It's not just what your boss thinks of you. We are really getting very strongly into 360 degree appraisals. There is input from managers, peers, subordinates and customers.' All the people who deal with the employee being appraised are telephoned and asked for their views on the appraisee's performance. The bank is in the process of formalising this and sending out forms for those giving input to fill in.

In appraisal interviews, employees chat with their manager. Nancy explains: 'You talk about last year and what went well last year, what feedback you've received from people. Positive points and areas for improvement are discussed. Targets can be set.' The employees being appraised have the opportunity to ask for such things as more training, promotion, or transfers. They can write down a list of their accomplishments and hand it to their manager at the beginning of the appraisal.

'Unfortunately, it's a top-down approach. We're trying to change this and get more of a dialogue going. I personally think that it's up to a group of people to say "this is what we want to be evaluated on".

'If you don't do it, a lot of things fester that the manager never tells the employee about. It puts some of the onus on the manager to sort things out,' says Nancy. Employees want feedback and input on their performance. 'In an ideal world appraisals wouldn't be necessary because you'd have been having an on-going dialogue all year.'

'It should be an honest discussion between two employees, but they are always a little awkward.' Managers often feel embarrassed about carrying out appraisals. Employees may feel nervous about being criticised. The manager can easily take command as they know what they are going to say. 'The employee hasn't had time to think. They should have time to prepare.'

During the appraisal interviews at First Chicago bank, merit pay rises are also awarded. This is usually discussed at the beginning of the interview and up to 5 per cent of the employee's salary can be awarded as a merit pay rise. 'They might be sitting there waiting to see how much money they're going to get. I don't think money motivates. There are so many other things that motivate. If you say to someone that they're doing well and making a good contribution to the team – that's the motivator.

'Some people establish a relationship with their employee that says, "I want you to do the best you can during the year and I'm going to do all I can to help you

Nancy Seever – human resources manager at First Chicago Bank

achieve tremendous potential. I'll listen to what you have to say because I'm on your side". Others say, "Gottya! Let me tell you what's wrong with you".'

Nancy would like appraisal interviews to leave employees feeling positive and motivated. 'We're all on the same side,' says Nancy, 'but some play the boss-subordinate role.'

Training managers how to do appraisal interviews is not a priority at the bank. Their training at present is aimed at management change, teambuilding, leadership and supervisory training.

Managers are reluctant to do appraisal interviews. 'If they're not tied to money they won't get done. They're awkward, so people don't want to do them. They're uncomfortable.' Many managers don't feel the need to give feedback to their subordinates. 'They think, "You're doing an OK job, if you weren't you wouldn't be here".'

QUESTIONS

1 What are the benefits of '360 degree' appraisals, rather than just one person judging performance?

2 What sort of problems does Nancy Seever mention that they have at First Chicago bank with appraisals?

3 What does Nancy Seever see as being the ideal appraisal interview?

4 How is performance-related pay implemented at First Chicago?

TASK

Devise a rating scale or set of criteria you would be looking for in the competent student. In groups of three, carry out an appraisal interview, with one appraisee, one appraiser and one observer. The objective of the interview is to discuss the student's performance at college over the past few months.

With help from the observer, discuss your individual emotions during the interview and how the interview could be improved in future to increase student motivation.

Evidence indicator

Conduct a survey of a small work group, which includes their personal attitudes to their work and the impact of motivation factors on their performance.

You will need to find out:

- what motivators their employer uses
- what each person does in his or her job
- how each person feels about his or her job
- whether the motivation factors affect work performance

SAMPLE INTERVIEW

Read the following case study on a small work group – the employee relations team at Fodens Trucks. Use the case to discuss:

(a) their attitudes to work
(b) the effect of motivators on their work
(c) which questions to include in your own questionnaire for the survey of a work group
(d) different types of work groups it may be possible to survey

Identifying the personal attitudes of a small work group and the impact of motivation factors on their performance

The organisation

Foden Trucks is an operating division of PACCAR Inc. of America. Foden Trucks have a new company headquarters in Sandbach, Cheshire, on a 60 acre site. At the Sandbach headquarters, they employ 500 people and build lorries to customer specifications. They are in a very competitive industry – in the 1960s there were over 60 manufacturers of lorries in Europe, now there are only eleven.

The motivation factors

1 Annual salary with wide salary bands. The salary is around average for the industry.

The small work group at Fodens. From left to right; employee relations manager, health and safety officer, personnel administrator, personnel officer

2 Performance appraisal. Interviews take place annually, goals and targets are set for employees during the interview. These are related to the company's aim for continuous improvement. Appraisal interviews for managers are linked to business goals. Their targets are related to strategic planning and they can receive incentive compensation (a pay award) for achieving their goals.

3 Company shares can be purchased at a special rate by employees.

4 Pension contribution scheme. Employees pay 5 per cent of their salary into the pension scheme and the company adds a greater percentage to it, giving a guaranteed pension upon retirement.

5 Weekly meetings are held to stress communication and co-operation between departments. All departments are interdependant and need one another's co-operation.

6 Promotion is from within whenever possible. The company occasionally give six month transfers to people to experience the work of other departments.

Sandy Massie, the employee relations manager, says: 'Pay awards are not made during the appraisal interview, but pay rises do depend upon the appraisal.'

The recession has made the possibility of promoting people more difficult, as there are fewer jobs. 'Most movement has been outwards rather than upwards, but we do try to give career moves to people,' explains Sandy.

There are currently no company-organised social events, although various departments do put on their own social functions. The company is planning to give everyone a turkey for Christmas.

Employee retention is very good and absenteeism is below the average for the industry at 3 per cent.

The work group

The work group consists of:

- employee relations manager
- personnel officer
- health and safety officer
- personnel administrator

Employee relations manager

The employee relations manager is responsible for all areas of personnel work – training, development, employee relations, recruitment. He has worked for Fodens for just over four years.

'I like the variety, it's very interesting. I'm not sure that meeting people constantly is one of the favourite parts of my job. Our role is as facilitators – I don't want to do the personnel work, I want the line managers to do it and I help them in any way I can. The supervisors are in on interviews and they mostly make the decision. That's a much better way of getting the correct mix.

'People come to work for the money. If you work hard here, they tend to pay you for it. I like to work for a company that is seen to be successful, not only in the UK/US market, but in a global sense. It can be fun to work here, which I think is important. Companies that are successful have a buzz, which we've got.'

'I do find the goals set during the appraisal motivating. The whole system is geared towards building, the Japanese idea of kaizen or continuous improvement.

'I like to see team success and that the whole team has achieved success. Some people are loners and it's very difficult to get them into teams. Those particular types need more encouragement to join in.'

Personnel officer

The personnel officer has worked at Fodens for four and a half years. She is involved with recruitment, and has some responsibility for training, various aspects of personnel administration, and joint responsibility for employee benefits and 'anything else that crops up'. She also manages the residential house within the company which is used for accommodating visitors to the company.

'I enjoy it, I like the variety and meeting people and being involved with people from their first contact with the company. I like having the responsibility. The job is interesting, and it's not working in isolation.'

'The appraisal interview has no real impact on my performance. I find it probably sets objectives for the year, but they get overtaken by day-to-day priorities and we just "do it".

'I don't have anybody sitting on my shoulder saying "do this, do that". My motivation comes from trying to do the best for people. I'd be letting them down if I didn't. We don't have formal sit-down meetings, but we get all the information about what's happening.

'We work as a team, our culture and experience says that people will be let down if you don't. People come in and work even if they're ill – there's such a strong team spirit. There is a "return to work" programme which allows people who have been away ill to return to work gradually in a less difficult job while their health fully recovers. There's great loyalty to the team. If you get on as a team, you enjoy spending time in the office.

'Promotion isn't as I would want. I don't see any opportunity for promotion in the present climate.

'I would like to see Christmas parties and social functions. The company doesn't support any social functions.'

Health and safety officer

The health and safety officer and occupational health nurse has worked at Fodens for just over four years.

'I work mainly on the shop floor. I'm responsible for health and safety, and the welfare of all Foden employees. We're a very safe company. We have a mature workforce and they know their jobs. The company does put a lot a financial backing behind the health and safety equipment.

'The company doctor comes on site once a week. After the personnel officer has chosen people, we do the medical. I'm in charge of all the safety equipment – such things as ear protectors and gloves.

'I carry out investigations of any problems and accidents. I do welfare counselling on the shopfloor. I go out and visit employees off sick or who are in hospital.

'I'm involved with a lot of people. It's different every day. Some days I do a lot of paperwork. I liaise between people and sort out conflicts. Most levels are accessible to me. I'm the one person who has to be seen to be unbiased, so no one has got any fear of me. I can communicate with both groups. I'm the secretary of the health and safety committee which has the union and management on it and I'll back whoever I think is right. I'm accepted by all groups and I'm independent. It's a very interesting job.

'I think most of us feel that for the amount of work we do, we're stretched. There used to be eight of us, there are now three and we're doing exactly the same work.

'Everybody pulls together in the busy times, but we can also relax together. If we'd got a personal problem, we could tell one another and it wouldn't go outside this office. We cover for one another if one of us has to go home because the children are ill.

'I get job satisfaction. I get thanks from people in the company. I do it for the welfare of others. The company have paid for me to train to be a safety officer, so they've pushed me quite far. Much further than nurses in other companies. They've sent me on lots of courses. And I've got a new bicycle for riding around the site.'

Personnel administrator

The personnel administrator has worked for Fodens for 13 years and has a daughter aged 17 months. She does the administration for the team, all the typing, the keeping of personnel records, holiday and sick pay and also does switchboard relief.

'I like the variation. I like the people I work with and being busy and having a lot to do. When you've finished a job, it's satisfying. I'm happy with the salary, it's quite good compared to other jobs I see advertised in the paper.

'The appraisal is not relevant, we talk about things as they happen. Goals are planned and set in the interview and then for various reasons we can't achieve them. For example, last year we had a big recruitment drive and took on an extra 120 people. We had 1,200 applications and it took up most of our time for five or six months. We'd anticipated a slight increase, but it wasn't taken account of in the appraisal goals because it was unexpected.

'I came back twelve months ago after having a baby. I'd like to be able to do part-time, but it's not available here. We work 8 till 4, so finishing at 4 o'clock is not too bad.'

WORDSEARCH

Factors influencing attitudes and performance at work

```
H  M  O  T  I  V  A  S  O  C  I  A  L  E  A  B  Q  P  R  T
B  I  M  O  T  I  V  A  T  I  O  N  S  N  F  Q  E  H  R  A
E  H  E  S  U  B  J  A  N  E  B  D  T  R  H  A  V  Y  O  U
H  U  Q  R  Y  F  R  C  N  T  E  B  A  I  A  V  I  S  T  S
A  A  T  Y  A  N  A  L  T  E  T  D  S  C  E  N  E  I  A  T
V  P  B  Y  D  R  A  F  N  W  A  R  K  H  U  E  E  O  T  A
I  S  J  E  H  N  C  L  G  G  S  H  K  M  W  E  I  L  I  T
O  X  J  K  O  O  A  H  C  L  K  E  A  E  U  D  M  O  O  U
U  P  N  Q  I  N  X  V  Y  N  H  R  T  N  S  S  G  G  N  S
R  N  P  S  O  O  A  G  O  F  U  N  C  T  I  O  N  I  V  N
P  A  Y  S  Q  F  R  I  F  U  N  C  Y  S  O  N  S  C  Z  O
R  H  R  O  L  E  T  C  W  M  K  P  R  P  O  D  E  A  R  I
P  E  S  T  S  A  E  I  O  A  I  E  Z  O  I  A  Q  L  R  T
P  U  B  G  U  T  E  V  O  R  I  W  T  W  T  F  U  N  I  A
F  U  N  I  F  R  P  E  A  F  S  G  L  E  A  Q  C  R  X  R
V  G  T  V  U  T  E  T  S  E  E  V  D  R  R  O  Q  Z  I  I
G  O  J  T  S  O  I  I  V  E  D  Z  F  K  I  R  K  U  R  P
M  W  L  S  Y  O  T  I  N  O  R  M  S  H  P  P  X  R  M  S
X  U  T  W  N  A  R  P  S  L  P  A  T  C  S  J  O  B  O  A
C  O  F  S  S  D  I  S  S  A  T  I  S  F  I  E  R  S  M  W
```

WORK	PERSONAL NEEDS	PHYSIOLOGICAL
HIERARCHY	ROLE	SOCIAL
NEEDS	FUNCTION	SATISFIERS
CULTURE	DRIVES	DISSATISFIERS
NORMS	ASPIRATIONS	JOB
POWER	BEHAVIOUR	ENRICHMENT
STATUS	MOTIVATION	ROTATION
TASK		

Element 15.1 Review test

Performance criterion 1
1 Define an 'attitude'.
2 How can management attitudes affect the nature of work?
3 What did F W Taylor believe that it was a manager's job to do?
4 Name the **five** needs identified in the hierarchy of needs.
5 How can employers help to meet people's esteem needs?
6 Define what is meant by 'organisational culture'.
7 Who has the most power in a 'power culture'?
8 In which culture are expensive company cars and luxurious offices important?
9 How are people's attitudes at work affected by conflict between their department and another department with which they have close contact?

Performance criterion 2
10 Name the **three** needs which McClelland identified.
11 Which theory identified 'satisfiers' and 'dissatisfiers'?
12 Is salary a 'satisfier' or a 'dissatisfier'?
13 Which motivational theory emphasizes expectations as an important factor in motivation?
14 How do motivators contribute to job enrichment?
15 What is job rotation?
16 What are the disadvantages of job rotation?

Performance criterion 3
17 In which types of job is it easy to monitor employees' performance?
18 What is 'piece work'?
19 List **three** objectives of performance appraisal.
20 What is performance-related pay?

Element 15.2
EXAMINE GROUPS AT WORK

PERFORMANCE CRITERIA

1 The nature of the groups commonly found in organisations are examined
Range: nature: formal: deliberately constituted by management, may be defined
with a specific task, function or status; informal: can form without
management support, can conflict with aims of organisation.

2 Processes of group behaviour are described
Range: processes: behaviour: working methods, quantity of work carried out;
norms: conforming, shared perceptions, common attitudes, beliefs about
working methods.

**3 The contribution of groups to achievement of organisational goals is
assessed**
Range: goals: organisational, long term, short term; group goals; compatibility
with organisational goals, conflict and resolution.

4 Approaches to developing effective teams are identified and compared
Range: teams: members who co-operate and voluntarily co-ordinate activities to
achieve group objectives group purpose; membership: team workers,
innovators, chair person, resource/investigators, catalysts; stage of
development: norming, storming, performing; progress in task; life
of group.

EVIDENCE INDICATOR

A simple group task or activity requiring co-operative effort and decision making.
Individual report examining group's development and performance, including
analysis of own contribution, experience and impact on group.

Performance Criterion 1
The nature of groups commonly found in organisations

People are social beings who need to interact with other people. In everyday life we come into contact with other people – when we queue for a bus, go shopping, or when we go to work. At some time during the day we will belong to a group. These groups will either be formal or informal in nature.

Formal groups are organised with definite and clear formal structures and rules. People in the group have a common purpose and they interact on a regular basis. Examples of formal groups include businesses, colleges or football clubs. Groups of employees work together, students attend lectures and learn together, members of football teams will practise and play regularly.

Informal groups are typified by their informal structures, rules and behavioural patterns. Examples of informal groups include the family and our group of friends.

TASK

What other groups can you think of that you belong to, besides your family and friendship groups?

It is important to make a distinction between groups and associations of people. People queueing at a bus stop, for instance, have a common purpose to get on the next bus. But the queue does not act as a group – it does not have a structure or a set of rules.

THIS AREA IS SO ROUGH EVEN THE BUSES GO ROUND IN TWOS

People can also be grouped together for statistical purposes. In market research, people can be classified as having the same characteristics and be grouped together in a social group. The National Readership Survey grouped people together according to social class, income and lifestyle. Lower middle class (C1) grouping includes people who work at supervisory, clerical and junior managerial positions.

Groups which are formed are distinct from associations because they have the following features:

● a clear membership
● people know they are in the group
● the members have a shared purpose
● there is a hierarchical structure
● the members will interact with each other
● members of the group can change but the group can still exist

Formal groups

Formal groups are deliberately constituted by management and can be defined with a specific task, function or status. An organisation such as a bank has groups of individuals working together to achieve certain goals. There is a formal structure set up by management which allows them to direct, co-ordinate and communicate the organisation's activities and resources to achieve those goals.

The directors of the bank will work as a group and decide upon the goals of the organisation. They will design the policies to enable the bank to achieve those goals. Lower down the management structure there will be those people who have to implement the policies. For example, it may have been decided that the aim of the bank is to increase customer care. The marketing manager may ask his or her workers to devise an advertising campaign informing customers of this initiative. The personnel department may organise its staff to set up training courses to train the bank's personnel on how to look after their customers. In the branches of the banks it will be the banking staff in their own distinct groups, working as cashiers or machine operators, who will be the people who finally have to implement the policy of improving customer care.

For this to happen in the organisation there has to be a hierarchy based on formal groupings called 'command groups'.

Command groups

These formal groups are made up of workers and their manager. The organisational hierarchy consists of a series of overlapping command groups where the managers belong to their own command group, as well as belonging to command groups made up of their fellow managers. The managers in this formal group will report to a manager at a higher level. The managers act as linking pins (*see* Fig. 2.1 on p. 90) between various formal groups in the organisation. This allows co-ordination between managers and allows them to carry out their functions.

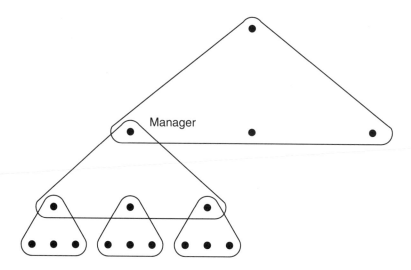

Manager

Fig. 2.1 The manager as the linking pin

Committees

Formal groups such as committees are set up in an organisation by management to deal with some type of activity. A group of individuals who form a committee are charged with a specific task. Committees can exist in all organisations at all levels. A fund raising committee may be the main committee in a charity, whereas in central government, select committees wield considerable political power. They require anyone to appear before them while they are investigating a particular problem. In local government there are committees which have specific responsibilities such as education, leisure or finance. In industry, committees might be formed to oversee the implementation of health and safety legislation.

The reason for the formation of committees is that they allow other members from the organisation to exchange ideas. Committees enable people to understand other people's problems and difficulties and lend themselves to better co-operation and co-ordination. Committees can recommend a range of suggestions to a problem and reduce the effectiveness of powerful self-interested groups. As members of a committee, people can be more honest and open because they feel protected by the committee itself. Any decisions are the decisions of the committee and not of individual members. When discussing a range of options, a number of suggestions can be put forward so that strengths and weaknesses can be fully discussed.

When people are involved in committee work and participate in decision making they identify more with the organisation.

A committee will perform well when:

- the guidelines of the committee are clearly defined.
- the committee's authority is precise and is recognised, i.e. it investigates and reports back, or makes suggestions and/or decisions.
- the size of the committee is manageable.
- the chairperson appointed is able to run the meetings efficiently and effectively.

Committees do have some disadvantages. They tend to be slow, it is difficult to get all the members together, and the discussion of topics will be slow if everyone's views are to be heard. Decisions may err on the side of caution or may be a result of compromise. No one person is responsible for the decision and by the time the decision is made, events may well have moved on and the situation changed.

Task groups

These tend to be temporary in nature and have a specific task to perform. For example, the police may set up a task force to combat a particular crime in an area.

Work teams

These can be formed as problem-solving teams where members work together to improve the quality of a product. The members of the team may come from the same department or from a servicing department.

Work teams can also be formed by the organisation to work together to make the product. They all learn the tasks involved and rotate from one job to another. This teamwork approach to production will become more important in the future as quality becomes the major force in competition.

Informal groups

These groups can be formed without management support and they tend to evolve naturally. The informal groups place a greater emphasis on personal relationships rather than a task.

The characteristics of the informal group include:

- A loose structure which allows greater flexibility.
- Membership by agreement with the group, which may be spoken or unspoken.
- Behaviour within the group controlled by the members of the group.
- Membership sought by individuals to satisfy their physiological and social needs.

The membership of the informal group will bear no relation to the formal groupings in the organisation. The membership will cut across sectional, departmental and managerial levels within the organisation.

Formation of informal groups

Informal groups are usually created for two reasons:

- to pursue a particular interest
- a friendship grouping

Interest groups are normally established because of a common interest the members have. People might group themselves together because they share the same skills – computer lecturers in a college may share the same table during their lunch, for example.

The life of the interest group will depend upon the reason for the formation. If the grouping has come about because the members have a common objective such as trying to modernise their staffroom, then as soon as the room has been refurbished, the group will disband. If the group find that it is taking longer than first thought to achieve their objective, or it appears that the battle is lost, the group may gradually disintegrate.

As an organisation gets bigger and the bureaucracy and management becomes less personal, people may begin to feel lost in the organisation. The organisation becomes more acceptable as people form friendship groups.

Another way to explain why informal groups evolve is to look at membership groupings:

Horizontal Members who form a group are of the same management level or status in an organisation. They do not necessarily work together in the same department but may share an interest. They may meet in a pub after office hours to discuss common problems at work.

Vertical Members in this group work in the same department but are at different levels. Informal meetings enable people to keep up to date with what is happening in the department and the organisation.

Lateral These groups are made up of people who cut across the boundaries of departments and levels. They can be formed because of a particular interest everyone has, or it may be a way in which people form alliances in an organisation.

Why people join informal groups

1 They give members the sense of belonging and security.
2 Informal groups maintain and reinforce the attitudes and shared ideas of the group members.

3 They help to maintain people's self-esteem.

4 The group can offer professional support to a worker. If a worker is having difficulty in coping with a task, other members of the group may pull together to help.

5 The informal group allows communication to flow more quickly. The informal network operates alongside the organisational (formal) channels of communication. This flow of information keeps the group informed on matters of interest to them.

6 People can accomplish their tasks more quickly because red tape is removed by the informal group.

7 People can advance their career more quickly. People find it easier to be 'in the know' by the use of informal channels.

Leadership

The leader of the informal group will be appointed by recognition awarded by the group's members. The leader is seen by the group as the best person to put forward their views because the leader reflects the attitude and aspirations of the group. The person who is the leader of the group is there because the group respect him or her due to his or her age, experience or personality. The person will be the group's representative when dealing with management.

The role of the informal group in an organisation

The informal group has an important role to play within the organisation because it is this grouping which influences the behaviour of individuals in the workplace. The group can apply pressure on individuals to behave according to the rules of the group rather than those expected from the organisation.

A new entrant to the organisation may well go through an induction and training programme in order to perform his or her tasks. However, the informal group will apply pressure on the individual to adhere to their informal practices. Someone who produces more than is accepted by the group will be told to 'slow down', 'not to spoil a good job', or that 'they will be putting people out of work'. If this fails to change the way someone is working then other methods may used, such as derogatory comments, sarcasm, hiding tools, spoiling work, or sending someone 'to Coventry'.

Conversely, the informal group will not accept behaviour from individuals whose work rate is below the norm, and again the group's response is to try to influence that individual's behaviour. The group will also carry out sanctions on those members who overstep the line in the relationship between workers and management.

Informal groups can be useful to organisations. For example, the group of computing lecturing staff may well discuss a common problem over lunch and during their discussions may well come up with a solution. During informal meetings of the group (after work in the organisation's social club for example) members may come up with new ideas which can be formalised back at work and if successful, save the company time and money.

The managers can use the informal communication network to their own advantage because it can actually improve communications. For example, a manager may see a member of a group over lunch and ask that person to send a mutual colleague along to see him or her to discuss a problem. This method of communication is far quicker that the normal channels of communication.

The managers can also use the informal networks to leak information of a sensitive nature to alert workers to a change in operations and gauge their response.

Why do organisations need formal groups

1 Groups are better at managing organisations

Individuals do not possess the skills and experience to manage an organisation effectively. A sole trader who operates alone is faced with all the specialist managerial functions (e.g., marketing, accounting, sales, production, packaging, delivery and purchasing) and has to perform all the functions well if the business is to succeed. He or she may not be able to do them well because of lack of skills and lack of time. A large organisation can benefit from internal economies of scale by employing specialists for managerial functions.

2 Groups can co-ordinate the activities of organisations

Groups can make sure that production is maintained through the efficient allocation of scarce resources and ensure that production is geared to the needs of its clients. The need for co-ordination is obvious when, for example, an organisation is about to launch a new product. The marketing department needs to co-ordinate its advertising and sales promotion with distribution outlets such as shops to ensure that they have sufficient supplies to meet the expected demand by customers.

3 Groups can complete complex tasks

Groups are able to complete complex tasks because there will be a wealth of experience and qualifications which an individual would not possess.

4 Groups can generate new ideas and solve problems

Groups of individuals, by pooling their knowledge and experience, are able to solve more problems. People tend to be more creative in brainstorming situations where individuals can bounce ideas off one another, solving problems or creating new ideas.

5 Groups can support individuals

Groups can represent and support individuals formally or informally within the organisation and help to motivate the individual. This support is necessary when the organisation is going through a period of change and people are unsure of the impact these changes will have on them.

Honda reaches accord in UK

The receptionist at Honda's manufacturing complex has not yet had to leave her desk to help screw widgets together on the engine assembly line. But, if asked, she is perfectly prepared to do so. Indeed, it would be expected in the unlikely event of a sudden shop-floor crisis at the Japanese car maker's £370m plant in Swindon, 80 miles west of London.

The receptionist would even be appropriately dressed. As a matter of daily routine, she wears overalls similar to those of Shojiro Miyake, managing director of Honda manufacturing in the UK and president of Honda Motor Europe. They are the same overalls that are worn by the remaining 844 employees and directors currently working at the 360-acre site.

She could find herself swapping spanners on the assembly line with Andrew Jones, the plant manager who was last week made a director of Honda UK Manufacturing. The plant inspects and tests some 40,000 Honda Concertos built for it by its Rover Group partner. The plant also makes more than 100,000 engines a year and has just started producing the first of what, by the mid-1990s, will be 100,000 Honda cars a year.

Jones makes it clear that if the need is sufficiently urgent, no one in the plant is too senior, or exempt for any other reason, from helping out on even the most humble tasks. He has no office or secretary. But then neither do any other of the plant's most senior employees, including Miyake.

There are other cultural aspects of Honda's Swindon operation which, like the status-shrouding overalls, have already acquired a familiar ring to Western ears through Japanese companies which have long preceded Honda in Europe.

Everyone at Swindon is on the same pension scheme, sick pay conditions and holiday entitlement. There is no reserved parking. Everyone uses the same changing rooms and canteen. There are no formal job descriptions and there are no workers or directors – only 'associates'.

Currently, only a handful of Accords are coming off the line each day – a result of what Jones acknowledges to be an 'obsession' with quality, and of the small teams grouped on the assembly line learning for themselves how best to organise their work.

Jones says it will be 12 to 18 months before the Swindon plant is producing at its single-shift capacity of 50,000 cars a year, so anxious is Honda to set high quality standards from the start. Nevertheless, the build-up is under way, and employment at the plant will pass the 1,000 mark in early January, *en route* to 1,500 jobs by the end of next year as single-shift capacity nears, and an eventual 2,000 in the mid-1990s.

'Teamwork' crops up in almost every sentence uttered by Jones. 'It is critical. So many people talk of good teamwork as if it's some kind of philosopher's stone. In our case it translates as an overriding objective to develop together. If you were to go out on the line, you would find no work study or industrial engineers timing everything – we expect our people to develop their own jobs and functions.'

Working in teams of four, they are said by Jones to have gained great breadth of understanding and knowledge from each other. Initial teams were formed by one Japanese person training one 'Brit'. Both would then train two more Britons. All four would train another four – and so the process continues today.

'Teamwork means that we reject class differentiation and job demarcation. We don't accept anyone as being more important than anyone else. If we are recruiting at a senior level, that recruit spends at least one month on the shop floor. So if you want high status, a secretary, and an expensive desk to keep everyone at a distance – don't come and work here,' says Jones.

All staff are involved in daily start-of-shift briefings and are fully briefed from weekly management meetings. At the start of each month all staff review with Jones and his closest associates the company's current position and operating activities as well as welcoming new 'associates'. There are also monthly 'birthday party' get-togethers in which all staff with a birthday that month meet socially, and to swap ideas with Miyake, Jones and other senior colleagues.

There are also regular 'Y-Gaya' meetings involving all groups of employees. The phrase stands for 'free, frank interchange of views'. 'The idea', says Jones, 'is continually to widen understanding and spread knowledge.'

There are now 52 'new Honda circles' – teams of six people looking for continuous improvement within defined areas that the team itself selects. They include new ideas, training, environment and safety. As an example, one 'associate' was burned while deep in the foundry area, undertaking maintenance. His circle devised a new system which now means that no one needs to enter the hazard area.

The sometimes roguishly self-named circles have plaques created in token of their achievements. Honda, says Jones, has no problem publicly acknowledging its gratitude to, among other teams, the 'Missionary Position' and 'Three Men and a Ferret'.

Adapted from: 'Honda reaches accord in UK' by John Griffiths.

Source: The Financial Times, Monday 9 November 1992

QUESTIONS

1 Why don't managers have status symbols such as offices, secretaries and reserve parking at Honda?

2 Why is production low at Honda?

3 How many different types of formal group are there at Honda?

4 What advantages are there to Honda of organising the work in teams?

5 What benefits do the employees gain from teamwork?

The processes of group behaviour

Group effectiveness

Groups are seen as a positive force in organisations. It is an accepted practice today to place people in teams – to give people something to relate to and to work for, other than their own task. People like working in groups. They feel less of a small cog in a large machine, and more of a large cog in a small part of a large machine.

The effectiveness of groups can be measured by how well the group perform their tasks (whether they hit their quota or targets, for example).

The factors which influence the behaviour of groups include the following factors:

- the individual
- the group size
- group norms
- the shaping of behaviour
- task and maintenance factors
- the cohesiveness of the group

The individual

The effectiveness of any group will be determined by the individuals in the group. Individuals need to have the necessary skills, talents and experience to carry out their task as well as being able to work with others and pursue a shared idea and purpose.

The abilities individuals bring to the group will depend on the reason for the creation of the group. In some organisations, group members will be doing the same repetitive task, such as inputting data into a computer. The skills of the operatives will be the same.

In other situations, there may be duplication of skills and abilities which is detrimental as far as output is concerned because individuals may leave work for the fellow workers to do or the duplication may lead to unhealthy competition within the group.

Where individuals have a wide variety of skills and abilities, the group will operate more effectively because these people will bring complementary skills. The strengths of one person support weaknesses in another.

The individual will have a role to play in the group which to a certain extent will depend on his or her age, skills, education and qualifications.

The role of the individual

Roles are patterns of behaviour which people expect an individual to perform. The behaviour reflects that person's position or function in society. Everyone performs more than one role during the day. A woman may be a wife, daughter, mother, customer and manager and in each case she is expected to behave in a particular way.

TASK

1 List the roles you have performed today.
2 List the roles you normally perform on a Saturday.

As you are the person concerned you are the 'focal person', and the people that you interact with are called the 'role set'.

At work a person will have to perform a number of roles. A person may be the sales manager and be the supervisor of a number of salespeople. He or she will also be a subordinate reporting to the marketing manager, and may also be the department's representative on the health and safety committee and chairman of the works' bowling team. Therefore, the way in which a person carries out a role will depend on his or her perception of the role. This perception will be determined by intelligence, training, expectations, past experience, personality and motivation.

As a society we have expectations about how people should behave. For example, doctors' and lawyers' behaviour is defined in legal and cultural terms. There are clear rules of behaviour and if these are broken, doctors or lawyers can be barred from practising their professions. When we visit a medical centre we expect a certain pattern of behaviour from the doctor when he or she carries out the consultation.

Role signs

People look for signs which help to clarify a person's role. The signs help people to be aware of how to behave when they meet another person. In hospital we might be a little perplexed if the person we thought was a doctor was wearing a brown coat instead of the normal white coat. We normally expect a manual worker to wear a brown coat. If we visited a medical consultant we would probably find him or her wearing a business suit instead of the white coat.

Other signs we might look for are found in the environment where the person is carrying out his or her role. The furniture in an office will give a clue to the role played – a junior manager may have a desk, a more senior manager may have a desk and carpet. If a manager has to share an office, it indicates that his or her role is not as important as the manager's who has his or her own office.

Role ambiguity

In some cases a person may become unsure about what his or her role is, and just how much responsibility and control he or she has. This ambiguity may cause problems for the person concerned, as well as for members in the role set.

If a manager is not clear about his or her job remit then it may cause a lack of confidence from subordinates. If he or she overstretches his or her authority, colleagues may be offended.

Role incompatibility

The role of a person may be seen in different terms by different people. Someone who holds a supervisory position is expected to behave in a particular way by the workers and in another way by management, so the supervisor is 'piggy in the middle'. The incompatibility is made worse if the supervisor sees his or her role as helping and supporting staff, but the senior management would prefer more direction from the supervisor.

Role overload

Individuals can have difficulty with the number of roles that they have to perform. The junior manager who is also a subordinate may face role conflict because there may be a difficulty in prioritising roles. Matters are made worse if there are pressures from the domestic roles he or she is expected to fulfill.

Role underload

Some individuals may feel devalued because they are not performing the role they think they are capable of. The person who has been passed over in promotion will feel rejected and that person's performance may deteriorate accordingly.

Group size

Group size is a major influence on a group's effectiveness. Too few members to perform the task is likely to put the group members in a stressful situation: too many and members will get in each other's way or will be underperforming, often due to communication problems.

The ideal size will depend upon the task the group has to perform. Size is important because of its effects on group leadership, group members, and the group process (*see* Table 2.1 on page 102).

The size of the group will influence the behaviour of the leader of the group. A small group may require less direction and control compared to a large group. For example, the proceedings within a meeting of a small group may be less formal compared to a large group. In the large group, people may only be allowed to speak at the invitation of the chairperson.

Table 2.1

Factors	Group size (number of members)		
	2–7	8–12	13–16
Leadership			
Demand on leader	low	moderate	high
Differences between leader and member	low	low to moderate	moderate to high
Direction of leader	low	low to moderate	moderate to high
Membership			
Tolerance of direction from leader	low to high	moderate to high	high
Domination of group interaction by a few members	low	moderate to high	high
Inhibition in participation by ordinary members	low	moderate	high
Group process			
Formalisation of rules and procedures	low	low to moderate	moderate to high
Time required for reaching decisions	low to moderate	moderate	moderate to high
Tendency for subgroups to form	low	moderate to high	high

As the group gets larger there is always the danger that subgroups may form which may have their own agendas which could be at variance to the formal agenda.

The larger the group the longer it takes to reach a decision. The decision reached is normally after much debate and can be a result of compromise to appease conflicting views from subgroups in the formal group.

The size of the group will change over time as reasons for the group's existence change. For example, a small team might be brought together to develop a new project. As the project develops, so the membership may increase to meet the extra demands and this increase in group size will change demands on the leaders, members and group processes. Management must be careful about who to add to the group so that the group does not become unbalanced.

When organisations face an economic downturn, the problem managers have to face is who to remove from the group. The aim is usually to reduce costs. The organisation may have a policy on redundancy such as 'last in first out', or those who stay are those the company has invested heavily in through education and training. Those who do stay are likely to experience disruption, and may have to take on additional duties which they resent or lack training for.

An aspect management needs to take into account when laying off a member from the formal group is that the person chosen may be a key member of the informal group. This may upset the composition and structure of the informal group. Costs may be reduced in the short term but the group could work less effectively and have more long term consequences for the organisation.

The optimum size of the group will include members who have a variety of skills and experience. The size of the group will influence the behaviour of those who participate in the group's activities. To some, a large group may appear intimidating and they may not want to be involved with group activities outside their own task. In meetings, they might not want to be involved in discussion. Others who have more self-confidence may contribute to the decisions and influence the group decisions just by their willingness to put forward their views. The group may reach a solution to a problem not based on the talents or experience vital to the decision but because of the dominating views of the more forthright people.

Group norms

A group norm is a shared perception of how things should be done, or is a shared attitude, feeling or belief. At work there will be norms which spill over from society and there will be those norms created and established in the workplace. The norms from society may include behaviour related to politeness and tact when interacting with others. The norms created by the group will be concerned with:

The task This refers to how the task should be accomplished, the time spent on it, the standards of quality and the units completed. Individuals who produce more than the group norm are referred to as 'rate busters'. Those who produce less than the group norm are called 'chiselers'.

Non-task activities This refers to those activities which are not task-related but occur in the workplace and are concerned with group standards such as the standard of dress to be worn in the workplace, the time taken for lunch breaks, what people do after they arrive at work and before they get down to the job.

Communication These norms establish how members of the group communicate with each other and rest of the workforce – the type of language, whether it is abusive, or if it is a language which includes words and phrases only understood by the group.

Attitude This refers to the members' general feeling about the organisation, the work and their behaviour to others, especially management. Anyone who says anything to management which would cause a problem for another individual in the group is known as a 'squealer'.

Norms only apply to behaviour and not to the thoughts and feelings of individuals. They tend to develop in relation to those factors the group deem to be important, such as pride in their work and the organisation, supervision, teamwork, planning and profitability. Norms tend to develop over time and are difficult to change. No one individual has any great impact on norms but a dominant individual may well influence them.

There are two types of norms:

Positive These norms influence the group behaviour which helps the organisation to achieve its goals. This may be that the workers take a pride in their work and the resulting output is of high quality and little waste is made.

Negative These norms work against the goals of the organisation. Examples of negative norms include stealing or the condoning of theft from the organisation such as inflating travel expenses.

The problem facing the new member of the group is that he or she will not know which behaviours are considered to be correct or incorrect, because there is nothing in writing to refer to and the rules regarding informal behaviour are unspoken. As time passes the new recruit learns, understands and follows the group rules.

One of the major problems facing management is introducing changes to the organisation which affect the way in which groups work. Many operations do not follow the rule book but people carry out their function following the precedents laid down over the years, i.e. custom and practice.

If change is introduced which does not recognise the informal operations of the group, management will find the changes are met with reluctance, hostility and resistance. Managers may be able to change the working practices of groups by a shared power strategy. This process is a normative re-education strategy and is based on empowerment and participation. Change is brought about by involving people in examining personal needs, values, group norms, and encouraging people to work together to plan change and give them the power to make decisions which affect the way they work. By this method management can influence the setting of group norms.

PROBLEM-SOLVING ACTIVITY

Imagine you have just won the state lottery and you are now a multi-millionaire. Deciding to pamper yourself, you book a world cruise. You are having the time of your life as you sail through the Pacific Ocean. You fall asleep one afternoon as you are soaking up the sun. You are wearing a T-shirt and jeans to protect you from the hot sun and on your lap is the book you have been reading. Next to your chair is a small table with a cool drink.

You wake up to find yourself alone in the sea and no ship in sight. The sea is dead calm and you can see an island in the distance. You swim towards it and finally lie exhausted on the white sandy beach. Checking yourself for cuts and broken bones you realise very quickly that you are naked except for your leather belt around your waist, fastened by a large brass buckle.

Somewhat shaken, you start to take in your surroundings. The island is deserted although there is plenty of vegetation and in the distance you can hear the sound of a waterfall, the squawking of birds and strange animal noises.

- How are you going to survive?

Your only assets are your belt and buckle.

- How many uses can you think of for your belt which will help you to survive on the island until you are rescued?

Now work in groups of four and share your ideas.

- How many ideas as a group are there? (Someone will have to record the ideas.)

Using the ideas from each other:

- How many uses can the whole group come up with?

While you are doing this activity, try to explain to the rest of the group how you ended up in the sea, alone and only wearing a leather belt.

1 When you got into groups what was the process for sharing the ideas? Who was the first person to share their ideas? Did you take turns in sequence around the table? How was the order of sharing ideas decided?

2 Did the person who contributed first become the leader of the group?

3 Did anyone assume the role of leader?

4 Who recorded the information? Why did this person do this task – were they elected, did they volunteer, or was someone appointed by the group?

5 Did everyone make a contribution to the ideas?

6 What was the procedure for contributing to the list?

7 Did the group have a discussion on each point?

8 How did the group agree on what should be added to the list?

9 Did anyone dominate the activity? If so, why did the group allow that to happen?

10 Were there any changes in leadership as the activity progressed?

11 Who was the person who reported back to the class? How was this person chosen?

12 Did you work harder on your own or in the group?

13 If you were going to do a similar activity again what would you do to improve
   • your performance?
   • the performance of the group?

The shaping of behaviour

Conformity

People who belong to groups have to conform or agree to the behaviour of the group. However, individuals can conform by outwardly agreeing with the group, while inwardly disagreeing. A new recruit may join an all male department where an aggressive masculine behaviour is expected by the group members. The new entrant may also display the same behaviour but not agree with it personally.

Internalisation is where people conform because they wish to follow the group's behaviour and this is done by the process of socialisation.

Socialisation

This is the process where a group will modify the behaviour of an individual who joins, and at the same time the new entrant will influence the group's behaviour. Socialisation is a continual process of adaptation by the individual to their physical, psychological and social environment through their interaction with other people.

Conditioning

People are conditioned into behaving in a particular way by the response to their behaviour. Behaviour which is accepted will be praised; behaviour which is unacceptable will be punished. The way an individual behaves in a formal group will be influenced by the conditioning the individual receives from the informal group. A person may prefer the praise from colleagues in the informal group rather than from the manager, so that the praise given by the manager may not have the intended effect. That person cannot be easily manipulated, influenced or controlled by rewards from the formal leader. The offering of incentives by management to individuals to work harder, improve quality, or produce more may have little effect if the individual operates in a group which does not value incentives.

Imitation

People learn how to behave by observing and imitating behaviour. Training is a form of imitation, i.e. being shown what to do. When a new person joins an organisation, how are they going to be shown what to do? Will they be taught 'off' or 'on' the job? Off the job training means that the entrant will be instructed outside the normal work environment and can be taught to do a job according to the regulations laid down by the company or the formal organisation. On the job training means that he or she will be allocated an instructor who is working on the production process and the new entrant is shown how to do the job as it is being done. This means that the new recruit is expected to follow the instructions of the worker while picking up the values of the informal group at the same time.

In a situation where the group is task-orientated, with members working together and sharing skills and experience, the newcomer will imitate the co-operative behaviour of the group members. Wanting to be like the others will be the motivator to work in a particular way.

Identification

Identification is the acceptance of another person's values and attitudes. People see others behaving in a particular way and will imitate their behaviour. They will want to be identified with that person. For example, the manager who always wears a dark suit, whose desk is always clear, whose door is always open, who has time to talk to his subordinates, and who does the job efficiently may well have the values a junior wishes to imitate.

Perception

Perception is the way in which people see things and interpret the behaviour of others. It is a person's viewpoint on a situation. The way in which a person understands situations depends upon his or her own values, needs, cultural backgrounds and circumstances of the moment.

People need to be aware of situations so that they know how to behave in them. They need to know what other people are likely to do. For example, when a person goes to a football match for the first time and his or her team scores a goal, he or she will know from the behaviour of the other fans that it is acceptable to chant, cheer and shout support.

If a person is formally introduced to members of a group, he or she will normally extend a hand to be shaken and smile at the person they have come into contact with. Over time, members of the group may just say 'hello' and smile rather than shake hands each time they meet.

What people see is not always as it seems. People may interpret the same situation differently, depending upon their experience of dealing with people and the situation itself.

In a room crowded with people a man may whisper something to a woman. This may give the impression to an observer that the two are conspiring. Someone else may think they are being rude, and another may believe something untoward is going on. In fact, the man is whispering to his wife that her slip is showing.

In many situations we only perceive information we wish to receive and reject all other stimuli. When we go to the cinema, we become engrossed in the film and forget the rest of the audience. People choose to perceive the things they want to pay attention to.

TASK

Sit in a room and tape the noises. Before playing back the tape list the noises you remember. Play back the tape and identify those noises you did not notice.

In some situations people only have part of the information and fill in the gaps unconsciously because they expect things to happen in a certain way. People tend to assume that because something is always done in a certain way it will continue to be so.

Look at Box A and look at Box B in Fig. 2.2. What is different about the boxes?

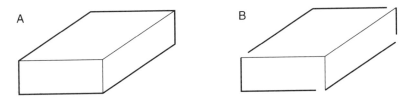

Fig. 2.2

In other situations we see what we want to see even though the evidence may be against it. Look at Fig.2.3. Which is the longer line?

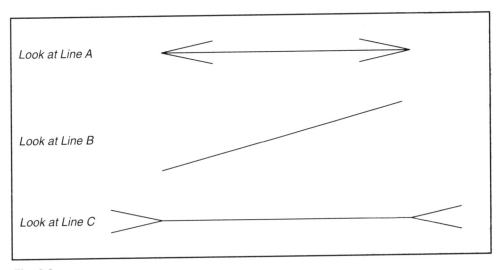

Fig. 2.3

Look at Fig. 2.4. What do you see?

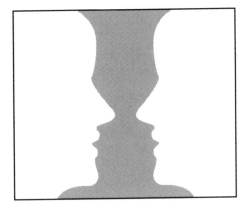

Fig. 2.4

Is it a vase or the profiles of two men?

What we see is the vase *or* the profiles. We organise the patterns so that we see one first, set against a background which we see later. The way in which a person behaves has to be set in context – this is why people are surprised when someone behaves out of character. The person is perhaps reacting to a situation he or she does not normally find him or herself in.

Understanding different perceptions

Perceptional differences occur when the way in which a person sees him or herself differs from how others see him or her. A manager may think of him or herself as democratic in style, able to listen to people's views and act on their suggestions, and always having an open door. Subordinates perhaps see him or her as someone lazy who has abdicated responsibility. This difference in perception can be illustrated by a comparison of views in Fig. 2.5.

The differences shown in Fig. 2.5 will help to explain why people may behave differently to their manager's expectations.

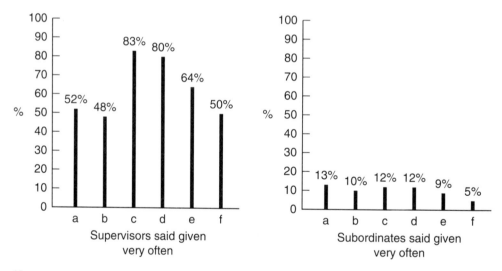

Key

a Gives privileges
b Gives more responsibility
c Gives a pat on the back
d Gives sincere and thorough praise
e Trains for better jobs
f Gives more interesting jobs

Fig. 2.5 Ways in which supervisors may recognise subordinates for high performance

Stereotypes

This occurs where individuals are identified with a particular group. Young people, old people, students, unemployed, unmarried mothers, male, female. The person is classified because of one feature, for example, age, sex, colour. This can create biased perceptions of individuals and create problems. For women, one of the problems they face at work is the lack of opportunity for promotion. They are faced with invisible barriers, and some women feel that they have been treated unfairly because of bias against women.

The problem facing a manager is that stereotyping makes it difficult for managers to assess the individual differences of people at work. This may adversely affect the organisation because the manager may select the wrong person for the task.

TASK

A. Consider the three sets of statements below:

1 (a) He is having lunch with the boss
   (b) She is having lunch with the boss

2 (a) He is not in the office
   (b) She is not in the office

3 (a) He is talking to his fellow workers
   (b) She is talking to her fellow workers

How do you interpret these situations? Do you draw the same conclusion for the man as for the woman?

B. Select a range of job adverts. Are there ways in which the advertiser discriminates, e.g. sex, age, gender or other?

Halo effects

This occurs when one attribute of a person creates the overall impression of them. The way in which a person behaves at a first meeting will create an impression which is difficult to change.

The first impression is the way people expect others to behave and eventually people will perform to the perceptions others have of them. The manager who tells his team they are the best will perform well whereas an individual who is always being pulled up for making mistakes although their individual performance is on a par with their team members may eventually make more mistakes than they do.

Conflict

Conflict can occur with perceptions. For example, if a manager values perfection, worries about small things and decides that his or her subordinates should have the same values by instilling discipline into them to make sure that everything is done to order, their performance may decline. This will be particularly true for those subordinates who enjoy new challenges and problem solving, and may feel as if they are being suffocated. A manager needs to be aware of individual needs to allow people to perform.

Task and maintenance behaviours

If the group is going to work well together over time, there are two types of activities which the group must perform.

1 **Task activities** are those which are directed towards reaching the goals of the group.
2 **Maintenance activities** are those concerned with keeping the group together as a social system and making sure it operates as a group.

It is normally the job of the leader to carry out these activities but all members of the group can share in them.

Task activities

Initiating	This is concerned with proposing tasks or goals and suggesting ideas and ways for solving that problem.
Seeking information or opinions	Seeking out information about the situation under consideration and finding out people's views, ideas and suggestions. Enables informed judgements to be made.

Giving information or opinions	People offer information, opinions and views on situations and are willing to make suggestions to help solve a problem.
Clarifying and elaborating	This involves the interpretation of ideas, clarifying points and proposing alternative ideas.
Summarising	This activity takes place after ideas have been put forward and discussions have taken place. It pulls together people's thoughts and ideas and offers solutions on the evidence offered.
Consensus testing	Making sure that the group accepts its decision.

Maintenance activities

Listening	Listening to other people's thoughts, ideas and suggestions. Giving full attention when someone else is speaking.
Harmonising	Reducing tension, bringing people together who are in disagreement.
Gatekeeping	Making sure that each member of the group participates in the discussions. Allowing relevant information to flow freely.
Encouraging	Supporting contributions from members, being warm and friendly to others.
Compromising	Looking for workable alternatives as solutions to problems.

Members of the group will also be involved in reducing activities which distract the group from reaching their goal. Disruptive behaviour by individuals may take place at any time during the life of the group and other group members should behave in a way which either reduces or eliminates the distractions. Disruptive behaviour includes:

- being aggressive
- blocking
- sympathy pleading
- withdrawal
- competing
- special pleading
- playing games or telling jokes
- seeking recognition

Group cohesiveness

How well the group works together will depend on how the members feel towards each other. This will be determined by the formal process the group works with as well as the informal norms established in the formal group. The greater the cohesiveness, the more chance that the group will achieve its goals. It also means that if the group get on well then they will operate more effectively and efficiently and will have a high positive work performance. It is one of the jobs of the leader to encourage group cohesiveness and this can be done through the following methods:

1 Making sure that the group have a general understanding and agree on the goals.
2 Allowing communications to flow freely between members.
3 Encouraging interaction between members.
4 Ensuring that the size of the group is not too large, which could lead to the creation of subgroups or the isolation of individual members.
5 Encouraging participation by all members of the group.
6 Ensuring that individuals benefit from being part of the group.

A problem with groups which become too involved with their work and one another is 'group think'. This occurs when the group becomes oversensitive, and its members shy away from criticising individual ideas to avoid any conflict within the group. The desire to hold the group together and avoid disagreements may lead to poor decision making.

In extreme cases, the group may actually all agree with one another on a project and outsiders who disagree or present evidence to show that the project is unworkable are ignored.

CASE STUDY

Teamwork at LoDan Electronics Inc

LoDan make cables and connectors for electronic equipment. Their customers are mainly companies which manufacture computers.

One hundred and fifty people are employed at the Arlington Heights branch of LoDan in Illinois. It is a small manufacturing company and has a very friendly and welcoming atmosphere.

Human resources manager, Danielle Rossini, designed a teambuilding programme especially for LoDan employees. 'My programme focuses on situations everyone can identify with.' Teams went through a two-week class in which everyone met for an hour per week. They were removed from their

Danielle Rossini

normal working environment and had classes in the meeting room in the offices at Arlington Heights. They were given everyday problems to discuss such as:

- 'The car has broken down, what do we do?'
- 'How can we make some toast?'

The problems were designed so that everyone could contribute and were not bound by their normal work roles.

There are 18 different teams and most of them consist of people who work in different areas of LoDan, making them cross-functional teams.

'In the past, people had no idea what others from different departments were talking about. The biggest thing teamwork has done is to open up lines of communication,' explains Danielle.

Previously, management made all the decisions; now employees have new powers to make some decisions. 'Now managers are leaders and coaches instead of dictators and diplomats. It's a completely different way of running a company.'

The 'No More Tangles' team

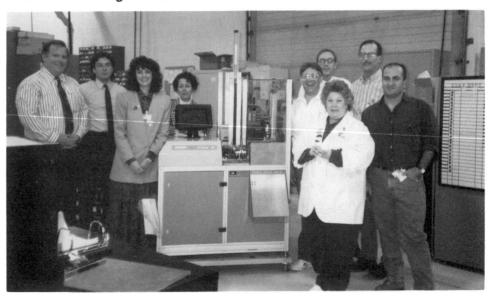

Rosaleen Dietrich is the teamleader for a problem-solving team called No More Tangles. Ten people formed the team one year ago with the objective of reducing the cycle time of a product. The product was a component for a police car. The cycle time is the time taken from the receipt of the materials from the supplier to make the product, to the delivery of the product to the customer. The No More Tangles team discovered that to complete this cycle took 57 different steps. The team reduced this to only 11 steps.

The team consisted of people from the warehouse, quality assurance, manufacturing, sales, engineering and human resources management. This brought in a lot of different perspectives as everyone in the team knew about different aspects of the process. Rosaleen and Danielle were from human resources management and they therefore knew very little about the technical aspects of the work. They brought a fresh perspective to the problem and their constant questioning as to why things were done in the traditional way made the people who knew the most about the process question it themselves.

The teamleader's function was to help the group focus on the task, to smooth things over when people took up defensive positions, and to make sure that the team met their goals. The method by which the number of processes was reduced from 57 to 11 was as follows:

- A flowchart was drawn, identifying all the processes the product went through.
- Those processes which did not add value to the customer were identified.
- The processes which did not add value were eliminated.

Processes which do not add value are such things as moving equipment around the factory and people walking to the stores department to collect materials – anything which does not directly contribute to making the final product.

One of the results of cutting out all non-value added steps is the introduction of a 'dock to cell' programme. Each product is produced in a small 'cell' factory. Goods are received, manufactured and shipped to the customer in the same cell. It is a self-contained area with all the necessary materials and equipment on hand. The same cell is used for the manufacture of similar products. There are five cells in total in the factory.

The problem took the team four months to solve. This same process has been applied to other product lines by the No More Tangles team.

'People on the shopfloor are excited to see what is going to happen to their product process,' comments Rosaleen.

The continual change, development and improvement in LoDan is keeping them at the forefront of their industry.

QUESTIONS

1 Why did teams at LoDan discuss everyday problems like how to make toast, instead of ones concerned with their work?

2 What benefits are there from having cross-functional teams (teams made up of people from different areas or departments of the company)?

3 What difference has the work of the No More Tangles team made to LoDan?

Performance Criterion 3

The contribution of groups to achievement of organisational goals

Goals

A goal is a future state, an expectation, something someone is striving to accomplish. Goals may be long or short term. George's goals in life may be:

LONG TERM: to start my own business, to live abroad

SHORT TERM: to pass my exams, to get into the diving team

Organisational goals

Organisations do not have goals, people do. Organisational goals are established by senior management. When senior managers change, the goals of the organisation often change as well.

Organisations often have more than one goal. They often make their goals known publicly and call it their **mission statement**. Mission statements are displayed on noticeboards, printed on company literature, and some American firms give their employees cards with the mission statement on it to carry around in their pocket with them.

The mission statement for Motorola Inc of the USA is:

We will grow rapidly by providing our worldwide customers with what they want, when they want it, with Six Sigma quality and best-in-class cycle time, as we strive to achieve our fundamental corporate objective TOTAL CUSTOMER SATISFACTION.

Each employee has a Total Customer Satisfaction card which they can keep with them at all times to remind them of the organisation's objectives.

Fig. 2.6 The Motorola objective card

Reasons for goals

1 **Goals provide a direction for members of the organisation**. Employees should know what their organisation is aiming for so that their efforts can be in line with it.

2 **Goals provide a standard for performance**. People know what is expected of them and what standards they need to achieve in their own work.

3 **Goals provide a basis for planning and control for managers**. Managers cannot make any plans without goals. If the organisation is not going anywhere in particular then there is no need to control the activities of the employees. The organisation will become more of a community and drop-in centre than a company which provides products or services.

4 **Goals reduce uncertainty in decision making**. It is very difficult for managers to take decisions if they are not sure where the organisation is headed. If they understand that costs are to be kept low as part of a short term goal, this will help them to decide on such matters as whether to have the offices redecorated or how to respond to a supplier increasing their prices.

5 **Goals help to develop commitment among employees to the activities of the organisation**. Employees often do not fully understand what is happening in their organisation or why it is happening. Making the organisation goals clear to all employees helps them feel part of the organisation.

6 **Goals provide a basis from which to monitor achievements.** When an organisation has goals, the members of the organisation have a direction to head for and they can measure whether they have arrived, or how far yet they have to go.

Long term organisational goals

Possible long term goals may be:

- profit
- survival
- growth

Like long-range weather forecasts, long term goals are far less certain than short term goals. There is a much greater vagueness about what we would like to be doing in five years' time than what we will be doing tomorrow. The long term goal is still necessary as it provides a direction for short term goals and allows planning to take place.

Short term organisational goals

Short term goals are part of long term goals. They are for specific time periods and their achievement will lead the organisation towards the attainment of the long term goal.

The owner of a new business may have the short term goal of surviving for the first year and beginning to make a profit after the second year. The long term goal is to be profitable by increasing amounts. It is necessary for the owner to draw up a plan as to how survival will be achieved for the first year. Ensuring that bank loans are not so large that the business will not be able to afford the interest repayments, that there are no sudden rises in rent during the year, that the company advertises its services and retains its customers are all points to consider in the plan.

TASK

A. Which of the following goals are long term and which are short term in the following list of goals for a new ice-cream parlour opening in a city centre site with three employees?

1 Provide a relaxed and pleasant atmosphere for customers.
2 Retain the services of the three employees.
3 Open a string of ice-cream parlours around the UK.
4 Take over all the competition in the city.
5 Provide the best ice-cream in the city at the lowest possible price.
6 Provide a family experience for all ages.

B. In groups, discuss the following:

1 Make a list of ten goals you think organisations may have.
2 What would be your long and short term goals if you were just setting up in business?
3 Make up a mission statement for your imaginary business.
4 What advantages are there to organisations emphasising their goals to their employees? If you have ever worked, did you know the organisational goals? What difference to your work did knowing or not knowing make?
5 List your personal long and short term goals for the next five years. What skills and experience have you at the moment which will help you to achieve them?
6 What skills need to be enhanced or learnt to enable you to achieve your goals?
7 What barriers or problems do you foresee which may hinder your progress in achieving your personal goals?

Group goals

Groups and teams within organisations should have clearly defined and well communicated goals. Plans should be developed for the achievement of the goals and the work should be monitored to ascertain how far the goals have been achieved. When changes need to be made, all the team should be informed of the reasons and the nature of the change.

The goals of every group or team in the organisation should be very clearly linked to the organisation's goals. Once long and short term goals have been decided upon, plans will be drawn up for achieving them. These plans will include all functions or departments in the organisation and the groups within them. For example:

- **Short term goal** – to increase sales by 5 per cent
- **Marketing team's goal** – to devise advertisements and sales promotions
- **Sales team's goal** – to increase sales by offering the new sales promotion strategies devised by the marketing team
- **Production team's goal** – to increase production by at least 5 per cent in order to meet the expected increase in demand

Other departments and teams will follow similar patterns of activity to enable them to meet the short term goal. If one department or group does not pursue their goal, the organisational goal will fail. The production department may not wish to work more hours to increase production. Unless there is adequate stock to meet the increase in demand, all the sales promotions and advertising campaigns will have been a waste of money and effort.

Compatability with organisational goals

If groups merely had the goal of achieving the task as their sole aim in life, there would be no problems or conflicts between the group and their role in the organisation.

Teams often have goals which may or may not be compatible with organisational goals:

The work objectives

Some groups have not defined their purpose and members are unclear as to the group's goals. The goal may have been clear at one time, but has now been overtaken by events or been forgotten. If planning is haphazard and people at lower levels of the group are not involved, there will be confusion and a shifting of aims between different priorities.

Development

Development means improving team functioning. People may be more concerned with the way individuals work together than with getting the job done. A weak leader may allow dominant personalities to put their own goals as priorities and neglect the task the group should be working on. Another leader may be demotivated as he or she has reached the maximum salary or promotion point and now wants an easy life. If this is the case, it is easier to allow the group to do as they think best with no guidance or co-ordination. Some groups may find that carrying out their work conflicts with the social aspect of being in a group as it takes them away from the work station, or they may need silence or to talk to customers instead of other group members. This may cause the work to be neglected or done quickly and badly in order that group members can return to one another's company and not feel that they have missed anything.

Status

Status refers to the team's standing within the organisation or the world as a whole. Individuals and groups may benefit in terms of salary, benefits, career plans and prestige from the reputation of their group. Certain groups such as researchers, or sales and marketing teams may be able to make a reputation for themselves both within and outside the organisation, more so than the wages department or accounts receivables. Some groups are motivated by 'empire building' which means that they manage to get more resources for themselves in terms of staff, accommodation and equipment. Their aim is not to achieve organisational goals but to look important.

Intergroup competition

Without any competition, the organisation may stagnate, with everyone feeling that there is no incentive to change or improve. Very high levels of competition between groups in the organisation causes a conflict situation in which people may feel anxious and tense. Competing with another group may become a group's main objective rather than achieving their organisational goals. Jealousy and rivalry may waste group and management time. Some groups may deliberately set out to sabotage another group's work, costing the organisation money or lost business.

Workers may compete with management for control over their situation. The Hawthorne Studies, carried out in the USA during the 1930s, found that one group of workers restricted their output, despite the existence of a piece rate system. Group norms dictated that all group members should only produce a certain amount. The workers themselves were controlling production, and they would not allow management to control it.

Conflict within groups

Group members may differ as to which task is carried out, the way the work is carried out and who does it. There may be more than one task to do and opinions may vary about which is the most important. The group may be too large, and different cliques or factions form which take up opposing positions. Personality clashes, arguments, people not speaking to one another or being absent due to unpleasantness are all detrimental to the attainment of organisational goals.

Resolution of the conflict between goals

Different problems require different measures to cure them. Some ideas for easing the problems described are:

1 Understanding of the organisational and group goals should be clear to everyone in the organisation. Good communication is essential.
2 Involving the employees in the setting up of goals helps them to feel committed to them.
3 Checks should be made, such as at appraisal interviews, that everyone, especially the manager or leader of the group, understands and is committed to the goals.
4 Social activities and staffrooms for breaks help people to feel that they do have a social life at work. They also separate out the socialising from the work.
5 Groups should be treated fairly and those campaigning for more or better facilities should not be rewarded at the expense of others.
6 Reward the achievement of group and organisational goals. Encourage cooperation and interaction between groups with a record of disharmony. Stress some 'common enemy', such as external competitors or the goals themselves, as an entity to be overpowered.
7 Rotate group members between other departments and groups so that they can experience the problems other groups have and appreciate the talents and expertise present in the organisation.

The contribution of groups to organisational goals

When groups work well they can contribute greatly to organisational success. They also help members to meet personal goals, such as their social needs.

Groups are useful as they can:

- contribute to the solution of problems in the sharing and development of ideas
- encourage creativity and innovation
- improve the quality of decisions taken
- increase members' commitment to tasks and the organisation
- raise motivation by doing things together
- help control and discipline members themselves without outside interference from management
- satisfy individual needs

The Body Shop

From left to right: Ingrid, Pat, Jill (assistant manager), Jane (manager)

Jane Henshall has been manager of The Body Shop in Hanley, Staffordshire, since a few weeks after its opening four years ago. There are 14 members of staff which include a cleaner and two part-time staff who work on Saturdays. Other part-time staff work 25, 20 or 16 hours per week. In the busy weeks before Christmas extra people are taken on and the staff total rises to 19.

The ten staff who were working in the store in July 1991 have formed a partnership and are buying the right to a franchise from The Body Shop. They do not have to finance it personally; the payments to The Body Shop will come from profits.

They have formed themselves into a limited company called Veer Ltd. 'We wanted a short name, something to show the change of direction,' says Jane Henshall. The store will remain The Body Shop with the same product range of hair and skin preparations.

'Part of The Body Shop philosophy is to empower staff and give opportunities for staff to develop themselves.'

Giving the business to the staff seems to be the ultimate in empowering the workers.

'The Body Shop benefit financially as they get back a percentage of profits year on year. Instead of having us as their staff, they've managed costs. We give them money to do our payroll – we're not part of their payroll, they act as an agency for us. We pay them the money for our bills, so they get revenue from us.'

Performance Criterion 1: The nature of groups commonly found in organisations

New employees, and temporary employees who become permanent, have the option to buy into the partnership scheme, although, in the Hanley branch there is no staff turnover. The one employee on Youth Training has her wages increased in line with other members of staff when temporary staff are engaged such as during the Christmas period. Everyone earns the same hourly wage regardless of length of service. 'They're doing the same work,' says Jane.

On the staffroom door there is a family tree diagram with pictures of members of staff on it. This was begun in 1991 when the partnership was first set up and the collective feeling of the team started.

The ten partners who are buying the franchise have entered into an agreement with The Body Shop which strongly affiliates them to the principles by which The Body Shop is run. One of the stipulations is that the partnership cannot worsen conditions of employment for their staff, but they do have discretion over the adoption of certain benefits.

'As a group, if we can't afford it, we don't have to have it. It needs to be decided democratically, and it might be either benefits or bonus,' says Jane.

At the last meeting of the board of directors (Jane, plus one other manager, two members of staff and a representative from the Body Shop International) the board discussed benefits. The Body Shop are proposing to introduce permanent health care insurance – for employees who do not work for periods of up to six months, salary will be paid at 90 per cent of the normal rate. Also The Body Shop is introducing pensions for employees with more than one year's service. It will also be possible to buy or sell extra weeks of holiday. At present those with one year's service have 22 days' holiday, 27 days after five years and 32 days after ten years. The payroll department of The Body Shop will add on or deduct money from salaries according to whether people wish to take more or less holiday than their annual allowance. Also, the possibility of introducing childminding vouchers was discussed. The management of Veer Ltd will probably implement a mixture of these benefits.

The board also discussed the current financial position, Sunday trading and public relations. As a result, Alison, the assistant manager, has been made public relations officer to concentrate on marketing the Hanley Body Shop. The Body Shop does not advertise, so Alison's job will be to promote the shop through media such as talks, make-up fairs, bridal make-up shows and sales. The local newspaper will be taking part in The Body Shop's endangered species competition shortly.

The Body Shop has three managers: Jane: manager, Jill: deputy manager, and Alison: assistant manager. Other staff are sales assistants, except for Ingrid who is a sales specialist and is also the shop's bookkeeper. Alison takes charge of cashing up and public relations. Jill orders stock and carries out the administration for the shop. These tasks are not exclusively undertaken by these members of staff. 'Everyone can turn their hand to everything,' Jane points out.

Jane does not consider that there is any conflict between groups in the organisation and the aims of the organisation. 'Like any organisation, some people get on with some better than others. We're such a small band of people that everyone has to get on or there would be ructions. I think we all get on with each other.

'You generally pull together. People often go out socially together. You do get little cliques. It sometimes can affect the work, but only in that those who are not involved in what is being talked about might be annoyed. It's not a problem. We're all quite close here and it's quite a social place to work.'

Pat, a sales assistant, says, 'The social events are open to everyone. They may not come because they have other commitments. We mould, it's like a family.'

Performance Criterion 2: Processes of group behaviour

Jane explains how the work is divided: 'My job is to oversee what goes on. Alison's job description is to do cashing up, cash control and security. Jill orders stock and I see that the stock ordering is done. They all know how to do one another's job. Everything overlaps, it's informal. There are certain people I would ask to change the window display and not others. It's making the most of people's talents.

'There's never nothing to do. After Christmas, everything is remerchandised, dusted, priced. People might feel bored but there's always something to do. It's a very interesting job. Having worked in other shops I can see that here there's more to it. We help and advise people, learn about new products, do our own refills, make up gift baskets. Staff do a lot with their own ideas. Some ideas are not compatible with what The Body Shop would allow, or are not salesworthy. We try something once to see whether it works, we take it off after a week if it doesn't sell.'

'Its hard work here,' comments Pat. 'It's not a glamourous job. We get involved with fund raising and lots of activities outside of work.'

Ingrid feels that all staff are sensitive to one another's feelings. 'When you've worked with someone for four years, you're open, you sense problems.'

The group of partners and employees have seen their relationship develop strongly over the last four years. 'Sometimes we've wanted to kill one another, but it's got a lot better as the four years have gone by. It has taken a while for relationships to build up,' says Jill.

Performance Criterion 3: The contribution of groups to the achievement of organisational goals

There is a mission statement in the Hanley The Body Shop and the company has a strong sense of social responsibility. 'As a company we do have a lot of moral mission statements,' says Jane.

The main goal for Jane and her team this year is to increase sales by 5 per cent on the previous year. Other goals are to reflect a flagship shop (creating the best image for the company), to provide good training for staff, to obtain a commercial return from each product range, to attain a multi-skilled staff team and to have a commitment to community projects which do not bring direct revenue to the company. Two members of staff from Hanley visit a special school each week to give massage to the children there. They also raise money for them.

'At the moment sales are one per cent higher than last year. If we have a good Christmas it might be 5 per cent, but I think we'll miss it: it may be 3 per cent.'

Jane has long-term goals for the company. 'I want to see at the end of six years a viable business, one that is businesslike in its running. We're asking people to run a business who've never run one before. It's asking them to become employers rather than employees and not everyone can make that step.'

Jane's team in Hanley undertook training when the partnership was entered into. Members of staff went on courses for business, stock ordering and bookkeeping. Jane conducted a four week course for all staff on profit and loss and bookkeeping.

Ingrid feels that going into the partnership has made people more co-operative and willing to work hard. 'Everyone feels more responsibility for the shop as a business since we became a partnership,' comments Pat.

QUESTIONS

1 What is unusual about the payment system at The Body Shop?

2 What is the task of the formal group of the board of directors?

3 Why is the management team of Jane, Jill and Alison less formal than the board of directors?

4 How is the work allocated between staff?

5 What are the organisational goals? Which are long term and which are short term goals?

6 Are group or individual goals compatible with the organisational goals?

CASE STUDY

Successful team building – an American approach

Brian Unger is the president and chief executive officer of Unger-Sirovotka Associates Incorporated, one of America's top accountancy practices which specialises in small and medium privately owned businesses. Brian has 14 employees in his office in Liberty, Missouri and has recently taken over a branch in Chicago, Illinois which has 24 employees.

'When my father started the business, he was in association with a group with about 60 accountants in it. They met and shared ideas on such regular discussion topics as marketing, personnel and data processing. From participating with people with wide ideas and experience, we said, "What's really important?" and focused on our main objectives. We compared and rated ourselves with other offices. My father and I were always in the top one, two or three.'

'These concepts were way ahead of their time and we co-operated with what could be thought of as competitors. The larger group has broken up now. The key idea that newcomers could not grasp was teamwork. They wanted to keep people isolated and not share information.'

Brian Unger – president and chief executive officer of Unger-Sirovotka Associates Incorporated

'Our original concept of teams was to assign bookkeepers to a particular accountant. There was a negative pressure of building teams to pit against one another. Teams argued that they should have particular clients and that built walls. The original idea was based on competition between teams.

'One of the foundational concepts that I know works and is not just applicable to my industry is not only having monetary incentives, but also the incentives which come from cross-interaction in the workplace.

'We want integration and total flexibility within teams. I slowly changed the teams when I took over. Some made the transfer, some didn't. It initiated from a lot of observation on my part.

'Now, all bookkeepers work for all accountants. There is cross-interaction, people know one another, and they share ideas on how a problem can be tackled. When specialisms become too narrow, others in the accountant/bookkeeper network don't know about the area. There isn't sufficient support and co-operation. We are working within the speciality of small/medium sized businesses – it becomes counterproductive to specialise within that. Cross-training and people being able to do one another's jobs is the essence of what gives us the ability to give service at a high level. We must have a real sense of what it takes to maintain service without peaks and valleys in the quality of the service. If you've got enough cross-training, you can move client assignments between bookkeepers. Everybody has an investment in the other person in the team. No one is indispensable.

'There are minimum standards to achieve for each employee to earn their basic salary, and after that, bonusing begins. There are different bonus schemes for bookkeepers, accountants, telemarketers, salespeople, data processors and clerical workers. Every time that I can pay bonuses I'm making money – I love to pay bonuses!

'Let's take the accountants. The assignment of the client is made at the accountant level: any bookkeeper could then receive that assignment. Every accountant receives in bonus 17 per cent of the gross monthly fees from the client, that's the base. They also receive a $100 bonus on collection of monies due. Most collect above 75 per cent of total accounts receivables each month, and it's often 80 or 90 per cent. There are probably only ten accountants in the United States who receive that proportion of the money owed to them.

'The accountants also get paid for production. If they complete 92 per cent or higher of their clients' financial statements for the prior month, they get another $100 bonus. They also get a $100 bonus each month if they have more clients and the fees due to them from clients have increased. Accountants also get an annual incentive based on production. They receive an annual bonus on general fee increases to all clients. This year it was 5.8 per cent on monthly billings.

'I also set up an incentive on completion of tax returns for every one completed before the due date. I have accountants that make a pretty good living.

'Another area of the team are the salespeople. My top salesperson made about $40,000 in his first year here and now, after four years, earns $120,000 a year.

'Everyone here knows what the pie is. Everybody knows what everyone else is making because they're all working on the same formula. Production figures are published monthly and people ask one another for advice on how to increase their output.

'The training programme for salespeople for instance, is an inside programme to give an overview of what the firm does. The new employees are experienced at working in sales when they arrive. The introduction is through an audio tape series and then working and sitting with people doing all the different jobs in the firm to see what they do. They go with the salesperson they're replacing for three days. I'll participate during those days to make introductions, give cheerleading-type encouragement and reviews. From that point they'll go to Chicago for two days and spend a day with each of the sales team there. This enables them to see three different sales styles.

'Part of teambuilding is to involve spouses so that they know the programme and the people they'll work with. It gives them the chance to assess me and how they feel about their spouse coming to work with us. This is the cornerstone for starting a new person – do they connect? I've evolved the business into having a group of people who have similar preferences but their own individuality. You can leave individuals to do their own tasks, but you've got to give them the tools to do it.

'I meet with accountants every week as well as having individual meetings with them. The bookkeepers have cross-interaction all the time. The accountants working with different bookkeepers get suggestions and solutions to problems from the bookkeepers' experience with other accountants. It's an on-going problem-solving exercise through vertical and horizontal interaction; it's instant feedback.

'I've moved myself and my staff from being perfectionist to near perfection. Did it really matter if it wasn't perfect? Their attitude improved if I backed off and gave them room.

'Everybody knows that I will give praise. People used to be unsure as to whether they were doing a good job. When I laid off negative criticism, the job was done better than if I'd done it myself. The first few times that shocked me and I thought, "Gosh, I'm not needed around here".

'One employee said it was the best place she'd ever worked because all the people here are so caring. Most of the staff I think would say that one of the real positives in minimising stress is that there is lots of flexibility in hours and how the job is done. We all have confidence that each person is going to get the job done. The hands-off approach reduces stress, and it increases the quality and productivity in each of the people. If I say, "This needs to be done in this time, this way", production drops.'

QUESTIONS

1 How did Brian's business benefit from co-operation in its early stages?

2 Why does Brian disagree with having competition between teams?

3 What are the benefits of groups co-operating within the accountancy practice?

4 How does Brian encourage co-operation?

5 Why did Brian feel that he wasn't needed in his own company?

6 With reference to an organisation with which you are familiar, how could you put some of Brian's management principles into practice?

7 What do you think Brian's long term goal is?

8 How is he achieving it in the short term?

Performance Criterion 4
Approaches to developing effective teams

Teams

The effectiveness of any group will be determined by the individuals in it. Individuals need to have the necessary skills, talents and experience to carry out their task as well as being able to work with others pursuing a shared idea and purpose.

In those groups which have individuals with a wide variety of skills and abilities, the strengths of one person can support the weaknesses of another. Meredith Belbin studied groups of managers attending various management courses. In 1981 he wrote a book about the different roles managers take on in teamwork. He identified people with different qualities who would be useful in a team.

The eight roles are:

- Implementer
- Shaper
- Resource investigator
- Team worker
- Co-ordinator
- Plant
- Monitor/evaluator
- Completer/finisher

Table 2.2 Summary of the eight roles

Type	Typical features	Positive qualities	Allowable weaknesses
Implementer	Conservative, dutiful, predictable.	Organising ability, practical, common sense, hard-working self-disciplined.	Lack of flexibility, unresponsiveness to unproven ideas.
Co-ordinator	Calm, self-confident, controlled.	A capacity for treating and welcoming all potential contributors on their merits and without prejudice. A strong sense of objectives.	No more than ordinary in terms of intellect or creative ability.
Shaper	Highly strung, outgoing, dynamic.	Drive and a readiness to challenge inertia, ineffectiveness, complacency or self-deception.	Prone to provocation, irritation and impatience.
Plant	Individualistic, serious-minded, unorthodox.	Genius, imagination, intellect, knowledge.	Up in the clouds, inclined to disregard practical details or protocol.
Resource investigator	Extroverted, enthusiastic, curious, communicative.	A capacity for contacting people and exploring anything new. An ability to respond to challenge.	Liable to lose interest once the initial fascination has passed.
Monitor/ evaluator	Sober, unemotional, prudent.	Judgement, discretion, hard-headedness.	Lacks inspiration or the ability to motivate others.
Team worker	Socially orientated, rather mild, sensitive.	An ability to respond to people and situations and to promote team spirit.	Indecisiveness at moments of crisis.
Completer/ finisher	Painstaking, orderly, conscientious.	A capacity for follow-through, perfectionist.	A tendency to worry about small things. A reluctance to 'let go'.

ACTIVITY

Which team member are you?

Which of the following roles (starting on p. 132) fits in with the way you act in groups?

THE TEAM WORKER

You help individual members to achieve and maintain team effectiveness.

Your strengths
- Observing the strengths and weaknesses of members.
- Supporting members in their strengths, e.g. building on their ideas and suggestions.
- Supporting members in their weak areas by helping them or by finding appropriate resources.
- Improving communications between members.
- Setting an example in team spirit by your actions as a team member.

Your weaknesses
- Competing for leadership of the group or for status in the group.
- Siding with one member against another.
- A tendency to do things in the group which the members or outsiders might disapprove of.
- You can sometimes have a tendency to show off.

Further comments
You can perform this role at different levels of status in the group. When you are acting as manager, you delegate to others and help other people improve themselves. When you have a junior status you often act as a behind the scenes helper. You are always helpful and useful to the team.

THE PLANT

You are the creative person in the team, and you can easily think up ideas for things to do and solving problems. You often say things like, 'Why don't we ... '

Your strengths
- You can concentrate on the main problem or issue.
- You think of ways for the team to achieve its objective.
- When the team is stuck with a problem, you enjoy thinking out all the possibilities and directions they could go in for a solution.
- Your timing is good – you often think of things exactly when they're needed.

Your weaknesses
- You try to do too many things, rather than just what you're good at.
- You sometimes try to steer the team towards things you're interested in personally.
- You sulk if your ideas are rejected and vow never to contribute to the team again.
- You are reluctant to suggest anything if you feel that the group is very critical or dominant.

Further comments
If you are manager, you tend to want to push your ideas through without listening to other people's points of view. The stress of all the hassle of being manager can stifle your creativity. In a more junior role, you are good at suggesting ideas and solutions.

THE SHAPER

You help to give shape and form to the team's activities.

Your strengths
- You can see the need to set objectives and decide upon priorities.
- You can take an overview of what the team is doing and you can help other team members to see what they are doing within the bigger picture.
- You are good at reminding the group about the direction they should be going in and summing up what they have achieved in terms of their original objectives.
- You can co-ordinate people's contributions and give meaning to the team's activities.
- You can stand back from what is happening and assess the team's progress. You can intervene when they are going off course.

Your weaknesses
- You can tend to overturn people's contributions too readily when you are manager.
- You can tend to be bossy.
- You can tend to compete with the plant and the monitor/evaluator.

Further comments
You are helpful to a group when you are subtle, but if you are a leader you tend to control the group too much. If you are in a junior position you need to time your contributions carefully, possibly in the form of questions, as to where the group is going with their current activity.

THE IMPLEMENTER

You are the person who puts people's ideas into practice.

Your strengths
- You make sure that people know what they are to do and the tasks of the team are structured.
- You sort out the practical details from the plan and attend to them.
- You tend not to get distracted from what you are doing, even when there are various demands upon you and you my face a number of difficulties.
- You work hard to meet your targets.
- You give practical support, help and guidance to other team members.

Your weaknesses
- You tend to be inflexible in your approach to the task. You are at your best when you are able to balance your perseverance and be adaptable.
- You offer unconstructive criticism of team members' ideas and suggestions.
- You complete for status in the team.

Further comments
As a manager your strength is your concern for clarification of ideas. You want to be able to see things in practical terms. You are able to create and to maintain a structure in a team.

As a team member you are conscientious and have great determination to make sure the task is completed to standards set and on time.

RESOURCE INVESTIGATOR

You are able to explore outside resources and develop links which may be useful to the team.

Your strengths
- You are able to get on with people quickly and easily. Through your contacts and friendships you establish links with people outside the team who may be useful to it in reaching its objectives.
- You are interested in new ideas and new methods which you have experienced from outside the team and are able to introduce them to the team, enabling it to keep up to date with all developments which are relevant to the team's work.
- You help to maintain good relationships and are able to keep the peace in a team.
- You are able to encourage fellow team members to make best use of their talents, especially during times of crisis or if the group is under pressure.

Your weaknesses
- Getting too involved with your own ideas at the expense of exploring others.
- Rejecting ideas or information before putting them to the team for their opinion.
- You tend to ease up when the pressure is reduced.
- Your enjoyment of other people's company means you are distracted and you waste time.

THE CO-ORDINATOR

You control and organise the activities of the team, making best use of the resources available.

Your strengths
- You prepare things beforehand. Your meetings are structured and organised so that the business of the meeting is done efficiently.
- You encourage individuals to play their part in the team by making sure each individual understands the objectives of the task and making sure that they know the best way they can help.

- You can identify weaknesses in the team and take action to rectify this. You will introduce new members to make up the deficiency. You will notice if someone has a disproportionate amount of work and you will be able to reallocate the work.
- You are able to co-ordinate the use of resources available, both in and outside the team.
- You are able to keep individuals working on the task in hand.
- You are a role model for people to follow because of your own qualities of commitment, self-discipline and perseverance.
- You are able to delegate when it is appropriate to do so.
- You know when to move from discussion to decision making.

Your weaknesses
- You tend to hog the limelight.
- You get mixed up between determination and obstinacy.
- You tend to compete with the plant and the monitor/evaluator and refuse to admit that people may have certain qualities and abilities which are better than your own.
- You may give up the role of leader if faced with strong opposition or total apathy in your team.

THE COMPLETER/FINISHER

You like to ensure that the team's efforts are as near perfect as possible and that nothing is overlooked.

Your strengths
- You are good at seeing mistakes.
- You should choose something to work on which needs finishing qualities.
- You are good at paying attention to detail.
- You help to raise the standard of the team's work by your vigilance and offers of help.
- You are very keen to meet deadlines and you help to remind the team when the deadline is approaching and make them feel that they need to get things moving more quickly.

Your weaknesses
- You can tend to see the details rather than the overall plan.
- You can be too critical and worry so much that it depresses the rest of the team.

THE MONITOR/EVALUATOR

You are good at taking other people's ideas and judging whether they will work or not.

Your strengths
- You can think critically and this can work in the interests of the team.
- You are prepared to experiment.
- You are good at taking other people's suggestions and building on them. You can make the original idea work by changing it slightly to make it more practical.
- You are good at convincing the rest of the team that certain ideas are not workable.
- You are good at working with the plant.

Your weaknesses
- You can be selfish in pursuing your own goals, rather than the team's goals.
- You can hurt other people's feeling when rejecting their suggestions.
- You can be too critical and sometimes refuse to accept other people's ideas.
- You tend to fight with the co-ordinator or plant.
- Your criticisms can depress the rest of the team.

Further comments
You are particularly useful to the group if you are critical but fair, practical and prepared to change. If you are a manager, you tend to dominate the team and reject other people's ideas.

At a junior level you may seem critical and threatening to colleagues: you need tact to make yourself acceptable.

THE SPECIALIST

The brains behind the project. This person has the specialist, technical knowledge in a particular field.

Your strengths
- You may be brilliant in your area.
- You may possess unsurpassed technical knowledge and experience.
- You instinctly know how the project should be tackled and what needs to be done.

You weaknesses
- You are not necessarily a team worker, and you may be a loner and an introvert, making you difficult for others to work with.
- You may have a limited range of interests.

Further comments
You are not a particular personality type, but the person who knows all about what the team is trying to achieve. You are therefore very useful to the team and this usefulness will be easy or difficult to live with, depending upon your personality characteristics.

GROUP BEHAVIOUR ACTIVITY

The dice factory

Aim: To build dice and study the process of group behaviour and team development.

Resources required: Paper, scissors, glue, paper clips, rubber bands, pencils, rulers, felt tip pens/crayons, clock, the die template (see page 138).

Method: The class divide into groups of 5 or 6 persons. Each group chooses a leader and an observer.

The facilitator is the buyer for the toy factory and the supplier of materials for the groups. The buyer decides how many dice they require for the toy factory and will choose the best quality and the lowest prices.

Objects of the activity
- Each group is to operate as a factory, producing paper dice.
- Each group is in competition with the other factories.
- Each group's objective is to maximise profits.
- The group is to supply a toy factory with dice.
- The buyer at the toy factory has the final say as to whether or not the dice produced are of the required quality.
- The group buys sheets of paper from the supplier at a cost of £10 per sheet.
- The group has to decide how many dice they can make and sell in 20 minutes. That number of dice must be delivered to the buyer at the end of 20 minutes.
- The group has to decide on the selling price of the dice.
- Each group is allowed 45 minutes to practise making the dice.
- At the end of the practise period, all groups make their perfect dice.

Rules
1 **Only completed dice can be offered for sale.**
2 **Any rejected dice will have a scrap value of £5.**
3 **Any sheet of paper used has a scrap value of £5.**
4 **Any paper not used can be resold back to the supplier for £7 per sheet.**

At the end of the 20 minute period, the winning group will be the one which has made the most profit.

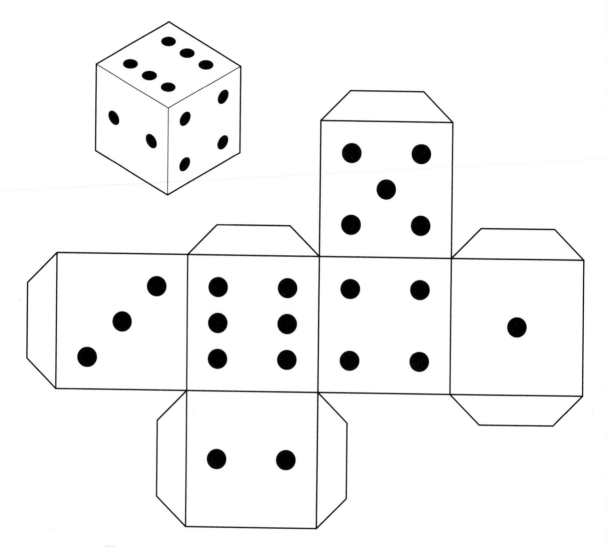

Fig. 2.7 Die template

Die template

1 Cut round the outline of the die in Fig. 2.7.
2 Crease all the internal lines and fold into a cube.
3 Place a little glue on the tabs, tuck them inside the cube and press gently, so that they keep your die firmly together.

Observer sheet

Your task is to observe the behaviour of each group member and try to identify which of Belbin's roles it fits into. (Members of the group may be performing the same role.)

1 What conflict was there within the group?

_____

_____

_____

2 What were the causes of the conflict?

_____

_____

_____

3 How well did the group communicate with one another?

_____

_____

_____

4 How well did the leader perform his or her role?

_____

_____

_____

5 How did the leader go about performing his or her role (what task and maintenance factors were evident)?

_____

_____

_____

1 Did you meet your target?

2 If yes, could you have done anything better?

3 If no, what went wrong?

4 Was there any conflict within the group and what were the causes?

5 Did any group member feel frustrated with the process?

6 What roles did group members take on?

7 Did you feel that any roles were missing?

8 How was the group membership chosen originally?

9 Did any informal groups or sub-groups form during the process?

10 Did you go through the stages of development of norming, storming and performing?

The losing team

The teams which are most likely to fail to meet their objectives are those which, according to Belbin, lack the following features:

Mental ability There needs to be at least one member of the team who can analyse the problem or be able to suggest ways forward for the team.

Negative selection The organisation recognises a deficiency in a team, i.e. the need for someone with specific skills, and decides to recruit. However, it reduces the field of applicants by the restrictions it lays down, such as the salary being too low or there being an age or experience barrier.

Personality The culture of the organisation will influence the behaviour of individuals. This may well be restrictive for some people to the extent that they do not perform to their capabilities. Some organisations may encourage specialists to the extent that they see the world from a narrow, rather than a global, viewpoint. This is a feature of the product-orientated organisation which concentrates on developing a product, then tries to sell it. Market-orientated companies first find out what customers want so that they can produce it for them.

Composition of the team The key players in a team have been identified as implementer, co-ordinator, shaper, plant, resource investigator, monitor/evaluator, team worker, and completer/finisher. Some teams may lack a key member such as a plant. They may have members carrying out a role they are unsuitable for or there may be a duplication of roles leading to competition. In some teams there may be those individuals who cannot operate well in a team because they are too individualistic or task-orientated. Some teams may have those individuals who have pushed themselves forward but are unable to live up to the standards set by the group and are incompetent and make mistakes. Unfortunately, the group is unable to help and support this person because perhaps they do not recognise their own shortcomings, or they cover up their trail so that no one can identify their mistakes.

Corporate cohesiveness Managers are given responsibility for a specific function such as marketing, finance or operations management. Problems arise for the team when the manager becomes more loyal to his area than to the organisation. This insular approach inhibits the ability of managers to see beyond their area and take an overview of the organisation.

The winning team

Belbin's research highlighted the following characteristics of a successful winning team:

- The leader of the team will be patient, able to instill trust, and know how to direct and use the strengths of the team players. The leader will not dominate the proceedings but will be able to pull the team together to focus on issues, especially when decisions need to made.
- A strong 'plant' – someone who is very creative and clever.
- A fair spread in mental abilities, i.e. having a mixture of clever and not so clever people. The latter, who recognise their own shortcomings, will look for alternative ways of fulfilling themselves.
- A spread in personal attributes, which offers wide team role coverage. Different types of team members provide a balance by offering varied skills and talents. This reduces tension within the team because individuals are not competing for the same role.
- A good match between the attributes of members and their responsibility in the team enables members to play to their individual strengths.
- The ability to recognise and counteract the shortcomings of the team, perhaps because it lacks a key player or has an individual who has a problem with his or her role. The team will help and support each other to reduce deficiencies.

Stages of group development

To get the best out of their groups, it is necessary for managers to understand how they behave during the formative stages of development. Managers can put a group of individuals in a room with a task and call them a team. However, before the individuals work as a team, the team has to go through a process of development – a sequence of events need to occur to encourage people to work together. B W Tuckman wrote an article in a journal called *Psychological Bulletin* in 1965 which introduced the idea that groups develop in a sequence. Tuckman highlighted four main stages of group development:

Stage 1: Forming

This is the initial formation of the group when it is clarified what the purpose of the group is and how it will operate. During this stage the hierarchical structure of the group, the leadership and the individual roles will be decided.

Time will then be spent by individuals to weigh each other up, and to ask questions to find out where each comes from and generally to see how everyone compares. Each member will be trying to create a favourable impression.

Stage 2: Storming

After the initial stage, people will have gained confidence, and members of the group will know each other better and be willing to put forward their ideas, argue their case or challenge someone else. It is during this stage of development when conflict and hostility will occur – but this is just a natural part of group development.

The initial operations of the group may be challenged and a more suitable structure and procedure agreed.

Stage 3: Norming

This stage of the group's development establishes the need for members to recognise that co-operation rather than hostility and conflict will enable the group to reach their goals. The group control the behaviour of individuals and reduce competition between group members. The group develops behavioural patterns and standards which become accepted as norms.

Stage 4: Performing

At this stage of the development the group has matured. Members can work as a team because the previous stages have brought structure and created group cohesiveness.

Leadership and the development stages of a group

The forming stage

During this stage the leader will be concerned with helping the group with the task.

The leader will help to clarify what the task is, set goals, and establish rules of operating, communicating and decision making. The leader must be able to demonstrate to the group the reason why each member is part of the group.

The storming stage

At this stage the leader may be redefining goals, modifying procedures and clarifying roles. He or she will be encouraging individuals and will have to manage conflict.

The leader must be prepared to listen to difficulties and encourage differences of opinion without causing conflict. He or she must be able to manage the group so that individuals participate, making sure that some do not dominate the group.

The norming stage

By this stage the group is becoming a cohesive unit and the leader needs to spend less time directing and so can become more of a team member, i.e. he or she has to 'let go' and allow the group to assume responsibility for its actions. However, the leader has to make sure that the group does not become too tightly knit so that it avoids conflict and disagreement – which will affect their performance.

The performing stage

By this stage the group should be operating as a unit and there is less need for control and support from the leader. This means the leader can target his or her energies in other areas.

Stages of formal group development

In 1965 Bernard Bass suggested an alternative approach to the formation of groups. Bass put forward the idea that group development is a four-stage process influenced mainly by groups learning how to use their resources.

The four stages of development are:

1 The acceptance stage

Members of a new group are usually very wary of other people and initially mistrust other people's views. Members are aware of their own strengths and weaknesses and tend to behave in a restrained manner so that they do not make mistakes or say anything that they might regret later. This stage of the group development is typified by formal behaviour of group members.

2 The communication and decision-making stage

Once the acceptance stage has passed, people feel more confident with their own performance and about being in the company of their colleagues. People are more open and frank in their discussion. Standards of procedure are established and a mechanism for some type of group decision-making strategy is developed.

3 The group solidarity stage

This stage comes more naturally as mutual acceptance and confidence in group members increases. Communication and decision-making structures are clarified as members of a group work together rather than compete.

4 Control and organisation

This final stage of the group development is where group solidarity leads to group control. Work is distributed according to individual abilities within the group activities. Co-operation, flexibility and informality is accepted at this stage.

Training for teambuilding at Allstate Insurance

Allstate is known in North and South America and Asia for home and life insurance. In the twelve years to 1990, the company grew at a very fast pace and achieved $1 billion turnover. Despite this rapid growth they were not very profitable, and in 1990 their new President, John Callahan, started a process of cultural change. The objective was to help employees respond in a quick and flexible way to the changing global market. (An example of how quickly the situation can change in insurance is that Allstate lost 2\frac{1}{2}$ billion in the 1992 Florida hurricane.)

As well as empowering people, Allstate introduced teamwork and reduced the layers of managers to result in a flatter organisation.

'People are the key to our future,' says Mark Lindner, Training Director. 'Any building we can rent or machine we can buy can be duplicated by our competitors.

A new product can be duplicated by the entire industry within months. Competitive advantage is through people. Experienced people are our biggest challenge, they feel they don't need to learn anything.' Allstate have people who have been with them for 20 years.

Teams get a bonus for good results. 'It's an experiment, we don't know if it's going to work,' Mark explains. People are used to being compensated individually. Team compensation causes emotional reactions; it's foreign to the American culture. Real teams are truly dependent upon one another. Survival depends upon the success of the team. People must interact to produce something beyond what we could individually produce.'

Teams were introduced quickly. An announcement was made to the employees that teamwork was going to begin at Allstate. Team leaders were trained first in leadership skills to help the leader to go back to his or her team and function differently.

'Saying that relationships are different and then doing things differently don't necessarily go together,' says Mark. Allstate had workshops for teams to discuss their relationships and what it would take to be a high performance team. 'We wanted to get away from applauding mediocrity and calling it good.'

During the training, people evaluated themselves and discussed their work. People had to try to accept critical comments. Teambuilding activities included physical activities in order to make the situation totally different to that at work. 'The quiet person had things to contribute,' comments Mark.

The workshop facilitators included Mark himself, people from a management consulting firm and employees who ranged from vice-presidents to secretaries. Teams went together to hotels for the training.

'There's support for what they've done when they get back together. We called it a workout instead of a workshop. They went to sweat, there was pain involved. With sport, you practice to be better when you're on the field – the same went for teambuilding training. They gave it their all and worked hard. It was not a holiday. People came in their sports gear.'

Allstate have been carrying out this training programme for four years and expect to be doing it for another four years. After the first 18 months, in June 1991, the president of the company said that it was 'the end of the beginning'. Some people are still not working as a member of a team, but the president is patient with them. He still hopes to encourage them to join in. He has said, 'The train has left the station, but if you run you can still get on board.'

TEAMS AT ALLSTATE

1 Mary Ann's team

Mary Ann Parchim is team leader for six people in the Re-Insurance LAN Unit. The team has been in existence for 14 months.

Mary Ann Parchim and her PC team at Allstate

'It can take three to five years to get the team working. We felt we were working as a team before it became official. We're very tuned in to one another.'

The team's role is the responsibility for personal computers at Allstate Reinsurance. All employees are on the computer network and have different needs and different computer skills. The team's mission is to make these people as productive as possible. The team offers them training in the form of a weekly class or one-to-one training. The team also does maintenance for PC support and is involved with external clients and brokers. On occasion, they visit the company's insurance brokers and train them at their offices.

Every Monday the team has a lunch meeting to catch up with one another. They decide what will be done in the coming week and who will do what. The team have one member who is much weaker than the others. They have given her considerable support.

'She is the type of individual who needed everything written down because she couldn't remember things,' explains Mary Ann. 'We started to document everything. She was also weaker on the technical side of the job. We brainstormed requirements for the team. All the parts of our jobs such as how to put a PC together, install memory, etc.' The team went through everything together. They rated themselves on each requirement for the job and then rated one another. There were some surprises as people found that others perceived them as having more knowledge than they thought they had, or less.

The team devised performance standards for core elements of their jobs – such things as answering the telephone by the third ring and resolving problems within

15 minutes of them occurring. They chose elements which were easy to measure. They have joint discussions to see whether performance standards are being met.

'I'm in the process of delegating more to the team,' says Mary Ann. 'If there are tough decisions, they come to me expecting me to make the decision. I now throw it back at them.' One team member said to Mary Ann, 'This is hard, I really liked it in the old days when you just told me what to do.'

Empowerment means that as well as being involved in making decisions, different people go to various meetings, according to their expertise. It also used to be considered a perk to go to trade conferences. Now people who have knowledge or can benefit from a conference can go, not just the team leader.

Allstate is looking at the idea of job banding – putting a group of jobs in the same pay grade. The team ideal is not very compatible with individuals wanting promotion. 'Promotion is still very important to these people. The team has a common business card, no one has a job title.' Sometimes people find the lack of a job title very difficult to live with. Also, the teams at Allstate do not have names.

'I still get mixed messages from management about teamwork,' comments Mary Ann, who often feels that the team could make decisions she has been instructed to take alone. Invitations to meetings have been specifically addressed to her in the past and she now takes a team member with her who has the right expertise. 'I've been to meetings where I didn't know what they were talking about, now they soon realise that the team member I take along is the person they should be talking to.'

Mary Ann wants to rotate the leadership of the team around other team members, 'but at this point I'm still the Mother Hen'.

The team have started a rotational assignment with the systems area who have greater technical expertise in computing than they have. Each team member will learn increased technical skills from the systems area during their six month attachment to them. Team members train at least one other member of the team to do their job, so that there is back-up for busy periods or absence. The written instructions for everything done by the team is kept on computer so that it can be continually updated.

2 Laura's team

Laura Fuesting is a team leader for Accounts Receivable. Their task is to collect insurance premiums for business insurance. There are 24 members and the team is two years old. Their job is to input and view information on the mainframe computer, open mail, post payments, take telephone calls and reconcile accounts.

Laura has divided the 24 team members into three groupings of eight to make the team more manageable. 'It's a lot of people to communicate with,' says Laura. Twenty per cent of pay is for overall department results, which is designed to encourage teamwork. Laura has appointed one person to be in charge of each of the three groups. There are still a lot of interpersonal problems and conflicts within the group.

'We've gone through team training which has brought an awareness. Classes have given people models to work with. We're not a high performance, self-managed team. It took a while for people to accept that I don't do the work, they do. I like the idea of teams but a lot of people don't. They would rather sit and do their own work.'

Laura feels that some people may never work as part of a team. Those who are prepared to try are those who address conflict and try to sort problems out.

'Some teamworkers are feeding off each other and sharing ideas. They say, "This works for me" and they show one another how they do things.' Since teamwork was introduced, the group's results are much improved. The amount of insurance premiums not received from customers has been reduced by half.

QUESTIONS

1 How are people encouraged to work as a team at Allstate?

2 How were people trained to be high performance teams?

3 Why does it take a long time for individuals to build themselves into a working team?

4 Why did Mary Ann's team get a good start on teambuilding?

5 How are standards kept high within the team?

6 Do Mary Ann's team experience any difficulties with teamwork?

7 What advantages are there to being a member of Mary Ann's team?

8 What differences are there between the work Mary Ann's team does and the work Laura's team does?

9 Why is Laura having more problems with her team than Mary Ann?

10 Do Laura's and Mary Ann's successes outweigh the problems they have encountered with teamwork?

WORDSEARCH

Groups at work

```
C A T P R O C E S S B E F K F O L G F P
H A E D E Y R I T H A I O P A S D F C E
A D A M K R G K N L A F M L H C E E B R
I N M D A C C C T D I P A A F O K I V F
R V W F L I S E V H I S E T I G J L J O
P G O U U V N M P H U V W R S N P E V R
E N R N B N L T G T D A I P O E T B C M
R I K C S S C J E W I Q U D V F A E I I
S M E T B I T T E N M O P D U F Q E R N
O R R E A R G G I I A N N V S A N U T G
N O R B A O G N V T O N I S P Q L O I S
G F U F C F O R M A L I C H I T T S T I
G N Q D F R O T T S H O R E G E E T E Z
G N V Q U F G H A K N I R N R H H H A E
N I G E E L V Y E O V W I B O D F E M C
I L O V Y E S A I M B M H R U R E E S S
M E I N F O R M A L R U M P P M M D E S
R C O H E S I V E O V E Q S S U V S N L
O L A U R A S S T G E O R G E M R I C M
N C S T A T U S B K F U N C T I O N B B
```

PROCESS	STORMING	TASK
CHAIRPERSON	MAINTENANCE	GROUPS
TEAMWORKER	NORMS SIZE	SHAPER
PERCEPTION	TEAMS	INDIVIDUALS
STATUS	PERFORMING	FORMING
INFORMAL	BELIEF	NORMING
FUNCTION	FORMAL	COHESIVE

Evidence indicator

A simple group task or activity requiring co-operative effort and decision making. Individual report examining the group's development and performance, including analysis of own contribution, experience and impact on group.

CHARITIES EXERCISE

The class should form groups of six to eight people. Groups do not have to be the same size. Each group should have an observer.

The group should sit around a table with the following information in front of them.

You are a local authority committee with £20,000 to donate among the following charitable and fund-raising organisations. Your group task is to decide how the money is to be distributed. Not all charities need to be included, and you are allowed to award all the money to a single organisation if you so choose. If you have not arrived at a consensus within 20 minutes, the money will be lost and no charity will benefit from donations.

Save the Children Fund	Pro Life Group
Oxfam	Cancer Research
RSPCA	local animal shelter
CND	Child Poverty Action Group
British Heart Foundation	The Samaritans
Salvation Army	Royal National Lifeboat Institution
Royal Institute for the Blind	Help the Aged

When individual and group feedback sheets have been completed, the group should discuss with their observer and facilitator how they performed and developed, including individual performances and impact on the group.

OBSERVER AND GROUP MEMBER FEEDBACK SHEET 1

As soon as the group starts their discussion, the observer should write the names of the group members in the appropriate boxes, according to how their contribution should be categorised. You may have the same name in one box several times. Some boxes may remain empty.

Role	Contributions	Name
Co-ordinator	Stating objectives Helping to establish roles Summing up group achievements	
Shaper	Shaping roles and objectives Pushing the group towards agreement	
Plant	Contributing ideas	
Monitor/ evaluator	Analysing the situation Assessing the contributions of others	
Implementer	Transforming discussion into practical steps Considering what is possible	
Team worker	Giving support to others Seconding another member's ideas Drawing quieter people into the discussion	
Resource investigator	Introducing ideas from outside Negotiating	
Completer/ finisher	Emphasising the need to meet the deadline Looking for errors and oversights Getting others to take the necessary actions	

OBSERVER FEEDBACK SHEET 2

Group development

How did the group's behaviour change during the 20 minute period?

_____

_____

Group performance

What was good about the group's performance?

_____

_____

What was unsatisfactory about the group's performance?

_____

_____

Did all group members contribute?

_____

_____

Were all the roles filled by a group member?

_____

_____

Would the group have benefited from a different membership carrying out all the roles?

_____

_____

Were any group members trying to carry out the same role?

_____

_____

Element 15.2 Review test

Performance criterion 1

 1 What is a formal group?
 2 What are the disadvantages of committees?
 3 What are the characteristics of informal groups?
 4 What are the advantages of informal groups?

Performance criterion 2

 5 What is meant by 'group norms'?
 6 What is the difference between positive and negative norms?
 7 How do people 'conform' in groups?

Performance criterion 3

 8 Why do organisations have goals?
 9 How do short term goals fit in with long term goals?
10 What is the main difference between long and short term goals?
11 Why might different groups within the organisation have different goals?
12 Why might some groups have 'status' as a group goal?
13 How might conflict arise within groups?
14 Suggest **three** ways of avoiding conflict between group and organisational goals.

Performance criterion 4

15 Why do teams need members to take on different roles?
16 What sort of person makes a good chairperson?
17 What do resource investigators need to be good at?
18 What will happen to groups without a plant?
19 What are the **three** stages of group development?
20 What is meant by 'storming'?

Element 15.3

EXAMINE BEHAVIOURAL ASPECTS OF MANAGING PEOPLE WHICH INFLUENCE PERFORMANCE AT WORK

PERFORMANCE CRITERIA

1 **Different management styles are identified and compared**
   Range: Styles: formal; informal; autocratic, democratic, consultative, *laissez faire.*

2 **The leadership role of the manager is examined and described**
   Range: Leadership role: task: responsibility for planning, organising and monitoring task achievements; individual/group; maximising contribution; recognising individual strengths and weakness, and building on the former; recognising maintenance factors and importance of motivators.

3 **Appropriate channels for effective communication are examined and described**
   Range: Channels: formal, informal, types: verbal, oral, written, non-verbal.

4 **Barriers to effective communication are investigated**
   Range: language, atmosphere, physical, timing.

EVIDENCE INDICATOR

A case study examining the mismanagement of a task over a period of time, examining the role of the leader and the communication channels used.

Different management styles

What is a leader?

History books refer to famous military leaders such as the Duke of Wellington, or religious leaders like Martin Luther and political leaders typified by Churchill. We have newspaper articles about present day world leaders, and magazines with features on leaders of fashion and music. We all have our own ideas of what a leader is, from our knowledge and experience. We come into contact with leaders in everyday life, such as at college or at work. Everyone therefore feels that they know what a leader is, but it is difficult to define the term. From our own experiences we might see leaders as:

- someone who leads from the front
- someone who speaks for others
- someone who sets an example for others

It could be said that a leader is:

Any member who influences the group.

However, this is rather vague, so the definition needs to be expanded to include:

Any member who influences the behaviour, beliefs and feelings of the other group members in an intended direction.

This gives an indication about leadership which can now be stated as:

The activity which changes the behaviour and attitude of a group to a directed purpose.

Formal and informal leaders

Leaders who are officially appointed to a position in an organisation, such as the managing director or the marketing manager, have positional or legitimate power and formal authority. They are formal leaders. Yet a person appointed as manager over a group of people may not be a natural leader. He or she may have difficulty motivating workers. He or she may be very good at administration or dealing with external clients, but poor at interpersonal relationships with staff.

Natural leaders may emerge in groups because they have power and authority which comes from an unofficial source. The basis for their leadership may be age, technical ability, years of service or referent power (people naturally refer decisions to them because of their charisma or expertise). They emerge as a group's informal leader and will carry out leadership roles in the group. They may be the person who helps the newcomer into the workplace or they may be the person who represents the group when dealing with their manager. When group members seek and take the advice of the informal leader, they are handing over decision-making power to him or her.

For the formal leader and the group to operate effectively, it may be in the interest of the formal leader to harness the power of the informal leader.

In some cases, the informal leader might carry out this role because he or she has been passed over for promotion and so finds that using power is personally satisfying. Or perhaps he or she may not *want* the responsibility which goes with formal leadership. For whatever reason someone carries out an informal leadership role, he or she is a strong influence on the group.

Informal leaders arise constantly in any group situation. A group of friends discussing where to go for an evening or on holiday may look to one particular group member to suggest ideas. This informal leader will quite naturally take

The informal leader

responsibility for planning and organising the event. This does not mean that he or she will do all the work involved, but he or she will co-ordinate the efforts of other group members.

Effective leadership

Effective leadership will occur when a person has the *authority* or the right to exert influence on the group and has the *power* or ability to change the behaviour of a group.

Authority

A leader is often able to operate in the group because his or her instructions are seen to be justified or legitimate. He or she has the authority to give instructions to others. Informal leaders have natural or charismatic authority. Normally, organisations have a vertical structure where authority originates at the top and descends through the organisation's layers. Each layer or rank of management has some authority but the scope of authority will diminish as it moves away from the top. In public companies, the chairperson and the board of directors are given the authority to run the business on behalf of the shareholders. These senior managers then delegate some of their authority to the next management layer.

Authority may be based on access and control of resources. Allocating scarce resources between competing uses will only be accepted if it is done by someone deemed to have the authority.

Natural qualities, persuasive powers and an air of confidence will give some people charismatic authority. Experts will be seen to have authority because of their specialist knowledge.

Authority will only operate when the subordinate accepts and complies with an instruction. If the leader gives what his or her subordinates consider to be a stupid instruction then the leader may be ignored. The subordinates may also fail to comply if they do not understand the instruction or do not have the necessary skills to carry out the request.

Power

A leader has already been identified as someone with the ability to influence the behaviour of a group in a particular direction and it is this 'ability' which is power. The extent of the ability to exercise power in the group depends on that person's *source* of power. Power will differ according to the methods employed to persuade the group members to comply with the leader's instructions. Below are examples of sources of power:

Reward power is based on the ability of one person to reward another for 'correct' behaviour. This can be done in the form of praise, or by recommending pay rises or promotions. Praise from the informal leader or merely just acknowledgement that the follower is considered to be a member of 'the gang' may be sufficient motivatation.

Coercive power is based on the ability of one person to punish another for 'incorrect' behaviour by withholding praise or merit pay rises, blocking promotion or even considering dismissal. Bullying and threats *could* work for an informal leader, but it is more usual for the informal leader to be popular and well-liked.

Legitimate power is found where a subordinate in the group acknowledges that the leader has the 'right' to exert influence. For example, the transport manager in a haulage firm has the right to issue the drivers their itinerary for the day and the driver has an obligation to accept the instructions.

Expert power is based on the belief that someone has a specific although limited subject area of knowledge which others in the group may not have.

Referent power is based on the individual style and qualities of a person. For instance, the popular leader may be able to motivate subordinates to follow his or her example. Other people feel it natural to refer to this type of person for guidance and advice.

The extent and mix of these powers will depend on the individual leader and the situation. The use of one power may reduce the effectiveness of another – if a person is disciplined for lateness by a manager this may reduce the referent power of that manager. From the viewpoint of the organisation, reward power is most useful because it can be exercised directly down the hierarchy. However, this does not mean that it is the best source of power to motivate individuals. Research indicates that the most important powers for organisational effectiveness are expert and referent power.

The formal leader

QUESTIONS

1 Define leadership and then decide how your definition differs from the ones on page 157. Is yours any less valid?

2 Think of different bosses you have had in the past. Make a list of good and bad things they did – this should give some dos and don'ts of good leadership.

3 Name the five types of power. How does the balance of power change for leaders such as President Clinton of the United States and Prime Minister John Major of Great Britain between when they are in office and when they are seeking re-election? What different types of power come into effect?

4 Think of some natural leaders in your personal lives. What is it about them that makes others want to follow them?

East 17

East 17   London Features International Ltd

'You have to make sure that when they have an interview with Smash Hits they turn up on time, that if they are doing a gig in Israel then they make the flight, when one of them needs their tooth pulling, when one of them needs someone to sort out his girlfriend problems and they need a quiet talk with you ...'

This is Tom Watkins, one of the most talked about managers in music. The man whose credits include the Pet Shop Boys, Bros and now East 17. 'One of the first things people always ask me about East 17 is if they are manageable. These kids are tough street kids. They come from an area of London very much like the area of London that I grew up in.'

Tom first met Tony Mortimer when he was a dancer for another of his signings, Faith, Hope and Charity. 'It was four years ago, and he bugged the life out of me with his tape ...'

Tom's real grudge was that Tony was on his own. He wasn't keen on signing solo artists. 'He was very persistent. Even when he was on the dole he would go away and make another demo. He finally came back with all the boys that are in the band, and played a tape with three tracks on it that were so good they were hard to resist.'

So Tom invited London Records round to listen to the boys.

When Tom works with a band he lives that band in every possible way. Levi the dog logos adorn cushions, caps, jackets and mugs scattered around his home. Watkins learned early that if you can woo the world with a pair of big black ears then simplicity is the key to branding a band. 'We made the dog fit into everything else – and like everything from a tin of beans to a pop group, you need to brand them, give it an identity. It has helped us sell the band through an array of merchandise.'

At the end of the day Tom is interested in finding talent and turning it into stardom. His one ambition is to get an act to conquer America. He believes East 17 are the ones. 'They are regarded as very street, very real and very English. They can do it.'

Adapted from 'E17's VIPs' by Tony Cross.

Source: Smash Hits, 9 – 22 June 1993 pp. 42–43. Reprinted by kind permission of Smash Hits magazine.

QUESTIONS

1 Do East 17 need a manager?

2 Have the band got formal and informal leaders?

3 What roles do Tom Watkins and Tony Mortimer perform for the band?

4 Why do you think Tom wants East 17 to 'conquer' America?

What do managers do?

The function of managers is to plan, organise and monitor the task and the people for whom they are responsible. Managers themselves will say that they make decisions. Yet when managers are observed at work, they flit between meetings, making phone calls, chatting to people, having a nice easy time and never seeming to achieve much. Are these managers being effective and doing what they are supposed to do? What is it that they're supposed to do? We need answers to these questions so that decisions can be made in organisations as to whether managers are needed, what sort of managers are needed, and how many. Managers are recruited, selected and trained according to knowledge or assumptions about what they do.

The informal style of management

Researchers who have observed managers have found that managers are organising, planning and monitoring (and achieving these things through talking to many different people), often on an informal basis. Their informal style can often be perceived by others as not being work at all, but managers perform their roles by gathering and giving out information, often in face-to-face situations. Managers are responsible for a part of an organisation and have authority over the people working there. They are enabling others to do their own jobs by giving information, making decisions on urgent matters and solving problems on the spot with little time for reflection. Playing the part of a linchpin – giving out and receiving information – provides the manager with an overview of what is happening in their organisation or department, so that they know whether objectives are being achieved, and can remedy matters quickly if they are not.

There is no specific job description of a 'manager' because managerial jobs are so different. The manager of the local leisure centre has a totally different job to the finance director of ICI, who in turn has a different job to the production manager at Nissan. The reasons they vary are because of different:

- types and sizes of organisations – public or private sector, service, manufacturing or extractive industries
- levels within the organisation – senior, middle, junior management or supervisory level
- functions in the organisation – personnel, accounts, marketing, purchasing, production or sales

The features of a managerial job which *do* seem to be common to most managers are:

1 Their day is made up of brief and varied interactions with people, mostly face to face. They are constantly interrupted and have very little quiet time in which to work. Many managers seem to be extrovert personalities who enjoy this hectic situation. They are doing their job by gathering and giving out information, planning, and finding and solving problems as they go along.

2 There is a choice available to managers as to what their job involves. Two managers doing identical jobs may spend their days in entirely different ways – one may prefer to communicate with subordinates and superiors through memos and reports while the other may spend time talking informally with people.

3 Managers always say *what* they manage rather than just that they are 'a manager'. They prefer to say, 'I am ... the bar manager, audit manager or hotel manager'. This is probably because being 'a manager' means very little due to the wide variety of managerial work which is possible.

Managers then, are 'doers' rather than 'thinkers', who carry out their work through interacting with other people in a brief and fragmented way. The decisions they make about the work are based on up-to-the-minute information which they gather from talking to people and which they would not possess if they sat alone in their offices working quietly.

Theories of leadership

The quest for knowledge on the subject of what makes for successful management and leadership has taken several forms. The earliest theories were the **trait theories** which looked at the personality characteristics of the leader. These proved to be largely unhelpful because successful leaders had very few characteristics in common. Next were the **style theories** which looked at how leaders and managers behaved. These led on to the **situational theories** which drew attention to the idea that leaders may have to behave differently in different circumstances.

These theories are summarised below:

- **Trait**: What type of person makes a successful leader?
- **Style**: What does a successful leader do?
- **Situational**: What should leaders do in different situations?

More recent research has turned away from theory to real life and focused on what managers *actually do*. Studies are being done on how managers spend their day and the difference between various levels of managerial jobs.

There is still no quick answer to the question of what makes for successful leadership. Situations, people, the task and the organisation all vary and at the same time interact with each other so greatly that there is no single recipe for success.

Trait theories

One of the most difficult problems facing organisations is choosing leaders. If we can understand what makes a good leader than the selection of personnel for leadership posts would be easy and straightforward. Early research looked at the characteristics of leaders.

The investigations in trait theories identified personal qualities common to successful leaders. It was hoped that the research would either show that some people were born with the necessary leadership skills and were therefore natural leaders, or if leadership skills were easily identifiable then people could be trained to become leaders.

TASK

- Think of five well-known people who you think were or are good leaders.
- List the personal qualities of each.
- Are there any personal qualities which are common to each figure?
- List the personal qualities of the five figures in rank order.
- Compare your list with that of your colleagues.
- Are any qualities the same in different people's lists?
- If the qualities are identified, can a checklist be made of the skills expected for an ideal leader?

After completing the task above, you will note that your results probably vary in content. If you attempt to define some of the personal qualities there is a problem as the meanings themselves are subjective. 'Ambition' to one person might be 'pushiness' to another.

The trait theory does not take into account those leaders who emerge naturally in a situation. Also, certain people may have some qualities identified as 'leadership qualities' and yet not be good leaders. Nobody can possess *all* of the traits. Famous leaders of the past have been found to be entirely different from one another, and yet all have been successful in their own field.

There are, however, some personality characteristics which have been found to be common to successful leaders:

- above average intelligence
- ability to use their own initiative
- confidence
- the ability to be objective and stand back from a situation, not getting so involved that they cannot see what is really happening

Also, certain physical characteristics have been found to be common to successful leaders – good health and plenty of energy.

Style theories of management and leadership

Style theories of management and leadership are concerned with leaders' behaviour rather than their personality traits.

The most common way to categorise leader behaviour is to look at where the focus of power lies:

- **Autocratic leaders** keep the power to make decisions to themselves.
- **Democratic leaders** share the decision-making power with subordinates.
- **Consultative leaders** ask the opinions of their subordinates, but make the final decision alone.
- **Laissez faire** means 'let it alone'. These leaders often allow subordinates to make day-to-day decisions about their jobs.

Most managers use all four styles over a period of time, depending upon the situation, but one style will tend to dominate and be their preferred style.

Autocratic

This style is sometimes known as **authoritative.**

These leaders take full authority and responsibility for their group. They structure the work situation for their employees and tell them what to do and how to do it. This style can be carried out in a positive or negative way:

- the positive stance encourages subordinates to work by offering rewards such as praise
- the negative stance forces subordinates to work by issuing threats and punishment.

Advantages of the autocratic style

- The positive or benevolent autocratic leader is often very pleasant to work for. Everyone in the group can feel confident and secure because they understand what they should do and get praise and recognition for good work from the leader.

'The trouble with all these computers is that they take away the sheer delight of bawling people out.'

- The autocratic style is satisfying for the leader as he or she can feel in control of the situation.
- This style allows for rapid decision making. A group of individuals, particularly with diverse opinions, will take longer to reach a decision, which may be detrimental to the organisation in situations where a quick reaction is important.
- People new to the organisation or people not very competent at their jobs will benefit from the certainty provided by this type of leader.

Disadvantages of the autocratic style

- People dislike the negative autocrat as the style can create fear and frustration.
- There is great dependence on the leader because he or she provides the structure within which to work. The work is done by subordinates to please the leader whether his or her style is negative or positive. Without the leader, the workers have no reason for doing the work.
- The autocratic style may stifle innovation and creativity from group members.

Democratic

This style is sometimes known as **participative.**

Authority is decentralised and decisions arise from consultation and participation between the leader and subordinates within the group. There is a team atmosphere, rather than leader and followers.

Advantages of the democratic style

- The democratic leader feels supported by the group: he or she is not making decisions alone as with the autocrat.
- Group members are encouraged to express their ideas and make suggestions which provide a greater diversity of solutions to problems.

'We need a committee meeting to make a decision on whether to have tea or coffee.'

- Group members feel greater commitment and motivation towards the task because they have participated in the decision. Group members can claim ownership of a decision which they participated in taking.
- Group members feel that there is respect for their own experience, knowledge and skills.
- Group members often have greater knowledge of events in the organisation and do not feel that they are 'always the last to know'.

Disadvantages of the democratic style

- The leader may not always agree with decisions made by the group. One of the problems of delegation is that others will always do things slightly differently to yourself. The leader may often feel slightly uncomfortable with the decisions taken.
- Group members need to be competent in the work in order to be able to contribute to decision making.
- Decision making is slower when more people are involved. When there is a wide range of opinion on a subject, it may be impossible for everyone to agree.
- Although the manager may be democratic, the subordinates may not be. Some subordinates may seize the opportunity to take more than their fair share of the power, and even unofficially take over from the official leader.

Consultative

The consultative leader often appears to be more democratic than he or she actually is. The leader informs the subordinates of impending changes and the decisions which need to be made within the organisation. Subordinates are encouraged to voice their opinions on any subjects raised by the leader. The leader listens to all sides of any argument and to anyone who wishes to express an opinion. He or she then makes the final decision and does not actually share his or her power with subordinates.

Advantages of the consultative manager

- Everyone is informed of events within the organisation before the final decision is made. Unpleasant news is given to the workers along with the pleasant, without anything final having been decided.
- People feel that they can openly discuss their individual problems, and those of the organisation and the group and that they will be listened to.
- No one is punished for expressing adverse opinions. The manager welcomes everyone's views on the subject under discussion.
- The time the manager devotes to subordinates and the amount of communication within the organisation is likely to be greater than within autocratic management.

Disadvantages of the consultative manager

- No real power sharing takes place.
- Newcomers and people attending the organisation for job interviews are likely to mistake the manager's soliciting of opinions and interested attention to their views as a democratic style of leadership. It may come as a disappointment when the passage of time reveals that subordinates' opinions are not always taken into account.

Laissez faire

This style is also known as **free rein**.

The *laissez faire* leadership style is a perfectly legitimate leadership style because the leader will carry out the functions of integrating, co-ordinating, representing and organising. There is a tendency to confuse this style with that of 'abdication' – the person who refuses to carry out his or her role as leader and avoids power and responsibility.

The manager of an adult centre which provides evening classes should have a *laissez faire* style. He or she does not need to visit classes in order to instruct the tutors on what to do. His or her role as leader is to decide upon what courses to run, to advertise them, co-ordinate timetabling and rooms, organise an enrolment evening, bank the money and perform many other tasks which the tutors would not see as their job. He or she is a distant figure whose role is so crucial that there would not be an adult centre without him or her, yet many tutors and students think of this sort of leader as superfluous.

Advantages of laissez faire

'No appointments for me today Miss Potts – I'm attending a funeral.'

Advantages of laissez faire

- Group members have autonomy over the day-to-day aspects of their job.
- Laissez faire style offers opportunities for personal growth to group members.
- This style often produces more successful results than the other styles when the group members are highly motivated and experts in their field.

Disadvantages of laissez faire

- A lack of direction from the leader could cause people to work at cross purposes or pursue irrelevancies.
- Group members often do not realise the amount of work involved in leading the group and may feel a lack of respect for the leader. Informal leaders may emerge, creating disharmony.

QUIZ

What is your management style?

Read each question and then tick the letter which best fits your response.

1 You've recently taken over a department where one member of staff, Dorothy, who is nearing retirement, cannot use the computer. Should you:
   (a) Tell her to go on a computer training course and make the arrangements immediately?
   (b) Have a talk with her and ask her opinion on the matter?
   (c) Take no action as she is getting close to retiring?

2 The staff car park is far too small and as personnel manager do you feel that you should:
   (a) Call a meeting with other managers to hear what they feel would be the best course of action?
   (b) Suggest to the managing director the next time you see him or her that it could go on the agenda of the next board of directors' meeting?
   (c) Go to the managing director and demand that something be done about it?

3 You are production manager in a sweet factory. Productivity is poor in the packing department. Should you:
   (a) Set the packers a target number of boxes to pack per day and give them a small bonus if they achieve it?
   (b) Arrange the packers into groups so that they can organise tasks as they see fit?
   (c) Wait for a few more weeks to see how things go?

4 The personnel director tells you, the personnel manager, to implement a staff appraisal scheme straightaway. Should you:
   (a) Wait and see what type of scheme the personnel director suggests?
   (b) Send round a memo to let everyone know that the appraisal scheme will be started immediately?
   (c) Call a staff meeting to discuss the proposal with the workers?

5 You are a production manager in a car factory. The board of directors has decided that you should organise the workers into teams which should meet every morning to discuss problems and how to improve quality. Do you:
   (a) Tell the workers about the teams required by the board of directors and leave them to sort it out?
   (b) Arrange times so that you can attend and chair all team meetings?
   (c) Put young team leaders in charge of the teams and let them organise the meetings?

6 You are the transport manager of a road haulage firm and each morning drivers are given their routes for the day. Do you:
   (a) Give the routes to each driver?
   (b) Call the drivers together to discuss the allocation of routes?
   (c) Pin the routes on a noticeboard and let the drivers choose their own?

7 You are the finance director of a High Street bank and you hear from a colleague that another bank is introducing worker participation in the form of allowing a bank clerk to be a worker-director and sit on the board of directors. Do you think:
   (a) Clerks should be allowed to contribute to decision making at board level?
   (b) It will be interesting to know how the other bank find the experiment?
   (c) Clerks have their own areas of responsibility and they have no place on the board?

8 You are working in a group on the design of a new advertisement for a jeans company and you have a very good idea which you think the group should use. Do you:
   (a) Call a special meeting of the group so that you can show them your plans?
   (b) Go to your manager and get your idea approved officially?
   (c) See what ideas the other group members come up with before you reveal yours?

9 You are manager of a sports centre and the centre needs to have a creche so that mothers can leave their young children while they use the sports facilities. Do you:
   (a) Ask the manager of the local nursery to come and organise it for you?

(b) Decide how it should be organised and call a meeting with those staff you've selected to run it in order to explain to them what they should do?

(c) Ask for interested staff to organise it as they see appropriate?

10 Again as manager of a sports centre, you find that because of Compulsory Competitive Tendering, you need to make redundancies among the staff. Should you:

(a) Select those staff to be made redundant whom you feel are the least competent workers?

(b) Tell the staff that a number of people must go and leave them to decide for themselves who it should be?

(c) Explain the position to the staff and ask for their ideas for reducing staffing levels?

11 You are the manager of a shoe shop and one sales assistant has been late almost every day for the past two weeks. Your area manager has informed you that something must be done about it. Should you:

(a) Give it another few days to see whether things improve?

(b) Give him or her a verbal warning and say that he or she will receive a written warning and then dismissal if things don't improve?

(c) Ask him or her if there are any problems with getting to work and try to sort them out if you can?

Score each letter you marked as follows:

Question no.	(a)	(b)	(c)
1	10	5	0
2	5	0	10
3	10	5	0
4	0	10	5
5	0	10	5
6	10	5	0
7	5	0	10
8	5	10	0
9	0	10	5
10	10	0	5
11	0	10	5

What does your score signify?

75–110
You tend to have an autocratic leadership style and prefer to make all the decisions yourself. This is suitable in situations where speed is essential or your subordinates

have little knowledge or experience in the job. Possibly, if your group of subordinates is very large and have very diverse opinions on the subject to be decided upon, it may be appropriate to take the decision yourself.

If you ticked (a) for Question 1, then perhaps you should take more notice of the feelings and opinions of others. Remember, it is just as important to manage people as the task in hand.

35-75

You tend to have a democratic leadership style and prefer to share the making of decisions with your subordinates. This is suitable in situations where there is adequate time for a longer decision-making process and the subordinates are knowledgeable and well motivated.

You believe in encouraging your followers to take part in setting goals and to contribute ideas and suggestions.

Alternatively, you may not take their suggestions very seriously and take the final decision yourself. In this case you are not democratic at all, but merely a consultative manager.

0-35

You tend to have a *laissez faire* leadership style and prefer to let your subordinates make their own decisions. This is suitable when working with people who are experts in their field or are highly motivated. *Laissez faire* can offer the greatest opportunities for subordinates to satisfy their needs.

If you ticked (c) for Question 3, then perhaps you are rather lazy about the task of management. Your subordinates will see you as work shy and your department will not be as effective or successful as it could be. If you don't like the responsibility which goes with decision taking, then perhaps a management job isn't for you just yet.

Extremes?

The extreme score for each style is:
    Autocratic style – 110
    Democratic style – 55
    Laissez faire – 0

Borderline case?

Possibly you react differently to each situation as it crops up, which is good.

Situational theories

Style theories consider that it is possible for leaders to behave in different ways. But being an autocratic or democratic leader may not be appropriate in every

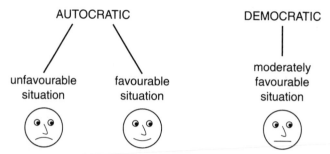

Fig 3.1 Fiedler's recommendation on autocratic and democratic leadership

situation. Often, it is necessary to wait and see what the circumstances are before deciding which style to adopt. Yet, to say that 'it depends upon the situation' is not very helpful, as no guidelines are given. There are countless possible different situations which could occur. Situational theories deal with them by putting all the different situations into categories, and give advice according to which category the situation comes under.

The situational theories move the idea of leadership away from being a personality trait (such as intelligence or charisma) or a style of behaviour (such as autocratic or *laissez faire*) towards a role to be performed or a job to be done (for example, supervising the unloading of a lorry or managing a post office).

Fiedler's contingency theory

A person may be very successful being democratic, having meetings and getting the whole team to contribute and feel committed to the work. In a different job and a different situation, there may only be one way to do the work, and it would be more appropriate to adopt an autocratic leadership style. The democratic leader may not do his or her job as successfully in all situations and may need to change his or her style to fit the circumstances.

Fiedler categorised different situations in which leaders might find themselves as:

- favourable to the leader
- unfavourable to the leader
- moderately favourable to the leader (a mixture of the two)

Fiedler recommended that leaders should adopt an autocratic leadership style if the situation is either strongly favourable or unfavourable to them and a democratic style if the situation is moderately favourable.

There are three factors which determine whether a situation is favourable or unfavourable for a leader. They are:

1 **Leader-member relations**
   How well the leader gets along with subordinates or group members, and the degree to which they feel supported by their members.

2 **Task structure**
   Whether the task is clearly laid down and structured. It may be flexible and there could be many different possible ways of completing the job. Or it could be clear-cut and programmed as to goals, procedures and measurable progress.

3 **Position power**
   How much power the leader has over such things as hiring and firing of the subordinates. The leader may be involved in recruitment and selection, the allocation of pay rises and promotions. The leader may also be responsible for giving verbal and written warnings for such things as lateness or absence. Some leaders have no power over any of these matters.

What is meant by a 'favourable situation':

- the leader is liked and trusted by the group (leader-member relationships)
- the task is clearly laid down and well defined (task structure)
- the power of the leader is high and he or she can reward and punish subordinates (position power)

What is meant by an 'unfavourable situation':

- the leader is disliked by the group
- the task is ambiguous and there are several possible ways in which it can be carried out
- the leader has no power to reward and punish subordinates

A moderately favourable situation is a mixture of favourable and unfavourable together. A popular leader may have no power to hire and fire and an unstructured task, so can therefore be democratic and ask the opinions of the group as to how the task should be carried out. This may be suitable when people are working in teams and on one-off projects such as designing computer systems. When the group members are experts in their own field or the problem they are working on is a creative one, then plenty of different suggestions and perspectives on the problem will be helpful to the leader.

Fiedler's approach is useful because it reminds us that there are occasions when it pays to be distant and task-centred rather than democratic. The main strength of the theory is that it points out that leaders need to be autocratic in certain situations.

The theory's advice on when to adopt a democratic style is more problematical. Mixing together the three variables of task structure, position power and leader popularity does not always provide a situation in which a leader can be democratic and share power with subordinates.

It is difficult to be democratic with a highly structured task as there is very little to discuss. If tins of dog food have to be taken swiftly from a conveyor belt and loaded into boxes, the ways it could be done are very limited. A democratic approach may be to let the workers reorganise their work in terms of job rotation so that people only have to do a certain task for an hour and then change over to something else – but this is not always possible.

Also, it is difficult for an unpopular leader to be democratic as the members may not feel co-operative enough to work with him or her. There may be a lack of trust in the leader or respect for the leader's expertise in the job. It is possible though, for the leader to be laissez faire and leave the members to do the task as they see fit. This would not be appropriate in all situations.

Events cropping up in addition to the daily routine can be dealt with in a democratic way. Workers can contribute to the solution of problems such as how to tighten security against burglars or shoplifters. They can provide suggestions on changes such as new layouts to the office or factory, what new staff should be told in an induction programme and how they should be trained.

Managers who are used to being autocratic and taking all the decisions themselves may forget that it is possible to involve staff occasionally. When changes are made in an autocratic way, staff can feel frustrated and that they are 'always the last to know'. This especially causes bitterness when the decisions are told to a few people, so that most staff find out what has been decided through the grapevine or rumour.

Managers who normally have an autocratic leadership style as a result of their situation can alter it in certain circumstances so that staff feel involved with and committed to changes.

Situational leadership theory

This theory was devised by American consultants Paul Hersey and Ken Blanchard in 1982.

Leadership style should be chosen according to the work experience of the subordinates (followers). For example, new and inexperienced workers in an organisation will need plenty of guidance and support whereas 'old hands' who have been working in the organisation for many years can be left to get on with their work.

The choice of leadership style is determined by the situation the leader finds him or herself in. There is one factor which determines the situation – the 'maturity' of the followers.

By **'maturity'**, Hersey and Blanchard mean:

- the amount of experience the follower has had doing his or her particular job
- how well motivated the follower is

The two definitions of maturity, though, do not necessarily go together. People who are new in a job may be willing to accept responsibility and are keen to achieve success in doing it. In the same way, people who have been doing their jobs for many years are not necessarily well motivated.

Hersey and Blanchard believed that both aspects of maturity (task experience and motivation) should be taken into account when deciding upon a leadership style.

Four different leadership styles were identified by Hersey and Blanchard. These can be listed as levels, depending upon experience in the job.

1 **Telling** (no experience)
   Specific instructions are given as to how to do the job, not only when the employee first joins the organisation but also while they are still learning their job. Communication is largely one-way – from boss to subordinate – and there is little personal relationship behaviour.

2 **Selling** (some experience)
   The leader continues to provide instructions as to how to do the job when needed. As the employee becomes familiar with the work, there will be more relationship behaviour. Communication becomes two-way and more open between the boss and subordinates. The boss will explain why the job is carried out in a certain way, which gives the subordinate a clearer understanding of the job and their role in the organisation.

3 **Participating** (experienced)
   The subordinate is now so experienced at the job that there is little task support needed and interactions with the leader consist of such matters as discussions on the wider role of the job and organisational politics.

4 **Delegating** (expert)
   There is very little communication with the leader. The subordinates are experienced enough at the job to complete it alone and they do not feel the need of emotional support from the boss in order to do the job.

The theory helps to give guidance to managers facing the dilemma of whether to adopt an *authoritarian* or *participative* style with their workers. The motivation of subordinates also has to be taken into account because unwilling subordinates may need more direction or attention from their leader than willing followers. Highly motivated people may be able to start at the 'participating' level rather than at the 'telling' level.

However, Hersey and Blanchard's theory does not consider different types of jobs, or that some organisations have such flat structures (lots of people on the same level all reporting to one boss) that it might be impossible for the leader to give all subordinates directions.

Some organisations have an overlap period of time when the person leaving shows the new starter how to do the job. Someone on the same level may act as mentor to the new person and the leader does not need to give any instructions.

The theory is useful however for pointing out that the varying amount of experience people have in doing a job will require different leadership styles. It also introduces the idea of using different leadership styles with each individual.

CASE STUDY

The Head Gardener hairdressing salon

Mark Shenton – manager, Head Gardener salon

The Head Gardener hairdressing salon has a relaxed and cheerful atmosphere and the clients experience a high quality service, provided by the young staff of this modern and fast-moving salon.

'There's a lot of know-how and experience here,' says manager Mark Shenton. 'People will pay a little more to have their hair done by an experienced stylist.' Mark is the salon's top stylist, and the most expensive.

Clients, who have often made their appointment weeks previously, enter the new mirrored and tiled salon and check in at the reception desk. Staff wear black and white. Clients sit and chat with their stylist about their hair, and receive suggestions and advice prior to being shampooed and conditioned. Coffee is offered and all clients and telephone calls are looked after quickly.

Mark is popular and approachable, and manages fourteen staff. Darren Hankey is the assistant manager and Christine David is in charge of staff training. Christine supervises those staff on the Youth Training Scheme.

The training centre above the salon is approved for NVQ Levels 1, 2 and 3, and participates in the National Preferred Scheme for training stylists. Staff being trained stay behind once a week for lessons with Christine, Mark and Darren. The salon has training sessions for senior as well as junior staff, and daytime use of the school above.

John English Ltd, who own the salon, give Mark the usual manager licence to run the business, using his own personality. When Mark first started as trainee manager, head office dealt with matters such as staff discipline, warnings, dismissals and pay rises. Mark has been running the salon for seven years and now deals with most things, according to company policy. Head office only pay the salaries.

Mark's day starts at 8.30 a.m. when he and Darren arrive to discuss the previous day's business, covering problems or complaints and whether they are reaching the targets set for them by John English Ltd. Their targets include the value of hair product sales, customer receipts and a given breakdown of services such as cuts and perms. If targets are not achieved, Mark gets a phone call from head office and is asked how he can improve the salon's performance in future. Mark works on a salary plus bonuses and commission geared to his salon's overall performance.

'Often the day begins with a mini five minute staff meeting,' says Mark. 'I can tell the staff about things like new products when they first arrive, so that it stays fresh in their minds.'

Mark also has more formal meetings with all staff at the beginning of each month. These deal with the results for the previous month and look at how the turnover on products such as perms, colours and cuts compare to the same month in the previous year. John English Ltd produce a monthly league table with salon placings. Mark says, 'If we're not at the top of the league table, we discuss what might have gone wrong, and how we might achieve top placing again.'

Mark holds these meetings after the monthly managers' meeting, when managers and more experienced directors exchange ideas and experiences.

Staff contribute ideas at the meeting and Mark says, 'It motivates staff. If we've had a poor month on perms, I say why I think that is and ask the others. They suggest ideas on what to do next month to improve.' Darren speaks at the meetings about the general running of the salon and Christine gives news on training. At the meetings there are awards for Staff of the Month and Junior of the Month as a recognition of good work, attendance and appearance. There are also Staff of the Year and Junior of the Year Awards which are presented on New Year's Eve.

Darren chairs a separate meeting for the junior staff. 'This is so that they can voice their opinions about things they might be reluctant to say to me,' says Mark. Mark also delegates the ordering of supplies (such as new shampoos and hairsprays) to a member of staff. Mark checks the order and the monthly stocktake and forwards these to company headquarters for processing. Part of Mark's role as manager is to interview and select new staff, and he also recommends pay awards for those staff he thinks deserve a higher salary. If there are discipline problems, Mark recommends that warnings are given officially. If he cannot obtain the desired improvements, he asks a director to interview the person, and often a change of workplace solves the problem.

As well as having his own clients, Mark is constantly interrupted by other stylists asking his advice. 'Mark, can you check this colour?' calls Lisa. 'Mark, can I borrow you for a minute?' asks Sarah, and Mark dashes off to discuss the best treatment for a client's hair.

'I enjoy getting involved with everyone else's work and spreading ideas around,' says Mark. Mark values the loyalty and expertise of his staff. 'It's easy to fall into the trap that it's all me, but I never forget that it takes more than one person to make it a success.'

QUESTIONS

1 How does Mark Shenton's situation fit in with Fiedler's Contingency Theory, in terms of:
   (a) Mark's position power?
   (b) relationships between Mark and his staff?
   (c) task structure?

2 What leadership style should Mark adopt in view of the situation he is in?

3 What might happen in the salon if Mark changed his leadership style and was:
   (a) completely *laissez faire* and let the staff organise the work as they wished?
   (b) completely democratic and involved everyone in the making of all decisions?

4 What leadership style does head office use with Mark?

Performance Criterion 2
The leadership role of the manager

For an organisation to be successful it has to achieve its aims. This means that departments, groups and individuals have to be planned and co-ordinated. Senior managers have to decide on the aims of the whole organisation and make sure that they are achieved. Middle and lower management are responsible for day-to-day operations. All managers have responsibility for a certain aspect of the organisation.

The role of the manager is to be responsible for:

- achieving a task
- managing a group of people

Although the task of a senior manager is different to that of other managers within the organisation, every manager has the responsibility of getting a job done through other people. The task allocated to any manager involves more work than one person can do. The manager therefore has a staff of people to whom they can delegate the work.

The manager's responsibility is to bring together the staff under his or her control in order to get the job done. Without achieving its goals, the organisation will lose its way. It will make a loss, or in the case of a non profit-making organisation such as a leisure centre or charity, it will not serve its customers as it should.

Achieving a task

Achieving a task, or getting a job done, requires:

- **Planning** – deciding what is to be done
- **Organising** – deciding how it is to be done
- **Monitoring** – checking that it has been done correctly

Fig. 3.2 Some reasons for poor profit

Planning

Planning involves:

- finding information so that all the facts are known about the present position and other possibilities
- deciding upon the objective for the group or organisation
- devising a workable plan

The first part of planning involves analysing a problem or facts about the present situation. The manager needs to know exactly what the problem is and where they want to be within a specified period of time.

If the problem in a jam tart manufacturing company is poor profits, there are many possibilities which could be investigated in the analysing (or finding information) stage.

Research may reveal that sales are low due to a lack of advertising. The customers (supermarkets) are not aware that the jam tarts are available and they are not ordering them.

The second part of planning is to decide upon objectives for the organisation or work group. Aims are *general*, objectives are *specific* and *measurable*. For example:

AIM: To increase profits
OBJECTIVE: To increase sales by 10 per cent over the next three months

These should complement one another, i.e. the increase in sales should bring about increased profit.

Planning is needed so that the aims are cascaded through the organisation and enable each level in the organisation to set its objectives accordingly.

When members of a team know and understand the objectives of the group they can share in the feeling of achievement when the group's objectives are met.

The third element in planning is devising a workable plan, which means considering the skills needed for the organisation, department or group to achieve their objectives, the availability of equipment and staff the required time and what co-operation between departments and other organisations will be necessary.

Organising

Organising involves:

1 (i) briefing the team on the aims and objectives of the plan and
  (ii) explaining why it is necessary

2 (i) allocating work to the appropriate team members and
  (ii) arranging any necessary training for them

3 obtaining any additional resources (more people, equipment, finance, buildings, machinery, materials, tools)

4 (i) deciding on standards of performance and
  (ii) devising a monitoring system to check that standards are met

An important element in organising the task is communicating to the group and individuals exactly what the plan involves and why it has been chosen. This stage will be less vital to the group with a **democratic** leader, as they will have already been involved in planning and will understand how the plan came about and the reasoning behind it.

A leader could call a meeting, have the agenda circulated, book a room, arrange photocopies of any necessary documents, organise coffee for mid-morning and give thought to the issues needing discussion, if appropriate to the situation. As well as creating a businesslike feel to the environment in which the decisions are made, such arrangements show that the leader cares about the meeting and the people there, so that staff feel valued. There are other ways of organising a decision-making process which may be equally appropriate to the particular situation – talking with people informally, for example, is a quick way to get people's opinions on a topic.

For many leaders, organising may be straightforward day-to-day activities such as drawing up rotas and timetables to decide when people work and what tasks they do, so that all jobs and times are covered adequately. However, the larger the task, the greater the amount of organisation needed. Imagine the organisation required to put on a pop concert. People have to be in the right place at the right time to take tickets, sell refreshments, operate the lighting and sound, provide backing music, and get the performers on stage.

Disorganised events, such as late deliveries, meetings where no one is sure why they have been called, conferences in cold halls, or customers arriving for appointments with the sales manager when he or she has gone out, all give the impression that the company is not worth doing business with, both to those outside the organisation and to the employees inside. The way the group is represented will affect the employees' work. If the leader gives the impression that his or her group is responsible, enthusiastic and effective, then information about the group's activities will be seen in that light. This means that those above the group in the organisation will:

- trust the group to continue their work without constant monitoring
- allow the group to have access to the necessary resources (finance, people or equipment) for which there is often competition with other groups in the organisation

Monitoring

Monitoring involves:

- testing procedures to see whether they meet objectives
- checking the work as it is being done to find out whether targets and standards are achieved
- observing the situation to check that the work is being done as intended before too much damage is done

The manager examines the results of the team's work as they start to emerge against the planned results. Actual results may be measured against planned results in terms of cost, outputs, standards, sales or profits.

Also, time is an important factor. Results should be achieved within a given time frame. If 100 jam tarts are needed by the customer at 8 a.m. the following day, then they must be ready by a certain time, to allow time for packing and delivery. It is also important to monitor resources at this point – is there sufficient jam and other ingredients? Are there enough cardboard boxes to pack them in? Are resources being wasted? Mistakes are often made during the production process and materials are thrown away. These mistakes cost money and mean that more resources will be needed to make a given amount of products.

It may be necessary to take some sort of corrective action during the monitoring process. It is not merely a time to count numbers produced or judge quality, although these activities certainly come into the monitoring process.

The final part of the monitoring responsibility is to evaluate the results. This means:

- checking that the job is being performed satisfactorily
- checking that objectives are being achieved
- checking that standards have been met

As a result of the review and evaluation process, the manager may decide to increase resources or use them in different ways to make the achievement of the task more effective. The manager may decide to move workers around to do other jobs, to use more temporary or part-time labour to meet peaks in demand, to use different machinery or equipment, or to move premises. There are many different ways resources can be organised.

QUIZ

Which part of the leadership role has gone wrong in the following situations?
Answer either: **Planning, Organising or Monitoring.**

1 Valerie has sent off twelve boxes of goods to a regular customer who always orders twelve boxes. Her boss Sue signed the documents to verify that it had been checked without looking at the order. If either Sue or Valerie had looked they would have noticed that the order was for fifteen boxes this month.

2 Trevor is the marketing manager for an ice-cream manufacturer. In the past he has carried out market research to find out whether consumers like the company's new flavours. This time, he considers the new chocolate flavour to be so good that it does not need any market research to confirm that it will be extremely popular.

3 Tony has started his own business importing china and ornaments from factories in the Philippines. Now that he has the goods in the country he is not sure what to do with them.

4 Eleanor is very busy and has been meaning to call a meeting of her department for some time. When she arrives at the office she is very angry because they are all sitting doing nothing when there is lots to be done – she just hasn't got around to explaining it to them yet.

5 Gordon has been drawing up rotas for staff to work in the bar in his nightclub. So many people wanted the same night off that he was very harassed trying to accommodate them all. Now he finds there is no cover at all for that one evening and he cannot go in himself.

6 Joanne has received several telephone calls from customers at her newsagents because they have not received their newspapers this morning. She is baffled because she wrote all the addresses on the papers for the new girl and gave her full instructions as to where to go.

7 Laura is the production manager in a toy factory. Today, no customer orders can go out because they have run out of boxes to pack them in.

Check your answers below:

1 Monitoring

It was Sue's job to sign the documents to verify that the order had been filled correctly by Valerie. She should be checking that standards have been met and that the job has been performed satisfactorily.

2 Planning

Without market research the company cannot know that there is a demand for their new product. It is Trevor's job to find out what the customer needs so that the company can meet those needs.

3 Planning

It appears that Tony liked the china and ornaments from the Philippines and ordered them without thinking about what might happen when they arrived in the UK. He is lacking information and objectives and he has not devised a plan.

4 Organising

The leader's job is to brief the team on the aims and objectives of the plan and explain why it is necessary. Eleanor has not done this, nor has she allocated work to the appropriate team members. Her being 'too busy' means that the work of the whole department has ground to a halt.

5 Organising

Gordon probably did allocate work to the appropriate team members, but due to the many changes to his original rota, confusion set in and the work was not allocated properly. Now he is faced with the prospect of having to close the nightclub altogether or employ someone unsuitable such as his Aunt Joyce.

6 Organising and monitoring

Joanne has done her planning and organising as far as she is concerned but the new paper girl obviously does not see the situation in the same light. The girl may have needed more training (organising role) and Joanne should check to see that the new employee can do the job and that it has been done.

7 Organising

Obtaining resources is part of the organising role. Arranging for sufficient boxes to be delivered is part of Laura's job. It may be that plenty of boxes were originally delivered and they have been spoiled due to poor quality packing or storage. In this case it would be the monitoring role which had gone wrong.

Managing individuals and groups

The manager's role of achieving a task, or getting the job done, is linked inextricably with managing people (*see* Fig. 3.3). People are employed for the specific purpose of helping to 'get the job done'.

Fig. 3.3 The main factors involved in managing people

Managing people requires:

- **maximising contribution** – getting the best out of each employee
- **recognising individual strengths and weaknesses and building on the former** – using the talents of each employee
- **recognising maintenance factors** – stepping in where appropriate to help employees
- **recognising importance of motivators** – using motivators to encourage people to contribute to organisational objectives

Employees can be viewed by managers as:

- paid 'hands' who have a specific job to do.
- members of the social system which makes up the organisation. They can and do interact with other members of the system and with the system itself. They are capable of contributing much more to the organisation than a 'pair of hands'.

The second of these ways of viewing employees – as people who are capable of contributing fully to the organisation – has been considered in leadership theories:

1 **Likert's Systems**
2 **Tannenbaum and Schmidt's Continuum of Leadership Behaviour**

These theories point out that different leadership styles are needed to encourage employees to contribute. They cannot give their maximum contribution to the organisation if their manager will not let them.

Development of style theory – Rensis Likert

Rensis Likert, born in 1903, was an American industrial psychologist who carried out research into how to use labour to the best advantage in industry.

Likert became very enthusiastic about the use of work groups and their participation in decision making. He considered that a democratic approach to the use of labour would result in maximum profitability, good labour relations and high productivity.

He expanded the idea of democratic/autocratic style into four different categories or 'systems', as illustrated in Table 3.1.

Table 3.1

	SYSTEM 1	SYSTEM 2	SYSTEM 3	SYSTEM 4
Category	Authoritarian style	Paternalistic authoritarian	Consultative style	Democratic style
Decision-making process	Imposes decisions	Keeps strict control and never delegates	Asks for and receives participation from subordinates but maintains the right to make the final decision	Gives some direction to subordinates but there is total participation and decision making by consensus
Motivation method	Threats of punishment	Rewards	Rewards and some	Commitment to group goals involvement
Style	AUTOCRAT	BENEVOLENT AUTOCRAT	CONSULTATIVE	DEMOCRAT

Although Likert considered the participative System 4 style of management to be ideal for a profitable and caring company, this has fallen from favour as there are some situations when a strong leader making autocratic decisions leads to the most successful outcome.

Nevertheless, Likert's ideas on the four features of effective management are being put into practice in many modern organisations:

1 Motivation of the workers through modern methods rather than rewards and punishment (autocratic).

2 Improvement of employees' self-esteem (benevolent).

3 The introduction of work groups committed to achieving organisational objectives (consultative).

4 The encouragement of mutual respect between work groups (democratic).

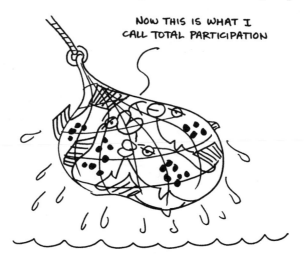

Continuum of leadership behaviour

Robert Tannenbaum and Warren Schmidt, both American psychologists, devised their 'Continuum of Leadership Behaviour' in 1958, which was intended as a framework to help managers decide how to behave in different situations. Although it does not actually give any advice other than to judge each situation differently, it points out that there are many different sorts of behaviours between democratic and autocratic, as shown in Fig. 3.4.

The continuum moves away from dictatorial rule to employees participating in the decision-making process and having greater control within the organisation. Tannenbaum and Schmidt do not say which style of leadership is best for different situations – they merely present these variations as possibilities.

Managers are not entirely free to change from one leadership style to another. It is part of the unstated organisational culture that all managers use a particular style, such as 'consulting with' or 'explaining to' their subordinates. If there is to be a change of style, then there will usually be a policy decision made by senior management that the style for the whole organisation will change. Managers with a different leadership style to others within the organisation will be seen as 'not fitting in' to the organisation. Their actions will be perceived by others as strange and unacceptable. However, if they are senior management, then others will follow their example and the organisational culture will change.

Managers cannot achieve their objectives if they treat their employees as commodities who sell their labour and nothing more. At the other extreme, managers cannot be expected to be totally caring and act as a parent to their employees. Managers are responsible for encouraging their subordinates to contribute fully to the organisation's objectives.

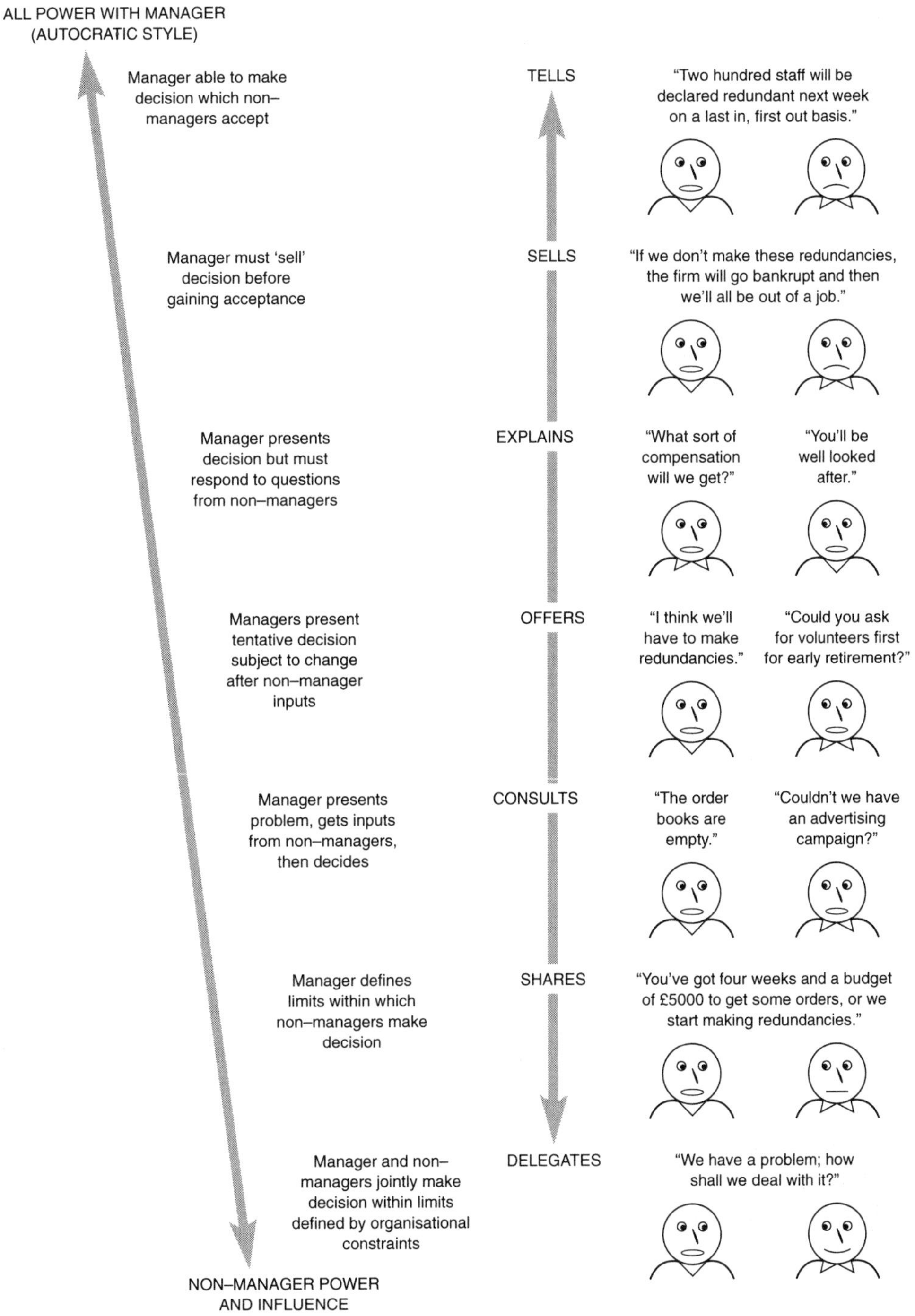

ALL POWER WITH MANAGER
(AUTOCRATIC STYLE)

Manager able to make decision which non–managers accept	TELLS	"Two hundred staff will be declared redundant next week on a last in, first out basis."
Manager must 'sell' decision before gaining acceptance	SELLS	"If we don't make these redundancies, the firm will go bankrupt and then we'll all be out of a job."
Manager presents decision but must respond to questions from non–managers	EXPLAINS	"What sort of compensation will we get?" / "You'll be well looked after."
Managers present tentative decision subject to change after non–manager inputs	OFFERS	"I think we'll have to make redundancies." / "Could you ask for volunteers first for early retirement?"
Manager presents problem, gets inputs from non–managers, then decides	CONSULTS	"The order books are empty." / "Couldn't we have an advertising campaign?"
Manager defines limits within which non–managers make decision	SHARES	"You've got four weeks and a budget of £5000 to get some orders, or we start making redundancies."
Manager and non–managers jointly make decision within limits defined by organisational constraints	DELEGATES	"We have a problem; how shall we deal with it?"

NON–MANAGER POWER
AND INFLUENCE

Fig. 3.4 Continuum of leadership behaviour

McGregor's Theory X and Theory Y

Managers hold different views about people. Douglas McGregor's book *The Human Side of Enterprise* (1960) sets out two extreme views of human nature which managers may take. The views are that people:

1 *do not* want to work (**Theory X** managers)
2 *do* want to work (**Theory Y** managers)

Theory X assumptions

1 Average human beings have an inherent dislike of work and will avoid it if they can.
2 Because of this human characteristic, most people must be coerced, controlled, directed and threatened with punishment if they are to put in adequate effort towards the achievement of organisational objectives.
3 Average human beings prefer to be directed, wish to avoid responsibility, have relatively little ambition, and want security above all.

Theory Y assumptions

1 The expenditure of physical effort and mental effort in work is as natural as play or rest.
2 External control and the threat of punishment are not the only means for bringing about effort toward organisational objectives. People will exercise self-direction and self-control in the service of objectives to which they are committed.
3 Average human beings learn, under proper conditions, not only to accept but also to seek responsibility.
4 The capacity to exercise a relatively high degree of imagination, ingenuity, and creativity in the solution of organisational problems is widely, not narrowly, distributed in the population.
5 Under the conditions of modern industrial life, the intellectual potential of the average human being is only partially utilized.

QUIZ

Are you a Theory X or Theory Y manager?

Answer **agree** or **disagree** to the following statements:

1 People are capable of contributing a lot more to their jobs than they do. Their brain power and ideas are not utilized.

2 People are capable of contributing a lot more to their jobs than they do. They do the minimum they can get away with.

3 Most people enjoy having responsibility in their jobs.

4 Most people want to be involved with creative problem solving in their jobs.

5 Most people want to be told exactly what to do and not have to use their initiative.

6 It should be made easier for employers to sack people who are not pulling their weight.

7 People like to work because it gives them the chance of fulfilment and job satisfaction.

8 People like the status and opportunities work gives them.

9 If people at work were not constantly watched, they wouldn't do any work at all.

10 The majority of people have only got the brain power to do menial jobs.

11 Most people would resign from their jobs immediately if they had enough money to live on.

12 Everyone hates the thought of having to go to work when they wake up in the morning.

Score your answers as follows:

Statement	Agree	Disagree
1	10	5
2	5	10
3	10	5
4	10	5
5	5	10
6	5	10
7	10	5
8	10	5
9	5	10
10	5	10
11	5	10
12	5	10

90 or more?
You are a **Theory Y** manager. You believe that people do want to go to work and do a good job. With your attitude to your subordinates you should be able to get the maximum contribution from them in terms of work, as you will encourage them to solve problems and contribute their ideas to getting the job done.

Less than 90?

You are a **Theory X** manager. You believe that people are lazy and need to be threatened to make them do any work. With these assumptions you will get the minimum out of your workforce.

The extremes of Theory X and Theory Y managers may not actually exist. As there is no 'average' person, there are rarely managers who fall into extreme categories.

QUESTIONS

1 Assuming there are such people as Theory X and Theory Y managers, which is it easier to be – a Theory X or Theory Y manager?

2 Do you think the following statements are always correct?

The Theory X manager is never wrong. If the work is going badly, it must the workers' fault because they are lazy. If the work is going well, then it is because the workers are so good.

The Theory Y manager is always wrong. If the work is going badly, it must be the manager's fault because he or she has good workers who do their job well. If the work is going well, it is down to those good workers.

3 How could you tell whether a manager held Theory X or Theory Y assumptions?

4 What sort of wording would a Theory X manager use in communications such as memos and notices to their staff?

5 Is it possible to be a manager with Theory Y assumptions in an organisation full of managers with Theory X assumptions about human nature?

Douglas McGregor's theory

According to Douglas McGregor's theory, Theory X managers are likely to treat workers as just 'paid hands', while Theory Y managers are likely to treat workers as people capable of contributing a lot to the organisation. They will encourage workers to participate in the achievement of organisational objectives.

Managers with Theory Y attitudes towards their subordinates will be more likely to maximise workers' contributions to the organisation.

There are various ways of doing this:

- employee participation
- training
- rewards/motivators

Maximising contribution through employee participation

There are various ways in which managers can encourage participation by employees with the aim of maximising contribution:

- empowerment
- work committees
- suggestion programmes
- quality circles
- industrial democracy
- employee ownership plans

Empowerment

This is a fairly recent idea, which is based upon organising workers into groups and giving them increased responsibility. This is often as a result of changes in organisational structure, such as removing layers of management. Workers can be made responsible for such things as improving their work processes, recruiting new staff, drawing up rotas, meeting targets, organising their own meetings, training team members, ordering stock, solving problems and dealing with customer complaints.

Groups can be empowered to do almost anything. They can be made up of people all doing the same job, people doing different jobs within the same department or they may be made up of people of different status from different departments (*cross-functional* teams).

Successful teamwork in Japan has involved cross-functional teams which all include a senior manager, access to the firm's resources, and a commitment to the project by all team members.

Empowerment should:

- ensure openness
- promote co-operation
- delegate authority
- manage performance
- develop people
- provide rewards and recognition
- encourage effective communication
- help resolve issues
- encourage innovation

Work committees

These are groups of workers and managers organised with the objective of considering and solving job problems. Many work committees replace trade unions in non-union organisations. They provide representation for the workforce.

Quality circles

Quality circles are voluntary groups which meet to solve problems, and produce ideas for improving productivity or working conditions. They meet regularly in company time and produce ideas for management to evaluate and implement.

The quality circle idea has now largely been incorporated into empowered teams.

Suggestion schemes

Suggestion schemes are a formal method by which employees can recommend work improvements. Often, a suggestion box is provided in the organisation and employees can post their written suggestions for consideration by management. Those suggestions accepted receive a payment which varies according to the value of the suggestion. Many firms have profited greatly through this system.

Suggestion schemes encourage individual contributions from employees and do not fit in with the concept of teamwork. Empowered teams give their ideas freely and team members can contribute to another member's idea to improve it. Suggestion schemes lack this face-to-face discussion.

Industrial democracy

This idea originated in Germany in the 1940s, when steel firms were required to have boards of directors with one-third worker representatives. British firms implementing the idea have usually had just one worker director, and the idea is now less fashionable.

Industrial democracy aims to encourage worker participation in management so that co-operation would replace conflict between workers and managers. The result should be increased understanding of one another's problems.

Employee ownership

The ultimate in employee ownership is a worker co-operative which is a company owned and managed by the workers.

On a lesser scale, many firms are encouraging workers to buy shares in the company so that commitment to the firm is increased. The intention is that employees will be encouraged to work harder as they reap the benefits through their share of the profits. Often, the actual amount of profits earned through employee share ownership is small and the employee may conclude that the same amount of profit would have been made whatever their effort.

Fig. 3.5 *Advantages of training to the organisation*

Maximising contribution through training

Training is any learning activity which is aimed towards gaining knowledge and skills for the purpose of an occupation or task. What do you need to know and be able to do in order to be a hairdresser, car mechanic, professional footballer, chef or bank clerk? Would you like to go on holiday in an aeroplane with an untrained pilot, or have your teeth looked at by an untrained dentist? People need training in order to be able to do their jobs. Most people can cut another person's hair or kick a football, but their performance would be very much enhanced by training.

Increasing an individual's knowledge and skills has advantages for both the organisation and the individual, as illustrated in Fig. 3.5.

Sufficient range of skills amongst employees

It is not sufficient that all the hairdressers in the salon can cut hair, as there are other skills which employees need to know. Someone must answer the telephone to callers wishing to make appointments, someone must shampoo, order new supplies, sweep up, or blowdry clients' hair. Training will ensure that all the necessary functions are covered by employees.

Harnessing work experience and on-the-job development in a planned way

Many people learn their jobs by 'watching Fred'. If Fred is an expert in his job and is good at explaining it to new recruits then this is an excellent way for them to learn. However, there may not be a 'Fred' in every organisation and new recruits could find themselves being instructed by someone who has picked up bad habits and incorrect ways of doing things. It is far better that a good employee is trained to be a staff trainer and has the procedures for training new recruits documented.

Improved product quality

The quality of a service, such as hairdressing, usually improves as the hairstylist receives more training when people are trained properly, fewer mistakes are made. Production errors result in low quality finished goods or services. If the quality of a product is too low for it to be sold to the customer, it is scrap and has to be thrown away, or it could be downgraded and sold less than full value, which costs the organisation more than if the work was completed correctly first time. Other costs of poor quality are the costs of refunds, repairs and replacements.

Improved service to customers

Customers will not have to check supplies for faults, make telephone calls complaining about the products or return poor quality products if supplies are always good quality. Well trained employees will also offer good service in the form of such things as answering the telephone promptly, being helpful and courteous to customers and delivering goods on time.

Increased motivation amongst employees

Those organisations which invest in training are communicating to their employees that they consider them to be important to the company's future success and that they wish to retain their services. Employee motivation and performance is enhanced and the workers will be able to maximise their contribution to the organisation.

Improved job performance and productivity

Intelligent and able people who are willing to learn cannot automatically perform skills without training. Not many people can speak Russian or drive a heavy goods vehicle – training and practise is needed to gain these skills. Training will enable people to do their jobs to the best of their ability and will also help them to do their jobs more quickly, thus enhancing productivity. Productivity is also increased by training workers to use new machinery and computerised equipment to speed up the work.

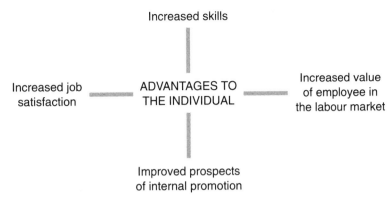

Fig. 3.6 Advantages of training to the individual

Development of knowledge and skills in the workforce

Having a skilled and knowledgeable workforce gives organisations a competitive advantage. It provides them with an asset their competitors may not have. Many organisations consider that their product can be bought from many other similar organisations and the way that they can attract and keep customers is through their people – their employees can offer an excellent service. This competitive advantage can only be maintained by training new and existing employees on how to give the best service. Fig. 3.6 illustrates the advantages to the employee of training in the workplace.

Increased skills

Individuals will benefit from working for a particular organisation if they are given training, as their own skills will be enhanced.

Increased value of employee in the labour market

Well-trained individuals will be better able to get a different job if they have to leave their present employment. Many organisations are now training their employees to be multi-skilled so that they can perform a range of tasks, or for everyone in a team to be able to do one another's jobs. This increases an individual's employability.

Improved prospects for internal promotion

Individuals who have been well-trained will be able to apply for other positions within the organisation, such as supervisor or manager, which untrained people are less likely to achieve.

Increased job satisfaction

Trained people who are using their skills and abilities will feel that their talents are being made the most of in their organisation. Their potential is being realised and they will feel more committed to the success of the organisation.

The importance of training

Organisations need to offer training to their employees for several reasons:

- New employees need to be introduced to the organisation and shown their specific job.
- Performance of experienced employees may be less than required by the organisation, and their skills may need updating.
- Organisational change – new developments such as the introduction of empowered teams, multi-skilling, total quality management and the reorganisation of work processes all need training for the employees to be able to understand and do what is expected of them.
- Individual needs – people may wish to change jobs, apply for promotion or be able to perform their present job more efficiently. These needs will often be discussed in annual appraisal interviews. If training can be given to meet these needs, the individual will feel more committed to the organisation.

Training and development should be integrated into wider business planning as it can make an important contribution to the achievement of business objectives.

Surveys of employers carried out in Britain by the Manpower Services Commission (now The Department of Employment) found that almost 70 per cent of workers did not receive any training in the 12 months before the survey. Organisations can avoid the costs of training by recruiting pre-skilled labour, contracting out skilled work or by producing products or services at the lower quality end of the market. These organisations are treating labour as a cost or commodity rather than as a resource to be invested in.

Maximising contribution through rewards

People will contribute to the organisation if they feel that they are rewarded for their efforts. The idea that we learn to behave in ways that produce rewards and avoid behaving in ways that produce punishment is simple. Yet managers often inadvertently punish people for doing their work well or for doing the right thing. If John notices that there is a mistake made on a customer order and tells his supervisor Jack, Jack may tell John to put it right, causing John extra work. Jack may be angry and treat the incident as if the blame lay with John instead of thanking him for noticing the problem. It would be far easier for John to say nothing when mistakes are noticed in future.

Organisational Behavioural Modification

The idea that rewards encourage behaviour and punishment discourages behaviour is based on the work of psychologists who studied learning or conditioning. Thorndike and Skinner put forward the theory that we learn to behave in certain ways, depending upon the rewards and punishments which follow the behaviour.

According to the theory of Organisational Behaviour Modification, our behaviour is reinforced by the rewards and punishments we receive.

Consequences of behaviour:

Receive something nice – *positive reinforcement*
Something nasty is taken away – *negative reinforcement*
Something nice is taken away – *punishment*
Something nasty is given – *punishment*

Reinforcers

Positive – pay rises, bonuses, praise, and recognition for good work will all positively reinforce behaviour

Negative – not having to perform disliked tasks or not having to work unsocial hours will negatively reinforce behaviour

Rewards do not have to be given *every* time the desirable behaviour is performed. People will carry on doing the football pools without winning every time. People will do a good job for occasional praise and recognition.

Punishment

Punishment can take the form of being given something nasty (such as a reprimand for being late), or having something nice taken away (such as losing the most interesting job in the office). People will behave in ways to avoid being given punishment.

Punishment should occur every time the unwanted behaviour occurs and it should also be immediate. If behaviour is neither rewarded or punished, it will not continue. If someone is doing something annoying and they are ignored, eventually they will stop. If someone is working really hard and they are ignored for a long period, they will consider it not worth their while trying so hard or continuing in that job.

If managers wish to maximise their employees' contributions they should be aware of the use of rewards and that correct behaviour may be being punished without anyone realising that this is so.

ORGANISATIONAL BEHAVIOUR MODIFICATION QUIZ

What might be the unintended results of the following managerial actions?

1 Deducting a day's pay from anyone who is more than 15 minutes late?

2 Giving a bonus for every week which is free of accidents?

3 Reducing the departmental budget by the amount not spent this year?

4 Reprimanding a member of staff severely for making a mistake?

5 Giving someone extra work who has finished all their own work quickly?

6 Allowing three days off with full pay and no sick note for anyone who is unwell?

7 Giving someone an enjoyable job to do first and an unpleasant one to follow for when they have finished the enjoyable job?

8 Paying double time overtime rates for those who have not completed the work assigned to them?

Answers

1 This encourages people to take the whole day off if they wake up late in the morning as they won't be paid for coming in.

2 People will not report accidents in order to get their bonus for the accident-free period. This may result in dangerous situations worsening.

3 People will spend all of their budgets in future as they have been punished for not spending this year.

4 People will hide their mistakes or try to blame someone else.

5 They will do their work more slowly in future as getting lots of extra work acts as a punishment for finishing quickly.

6 Staff will be encouraged to take time off occasionally and claim that they were sick.

7 The individual will make the pleasant job last as long as possible in order not to have to do the unpleasant job.

8 People will spin out their work so that it is unfinished and they can earn extra money working overtime.

Recognising individual strengths and weaknesses

The people who come under one manager's control all differ tremendously. The computers and equipment may be standardised, but the workers all have different interests, talents and personalities. They also have different ages, experiences of life and other careers, different attitudes and ideas.

These differences can be used by the manager to make a team which can cope with almost any situation or problem. People all doing the same job can help one another as some will be better at certain aspects of the job than others. They can teach and encourage one another, which all helps the team to attain the highest standards and keep improving. As well as achieving the task, team members need to be able to get on with each other. Different personalities aid this process as not everyone can be the 'life and soul of the party' – too many similarities often cause clashes.

How then do managers recognise these strengths and weaknesses to build a successful team?

Recruiting people with talents needed within the team

A candidate's application form and response to questions during interview will give clues as to his or her talents and weak areas. The proof of these will actually come when the person has been working for the organisation for some months, but recruitment provides a good indication. Some managers unconsciously choose candidates who have similar personalities to their own – this will seriously restrict the strengths of a team. The manager should be aware that a variety of strengths are needed.

Appraisal

An annual talk with each employee enables the manager to get to know him or her better. The employee may have unsuspected interests and ambitions which the manager should know about. Also, the employee may rarely come into contact with the manager and it may be the manager's first opportunity to hear in private about the employee's achievements and talents. The manager can use the information gained during appraisal interviews to encourage workers to try different tasks or change the jobs they are working on. The appraisal is also a good time for identifying training needs and opportunities which will build on strengths and help to remedy weaknesses.

Day-to-day contact

Many managers work very closely with their subordinates and know who is good at different aspects of the job. They have witnessed their work and know who to ask to do something artistic, who would be the best person to give a talk to an outside organisation, or who would be able to show the new recruit their job. They can use these strengths in their employees when they have seen what they can do.

However, some managers have many subordinates and do not often 'walk about' to see what people are doing. Others have employees who do their job out of sight, such as salespeople. In these cases, informal chats to find out how an employee is getting on could reveal their strengths and weaknesses. Going with them to visit clients or see them do their jobs occasionally is another possibility for finding out about their strengths. The manager could also ask for reports, oral or written, from people who work more closely with the employee. These reports could be from customers, suppliers, peers, bosses or subordinates.

Also, more senior managers may have middle or junior managers below them who are not as good at their jobs as they might be. These people may be suppressing talented people because they need them to carry out the work of the department. Senior managers may be able to take action to rescue the person who is 'too good to be promoted', and find ways of giving them the recognition they deserve.

Building on strengths

Once a person's strengths have been recognised it would be a pity not to use those talents. The manager should ensure that the employee has plenty of opportunities to practise his or her skills, and improve upon them with training and increased educational opportunities.

Each person should be consulted as to how he or she would like his or her talents used. Some people may not even realise that they are particularly good at one aspect of the job and this needs pointing out to them through the use of praise and recognition. Their confidence will improve and the organisation will benefit.

Recognising maintenance factors

The social processes involved when people work together need attending to. Machines need checking to ensure that they still work, otherwise they might suddenly break down at some crucial moment when a customer order needs urgent delivery. In the same way, groups are made up of human beings who have opinions, insecurities and fears, prejudices, likes and dislikes. They are just as likely to stop working and cease to function because of conflicts and personality clashes as the machine that is not regularly oiled and cleaned.

For any group to be effective, someone in the group must perform the maintenance factors. It is the responsibility of the leader to see that they are done.

Fig. 3.7 *Maintenance factors*

Autocratic managers will probably carry them out themselves, whereas democratic managers will allow group members to perform them.

Encouraging

People need to be made to feel that they are accepted and valuable members of the group. If someone is verbally attacked or criticised by other members for putting forward an idea considered to be unacceptable, he or she will feel discouraged. This needs to be put right, otherwise the person may withdraw from the group and reduce participation to a minimum. Members do not have to actually attack one another for discouragement to set in. Ignoring a member will have a discouraging effect. Someone in the group should acknowledge each member's contributions, or ask the opinions of those people who are not contributing.

It is more valuable to the group if different people take on the 'cheerleading' role of giving encouragement to group members. People feel supported if someone is shouting for them on the sidelines.

Compromising

There may be opposing opinions in a group as to how the work should be done – who does it, how much they should do, when and how it should be done. The opposing views could ultimately become open conflict with the result of the team falling apart. The leader can help to resolve the problem by:

- accurately judging the point at which tensions are turning to conflict
- adopting a bolder style if timid by nature
- separating out the issues involved from the personalities of the group members
- paying attention to the feelings of the people in the conflict
- judging whether or not to allow people to express their negative emotions

- bringing in a third party to help solve the problem
- setting a time limit for the settlement of differences

Either the third party or the manager can act as a consultant in order to negotiate a compromise solution to the disagreement. In extreme cases, the team membership may have to be changed, but generally if people value the task they are working on, they will make adjustments and come to an agreement.

Peace-keeping

An untroubled working relationship between all group members is far more productive than having constant debates and arguments which may really be focusing on personal dislikes rather than the task. Part of the leader's function is to get team members to see the good in one another and be positive about each other's strengths and capabilities instead of dwelling on one another's shortcomings.

The effective group will have a high level of mutual trust, respect for one another and affection between members. They will also be able to tell one another if there are problems with their work without them feeling personally attacked. Everyone's main concern should be getting the job done in the best way or finding the best solution to the problem, rather than having their own ideas accepted.

The calm and unflappable leader who has a grip on the situation will be best suited to keeping the peace between group members. Leaders who adopt a democratic or laissez faire style may have more problems with keeping the peace than autocratic or consultative leaders. If the democratic or laissez faire manager has group members who are manipulative or power-seeking, the balance of power sharing can quickly change away from equal shares towards the power resting with an informal leader.

Clarifying/summarising

Group discussion may go round in circles or be dominated by one person. Part of the function of the leader is to state where the group is in terms of reaching a solution, what should be done next and what else has yet to be decided upon. This summary helps to make clear in everyone's minds what has happened so far. Often, people are talking so much themselves or are too busy thinking about what they are going to say next, that they do not listen to the discussion as a whole. This leaves them confused about what has actually happened. A person's presence at a meeting does not necessarily mean that he or she sees what happens in the same light as everyone else.

Clarifying and summarising does not only take place within a meeting. Any task will be performed better if someone clears up confusions by stating what has been achieved so far and what has yet to be done.

Standard setting

Groups can become complacent, with a feeling of 'that will do' about their work, if there is no one to set standards for them. Sometimes the leader sets standards, because he or she is the best person in the group at that job, or it may be that the group set themselves standards of performance. These need to be challenging enough to keep people's interest and give a sense of achievement when accomplished.

It is not sufficient for a group to feel that they have maintained the same high standards over a number of years. Competitors outside the organisation may also be increasing their standards and the point will be reached at which the internal group's standards are quite low compared to their competitors. Standards therefore need to be continually rising.

Recognising the importance of motivators

In order for group members to be motivated, they should have:

- a job in which they are interested
- a feeling of achievement and satisfaction from doing that job
- recognition for their work, in the form of praise or acknowledgement that they have done the work well
- opportunities for promotion

The leader can influence many of these factors and improve the motivators if they are not satisfactory. Jobs can be made more interesting by changing them to include more interesting tasks. People can be consulted as to the things they prefer to do at work and jobs can be changed to suit them. The manager can give praise and recognition, as well as encouraging the team to praise one another. The manager may have little influence over promotion prospects, but responsibilities can be given to various people instead of all the delegation going to one person. Some managers can reorganise their departments and give people different job titles to make them feel that they have achieved promotion.

Pay

Pay can also be an important motivator when it is linked to performance. People can be rewarded as individuals through piece rates, bonuses, performance-related pay and commission. Group bonuses can also be given to reward people for working together. This encourages people to co-operate with one another and help one another, and raises standards within the team. It also discourages scheming and people withholding information and knowledge from one another.

The group

People's motivation will also be affected by the group they work with.

A satisfied group

A satisfied group is not necessarily a productive group, although it helps. Individuals will value membership of a group if:

- they like the other members and are liked by them
- they approve of the work of the group
- they would like to be identified with the group in the organisation

People can still be satisfied with their group, even when they do not particularly like one another. The group members may meet other needs, such as esteem needs, if it is a prestigious group in the organisation. Liking and friendship needs can be met elsewhere in an individual's life.

Standards and feedback

Standards need to be high to give people a feeling of achievement when they are reached. The standards should be realistic and acceptable to the group. It should be made very clear when the standards have been reached – people need feedback so that they know how well they have performed. Feedback is a vital ingredient in motivation. People have been motivated to work harder just by being told the results of their efforts. Factory workers have produced more when a blackboard with their production figures was placed on the shopfloor and airline enquiries telephone operators have increased the number of bookings when they were told the number of bookings compared to the number of enquiries.

Involvement

The group and the task should be important to the individual in order to justify his or her acceptance of the extra responsibility that involvement brings. If the individual does not feel committed to the task, he or she will merely attend meetings and go through the motions of the job without participating fully.

The task

The task itself is an important motivator for the group. Often groups can become comfortable 'homes' for people. They meet friends and socialise, discuss problems and feel accepted. Similarly, differences and fights between members may become more important than the task and a person may feel that his or her main objective is to defeat another group member.

The leader can emphasise the task as being far more important than individual needs. Failure to accomplish the task may threaten the survival of the group. Success may bring rewards and improve career prospects. It is the responsibility of the leader to ensure that the group see the task as important and worthwhile.

CASE STUDY

Signal Radio

Signal Radio is an independent local radio station which is self-funded by advertising revenue and sponsorship of items such as Traffic and Travel News. The station is ten years old and since 1990 has included new services of Signal Cheshire and Signal Stafford. They also run a TV Facilities House in Knutsford, Cheshire for making commercials, programmes and videos.

The manager

Chris Hurst is sales manager for Signal Radio. The Sales Department sell advertising airtime, sponsorships and roadshows. They have a professional staff

Chris Hurst – sales manager for Signal Radio

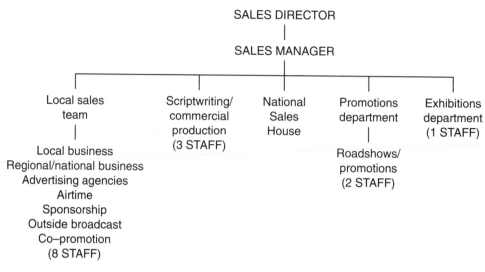

Fig. 3.8 *Structure of the sales department*

of commercial producers, scriptwriters and technical operators to make advertisements for clients, and to stage exhibitions and outside broadcasts and promotions. Their latest co-promotion is a venture with a local nightclub, Valentinos. The nightclub are putting on a show with the group East 17 and Signal Radio will advertise the event and share revenues with the nightclub. In the year 1992/93, Chris and his team made over £1 million worth of sales for the radio station.

Chris's boss is sales director Glyn Owen. The sales department is structured as in Fig. 3.8.

Seventy per cent of Signal Radio's advertising revenue is generated locally, the other 30 per cent comes from national advertising. The National Sales House in London co-ordinates national airtime sales for more than 100 local radio stations in the UK.

The leadership role of Chris Hurst

Task: responsibility for planning

'With sales it's quite simple. At the start of the financial year I'm given the targets I've got to work to; the sales they want to achieve for the year. I then split the target into monthly figures which are forecasted, bearing in mind seasonal fluctuations.'

The best times for selling advertising airtime on radio are in August when new cars are on the road, and at Christmas and Easter. One of the worst months for making airtime sales is February.

'It's not an equal split. I split the monthly targets between the sales executives, taking into account their experience and capabilities, and also the potential of the area they cover.'

Each sales executive is given responsibility for a local geographical area. They are also responsible for a financial target, which are target sales for the coming three months.

'It gives them a clear definition of where they're going and what they're expected to achieve. This year I argued with my managers for a more realistic approach to targeting, based on a 5 per cent increase on last year and got it. We're two months into this financial year and we've reached target in both months.'

Targets are given to executives only three months in advance as staff change fairly frequently. Working in radio is an excellent stepping stone for advancement to other jobs in the media and people often get promotion and move on. New sales-people are understandably often weaker than the experienced staff.

'I adjust targets for new members of staff and mine gets loaded to make up for that. I have kept a team in place for 18 months, but there is a natural progression from newspapers to local radio, national and then television. One of our staff has recently left to take up a job as sales director at another commercial radio station. I would give a new member of staff three to six months to come up to strength, which is quite a considerable time.'

Forecasts as to what will be good or bad months are not always accurate. In November 1992, the closure of local coal mines such as Trentham and Silverdale were announced. Business and local confidence was knocked and many shopping centres cut back on late night shopping evenings because they felt that people would not be buying much. Traders were not prepared to commit themselves to advertising campaigns. The sales department at Signal offered special packages and discounts to encourage businesses to advertise with them. Despite this, sales were below average.

Retailers tend to use radio for their advertising and these businesses are enthusiastic to run their commercials at the end of the week and the weekend. This leaves the earlier part of the week with plenty of airtime. Differences can be as great as 60 minutes of airtime used as advertising on Mondays and 120 minutes on Fridays.

Planning involves creating special packages to encourage businesses to go on air. The outside broadcast rate can be more than halved from £2000 for a three hour show to between £1000 and £700. When companies sponsor an outside broadcast they receive half a day of very concentrated advertising on their firm and any associated companies who wish to participate by advertising.

'Another area we planned was telesales. I identified that at the lower end of the advertising scale there were companies who could only afford to spend £100 to £200 and they were not being catered for.' The job of the telesales person is to ring companies and offer them advertising airtime as a simple, easy to understand package. The package includes a number of different adverts spaced over several days.

Chris's team has also come up with themes for advertising breaks – such as 'Signal Radio's Guide to Home Improvements'. Telesales ring all the home improvement companies and ask them if they wish to participate by advertising. The home improvement theme is then slotted into the early days of the week.

The sales department also keep printouts of all clients who have advertised in each month. They contact them in the same month of the following year to enquire whether they are interested in advertising again. In this way seasonal 'one-off' advertisers can be tracked down and not lost year to year.

Task: responsibility for organising

There are two sales meetings per month. 'You have to be very careful. Some managers use meetings to check up on what people are doing, which isn't the way I see a sales meeting. It should be to motivate and hype people up.'

Chris motivates his team by giving them as much information about new products as he can. 'I hand out packages and explain the reasoning behind new discounts, so the team understand why we're offering new things.'

Chris also reminds his team of how radio can respond to a client's demand. New packages can be formulated very quickly – they once had a client's advertisement on radio within six minutes of receiving the order.

The meetings start with a discussion of how each sales executive fared in the previous month. Chris reminds them of what to take note of during this particular month, such as contacting the local Chamber of Trade.

Mid-month figures are then looked at to see how far off target each sales executive is. Chris gives them lots of ideas as to how they can improve their sales – he sees this as 'getting them fired up'.

Chris receives the sales figures twice weekly, on Tuesdays and Thursdays. The figures show the sales to date of each sales executive, for the current and previous month.

Sales figures are displayed on a flip chart in the sales office. Every sales executive's name is listed, together with their target figure and their actual figure for the present month. Chris has by far the largest sales himself. The month on display showed his target to be £21,000 worth of sales and he had actually made £28,000. He believes in leading by example.

Chris does not believe in reprimanding people for poor results during a sales meeting. 'I have a quiet word with them in my office. It's a very small team and I talk to every sales executive every day. I feed them ideas. If they say they're having problems motivating a client to spend money on advertising I can give them information on forthcoming promotions. We could do a business feature interview and put the company on as a local business story. Everybody's got an ego and if we give them on-air coverage, it might mean the difference between getting an order and not getting an order.'

Task: responsibility for monitoring

Monitoring is done on sales figures. 'I have appointment sheets as well so I can monitor where people are going. Some companies have huge call-out sheets but I'm not a fan of clogging the team down with paperwork. They're there to be great sales people, not clerks. Their job definition is to achieve sales figures and that's what they're judged on.'

Chris periodically accompanies all sales executives to see clients and watch them 'pitching'.

Radio audiences are monitored on a national scale so that every station knows how many people listen to their local radio and for how long. Radio stations also know the breakdown of what socio-economic class their listeners belong to and how old they are. 'It's only the over 65s who stop listening to local independent radio, all other ages listen.'

The leadership role and responsibility for the individual/group

Maximising contribution

'There's no set formula. It's a team of individuals, they're a very diverse team. We like it diverse because some clients don't respond to extroverts, just as some don't respond to introverts. If someone fails with a client, we send out another sales executive with a different personality to see that client. You have to handle each member of staff in a different manner. Different things motivate different people.'

Sales executives all receive a basic salary and commission. Commission is earned after a target level of sales is achieved. Commission is 5 per cent after a given level on individual sales and 10 per cent above an individual's target, provided the group's target has been reached.

'I'm a fan of commission. Some people can earn a lot of commission. It's what it means to your life. I've just moved a good sales executive onto a more lucrative area than she was on before. She'll take home £1000 commission this month. That will change her life. If she works very hard, she could double her salary.'

The sales executives are also given responsibility. There is a deputy sales manager and two senior sales executives. 'I delegate and give them responsibility. You have to respect their decisions. It's not only money, it's self-esteem, a feeling of belonging to the team. If we hit target, we all go out for a sales team meal. We also do things like go-carting together; it's teambuilding.'

Sales executives also receive recognition from Chris for good work and clever ideas. He believes in them explaining their ideas to the sales director and giving them credit for their ideas.

Recognising individual strengths and weaknesses

During recruitment of new staff, Chris aims to employ someone who has talents which may be lacking in the existing team. There are three main skills in selling: finding new clients, keeping up the relationship with existing clients and maximising sales to both, and being able to 'close the deal' (spot 'buying signs' when the customer is ready to buy). Chris thinks that a good sales executive has got all these skills.

Chris has recently moved another sales executive away from a difficult area where there was not much new business and put her in a different area. Now she is 'performing like a star', says Chris.

Chris has employed a very experienced sales executive with an aggressive personality to take over an area where sales had been poor. Within six weeks she had sold sponsorship of the weather, traffic and travel, and the breakfast show.

'A lot of selling is down to confidence. You can tell before they visit a client whether they're going to succeed or not. If they believe that we've got the right products for that client, they know they can sell. Few clients can resist. But you can't always move people. You can train people to improve on their weak areas. The sales team swap ideas as to how to solve problems.'

When Chris took over the sales team two and a half years ago, he reorganised the layout of desks in the office. They now all face one another like one big desk. 'They listen to each other's telephone conversations, and if they can help with ideas for selling they write in big letters on a note pad and hold it up for the person on the phone to see. If someone is on the phone and needs details of rates, the others will get the file for them.'

The sales team receive a larger group commission than individual. The payment system for commission has been simplified so that everyone can understand it more easily.

'It means a lot to everyone if the team hits target. One of the best way of motivating people is peer pressure to improve themselves. Part of the good sales executive's job is to help others and push them forward.

'A role model is not a bad thing, which is why I sit out there with the team. It needs vibrance and people shouting, people talking about their commission. There are printouts showing everyone's sales. If you've sold nothing all week it shows. It's extremely pleasurable if you're the top seller.'

Sales executives receive a star if they reach their target. 'A twelve star executive is in a better position to negotiate salaries.'

QUESTIONS

1 How does Chris Hurst plan, organise and monitor task achievements?

2 How does he get the best out of individuals and the sales team as a group?

3 How does Chris recognise maintenance factors?

4 How are the following motivators used at Signal Radio:

- job satisfaction
- promotion
- recognition
- the job itself
- achievement

5 Explain what type of management style he uses.

The Ohio State and Michigan Studies

The role of manager or leader involves overseeing:

- the task
- the people

It is possible that some leaders may put more emphasis on one than the other. A manager may be very good at getting the job done well and on time, but in the process may upset staff and have a high rate of staff turnover and absenteeism. It will be expensive for the organisation to employ this manager, as despite the good work produced, the long-term effects will be low morale and the continual cost of recruiting new people and sorting out the grumbles of the existing staff.

Alternatively, a manager may enjoy people's company and not worry very much about getting the job done. The staff may have full attendance and enjoy going to work 'for the company' or 'a good laugh', but they will not be getting the task done to the best of their ability.

Managers need to achieve the fine balance between these two roles of getting the task done and making sure that the staff are happy.

The Ohio State and Michigan Studies were two different research studies which looked at the behaviour of leaders and whether they emphasised the task or the people in a situation. These two major research programmes were carried out at Ohio State University and the University of Michigan by a variety of different research teams from the late 1940s through to the 1970s.

Ohio State

These investigations began by attempting to identify the differences in the behaviour of leaders. Two factors emerged as the major differences:

- People orientated ('Consideration Structure')
  Includes behaviour between supervisor and subordinates which indicates trust, respect and warmth.
- Task orientated ('Initiating Structure')
  Includes behaviour in which the supervisor organises group activities without consulting the group as to their opinions on how it should be done.

The researchers found that leaders high on consideration had subordinates who were satisfied with them, had fewer absences and lower grievance rates than leaders low on consideration. According to these studies it is possible to be high or low on both people and task orientation.

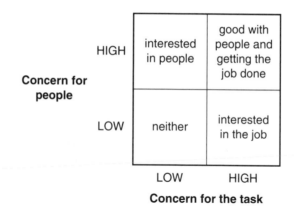

		LOW	HIGH
Concern for people	HIGH	interested in people	good with people and getting the job done
	LOW	neither	interested in the job
		LOW	HIGH
		Concern for the task	

Fig. 3.9 People and task orientation

Michigan

Researchers looked at what type of behaviour made leaders effective. They called the differences they found in leader behaviours *'production centred'* and *'employee centred'*.

- Production centred leaders:
  - set rigid standards for the work to be done to
  - organised tasks in detail
  - dictated exactly how the work was to be done
  - supervised subordinates' work closely

Task centred leadership

Employee centred leadership

- Employee centred leaders:
  - encouraged the workers to participate in setting goals and other decisions about the work
  - inspired trust and respect in the workers

The leaders who were most effective in terms of high production were:

1 Employee centred rather than production centred. The focus for communication between supervisor and worker is *'How are you getting on?'* rather than *'How is the work coming along?'*
2 Less likely to supervise the work very closely.
3 More likely to be doing different work to that of their subordinates (although this was not found to be true in all the studies carried out).

According to the Michigan research, the more effective leaders:

- have relationships with their subordinates which are supportive and make them feel important and worth while
- use group rather than individual methods of decision making and supervision
- tend to set high performance goals

Although the style theories are useful in drawing attention to the various ways in which a leader might behave, they do not provide any guidance for managers as to how to behave in different situations. It is probable that it is more appropriate to be autocratic or task-centred at times of danger and emergency, such as, a fire chief directing firemen at a fire in a large chemical factory. The people-centred style is suitable for circumstances like the solution of a complex problem such as the design of a staff training programme to prevent shoplifting in a retail store.

Appropriate channels for effective communication

Formal channels of communication

Formal channels of communication are those systems of communication created by an organisation. The formal structure of an organisation will help to determine the formal channels of communication.

Formal communication channels allow the information to flow within the organisation by the routes shown in Fig. 3.10:

Fig. 3.10 Communication channels

Vertical communications

Internal communications flow down the organisational pyramid. Policies are determined at boardroom level and are passed down to the next level. Senior managers pass on information, instructions and decisions to the middle managers until the relevant communication reaches the shop floor.

Information relating to production is sent up from the lower levels of the pyramid, enabling managers to monitor progress and to see how their areas are performing against planned targets.

The vertical formal channels of communication are usually illustrated by organisational charts.

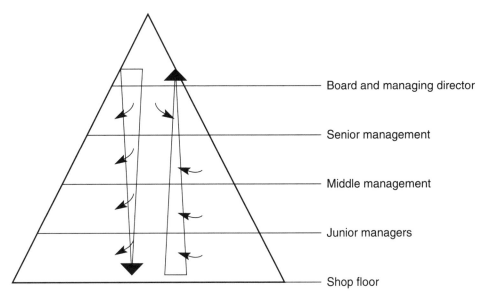

Fig. 3.11 The organisational pyramid

Problems with vertical channels of communication

The main problems relating to vertical channels of communication are:

1 The filtering of information

This can affect information going up or down the organisation. The manager usually decides to pass information downwards on a 'need to know' basis. This means the manager decides what information to leave out when passing on information. However, the manager may decide to pass on information slowly to reinforce or enhance his or her position of power. Information sent upwards will also be filtered as the person responsible for sending the information may restrict information, if it is critical of his or her performance. This is more likely to occur when a subordinate is hoping for promotion. One form of filtering of information is when people lie or modify the information to suit their own circumstances.

2 Failure to pass on information

This may arise because managers do not understand the scope of information which is required by subordinates at a lower level. This makes it difficult for the subordinates to operate efficiently. Knowledge is power and some people either will not share information at all, or share it only with a select few people.

3 The length of the chain of command

The number of layers the information has to pass through can mean a long time lag before people receive the information.

Lateral communications

Any organisation which is going to succeed makes decisions from the information it has at its disposal. Any information which is withheld will make the decision-making process slow and inefficient. Information must flow throughout the organisation between departments and across boundaries. Each member of the organisation must treat others as customers and try to meet their needs for information.

In any organisation there has to be cross-department communication, or the work of the marketing department would not be passed on, production would not know what to produce and the wages section would not know how much to pay out. Lateral communication informs, supports and co-ordinates activities across the organisation. The importance of lateral communication is shown by the use of formal channels with cross-functional activities, and the creation of cross-department committees and teams.

Problems with lateral communications

1 Filtering information

This will happen when departments do not have a close working relationship and there is a certain amount of jealousy. The information passed on will only be that which is sought and is essential to the operating of that department. Other information which may be useful is held back because it was not asked for. Other information may be passed on which enhances the image of a department but does not contain all of the relevant information.

2 Failure to pass on information

Here one department may fail to pass on information, because it deliberately withholds it or because it fails to realise the importance of the information to the other department. The conflict which may arise could be caused by inter-departmental rivalry.

3 The length of the chain

The longer the length of the chain, the longer it takes for information to be processed. In a longer chain more people get involved who can modify the information. Later on this can cause interpretation problems.

4 Which boss?

People work in particular departments and know who their line manager is. Problems arise if they have cross-departmental roles. They may have problems working for two managers especially where the line manager is in a more junior position to the manager. Who do they serve first and is the information to be passed on acceptable to the line manager?

Communications networks

The effectiveness of the working of groups will depend to some extent on the structure of the group and the channels of communication they use. The following figures represent structures and channels of communications between group members. The more formal structures are represented on the left and the structures become more informal towards the right.

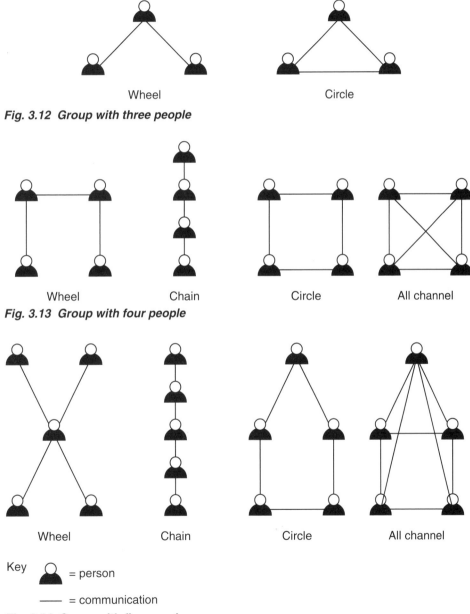

Wheel   Circle

Fig. 3.12 Group with three people

Wheel   Chain   Circle   All channel

Fig. 3.13 Group with four people

Wheel   Chain   Circle   All channel

Key   = person

—— = communication

Fig. 3.14 Group with five people

The **wheel** structure shows a situation where communication is centralised, i.e. there is someone at the hub of the wheel who acts as a gatekeeper. This is the person who allows the information to pass on to the other people in the structure and as such holds a very powerful position. From this central position he or she will gain job satisfaction because he or she will have a complete picture of what is going on. Those on the rim of the wheel can tend to feel more isolated and frustrated.

The same feeling of isolation and frustration is felt by those who work in a structure called the **chain**. The person at the centre should act as a sifter, only allowing information to those who need it, and enabling people to concentrate on their own specific tasks. Problems arise when the central person becomes swamped with work, or that person has not got the necessary skills or experience to carry out the task. The system becomes inefficient as the work piles up, and wrong information is given out or kept back.

At the other extreme is the structure known as the **circle,** where information flows freely between each member of the group. This structure will tend to be more informal than the wheel, but the group members may find that they are receiving information which they do not always require.

Informal communications

The grapevine

Organisations have their formal channels of communications. Running alongside them are the informal channels, such as 'the grapevine'. The grapevine carries formal and informal communication about the organisation and the people in it. The information is normally passed on orally at face-to-face meetings between individuals and groups. However, with the networking of computer-based work stations and the speed of telecommunications, the grapevine has become faster and more sophisticated.

Causes

Everybody who works in an organisation will be involved in the grapevine to some extent because people talk about work and what is or isn't happening. People might have a short informal break from their task, go to the canteen, or find themselves in another situation where they can pass on comments and share experiences.

The grapevine becomes most active when something important is about to happen or is actually happening – for example, a manager is replaced, some workers are about to be laid off or the company is about to be taken over. As soon as the news breaks, the grapevine is in operation and information travels very fast.

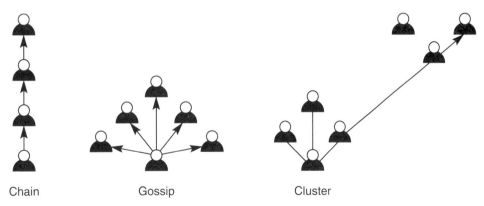

Chain   Gossip   Cluster

Fig. 3.15 The grapevine

Features

The grapevine will always start off with information which is true, but its weakness is that it lacks the full story. This gives the opportunity for people to jump to conclusions and to fill in the gaps in the information. This is how a story becomes distorted.

The grapevine is not held back by the barriers found in formal communication channels. It can cut across departments, jump over managers and move rapidly in all directions, the flow of information made easy because people want to know it and pass it on.

The flow of information through the grapevine is dependant upon the informal communication network. Within the network there will be the originator of the message and those who he or she passes the information on to. It may be that the grapevine operates as the chain, where one person passes on the information to another person, who passes it on to someone else. Eventually the information becomes outdated as events overtake the grapevine or a person does not pass the story on.

The originator is often a gossip, who passes on information to everyone they meet, either in the office or at lunchtime. However, information is usually passed on in a selective manner because the grapevine is a secretive method of transmitting information. This choosing of people who receive the information means that it will cluster around those people who belong to informal groups.

The grapevine can also be sensitive because by its very nature it can be selective. It can miss out individuals who may be part of the grapevine message.

Managers and the grapevine

Managers cannot ignore the grapevine because it can cause harm to the working of the organisation. The grapevine distorts information and can start to undermine the confidence of some individuals. The grapevine will operate well in situations where managers tend to be autocratic and hold on to information, and can cause problems which the managers may have to spend time dealing with rather than their real work. The grapevine is less powerful in organisations which are more open.

However, the grapevine is a source of information to the manager because it gives him or her a means of finding out how people really feel about the organisation or what is happening at that time. The manager can use the grapevine to his or her own advantage because he or she can feed it information which may reduce anxiety and worry among staff. Also, if the manager is facing a difficult situation, he or she can leak information to the grapevine to see how staff react. From the response of the grapevine the manager can work out alternative strategies.

Types of communication

The method chosen to deliver a message will be determined by:

- the sender
- the message
- the receiver

The sender

When choosing the type of communication, the sender has to take into account both the message and who is going to receive it. The method chosen will depend to a certain extent on the individual preferences of the sender and the purpose of the communication. Some people prefer to deal with situations face to face and are reluctant to put things in writing. Others are happiest when everything is written down.

The nature of the job will have an influence on the type of communication used. For example, people working in the personnel department may spend most of their time in face-to-face interviews and keep written records. The accounts department may deal mainly with written forms of communication. The position of the sender in an organisation will help to determine their methods of communication – managers may meet their immediate subordinates in meetings but deal with lower levels through written messages.

The message

The message itself will have a bearing on the type of communication used. If someone is about to be laid off from work they are unlikely to hear about it by letter in their pay packet. However, someone who is resigning from their position will be expected to do it in writing. Confidential information can be passed on orally or in written form. Reports to managers or to shareholders will always be in writing.

How quickly the message needs to be conveyed should also be considered. The telephone is normally the fastest but with today's technological advances other means such as using the fax can be just as quick. The sender of the message also has to think of the cost involved. Is it cheaper to talk to all the workers in a hall or should they each receive a letter? Another consideration is what convention has been used in sending messages previously? If workers are to be rewarded for long service, how should they be congratulated – by letter, by an awards meeting? What has been done in the past? Some information has to be in written form because of legal requirements, such as a person's contract of employment.

The receiver

When messages are sent the sender has to remember who is going to receive them. Is it one individual or a large number of people? With individuals, do they respond better to oral communications or do they prefer to receive written instructions?

When organisations are communicating with their customers, they have to be aware of *why* they are communicating. If it is to ask them to buy their product then the organisation will probably use advertising and sales promotional techniques. To some customers advertising is a reassurance that the product they have bought is the right one.

The people who receive the message have got to be able to understand the message so the way in which it is conveyed is important. Three-hour lectures may be the easiest way for the lecturer to get his or her message across to 300 students, but the majority of students will be exhausted after 20 minutes and may not concentrate on the rest of the lecture.

Communication methods

The choice of communication methods includes:

● written
● oral

Written communication

The written method of communication is chosen for a variety of reasons, an important one being that it provides a permanent record of events. This means that in future people can check on events to see what happened and what was agreed. The written record is less likely to be misunderstood because people are careful in what they write. They have time to think about what they are writing and this enables them to present information clearly and unambiguously. There is less likely to be misunderstanding compared with oral communications. Instructions can be clearly written down and people can refer back to the information as many times as required. This ability to reread information gives the reader time to absorb and comprehend, whereas when a lot of information is given orally, the receiver will have difficulty remembering what was said.

Written forms of communication enable information to be analysed and evaluated more readily. The information can also be displayed in a variety of ways, which makes it easier to understand.

Examples of written communications include:

- annual company reports and accounts
- bulletins
- employee handbooks
- employee newspapers
- house journals
- letters
- memoranda
- minutes of meetings
- noticeboards
- pay slip inserts
- reports

Annual company reports and accounts

This is the statutory report all public limited companies have to present each year to their shareholders. It includes a set of published final accounts which include the balance sheet, the profit and loss account and the cash flow statement. Directors write a report on the company's performance in the context of a comparison with past years, competition, and the business environment in which it operates. The directors also make a summary of the expected performance for the following year.

Bulletins

Bulletins are used by organisations to pass specific information on quickly. Some organisations have bulletin boards on which new information is pasted on a regular basis.

Employee handbooks

Organisations give employees handbooks about the organisation. These are especially useful to new entrants because they give information on the organisation, as well as employment matters, policies such as equal opportunity, and procedures relating to grievance or claiming sick pay. They may also include sections on the social amenities. The handbook is a useful reference source but it does need regular updating.

Employee newspapers

These are published on a regular basis, usually weekly, and are a way in which the management can keep the workforce up to date with events happening in the organisation. It helps the workforce understand what is going on in the organisation and helps workers to identify with the organisation. It will present news on social events and the company's clubs and societies. Workers are able to read about the fishing club or how the company's football team is doing.

House journals

These carry out a similar function to the newspaper, but they tend to be published less often and are more 'glossy' in appearance. They provide the workers with an update on policies and feature more indepth articles on the operations of the organisation.

Letters

These are the usual way in which an organisation keeps in contact with its customers and suppliers. The letter has to be formal and businesslike, following the general rules on layout, presentation and salutations.

Memoranda

These are internal informal communications and usually contain very brief messages. They are one of the most widely used methods of communication in organisations.

Minutes of meetings

Minutes or summaries of what was said and decided in a meeting are often recorded. The minutes of a meeting are normally circulated to the members and in many cases the minutes are published. Minutes enable people to see the progress of a meeting and let new members know what has gone on before.

Noticeboards

Most organisations have a noticeboard where bulletins can be posted. If it is regularly used, the noticeboard can be an effective means of communication. As well as being used for official notifications, the noticeboard is also useful for workers who perhaps want to sell something or a club who want to advertise for new members.

Pay slip inserts

This means of communicating to the workforce guarantees that the workers will get their communication. However, the workforce may view their pay slip as private and resent it being used for other purposes.

Reports

Formal reports are normally requested on a specific topic. The managing director, for example, may be asked to report to the board of directors on the launch of a new product. The report is written and presented in a particular style and layout.

Oral communication

This is a direct form of communication between people and as such allows for immediate responses and feedback. Oral communications can also benefit from people being able to see the other person and observe their reactions. This method of communication is more flexible than the written word as people are able to change their position in a discussion or are able to persuade people round to their point of view. Oral communication allows for participation and contributions from the people present.

Examples of oral communication include:

- briefing groups
- conferences and seminars
- departmental meetings
- face-to-face conversations
- inductions
- interviews
- joint consultations
- telephone calls

Briefing groups

Departmental managers may call their section heads to a short briefing meeting at the start of each morning. This update enables everyone to know what is happening in the department on a daily basis and helps to remove communication barriers. The section heads can then pass on messages to their own group members.

Conferences

This method of communication is used by professions such as medicine, education and management. The people attending are often doing the same type of job but from different organisations. Surgeons may gather to hear about the latest surgical techniques while personnel managers may listen to accounts of research and events in their particular field. They are normally on specific topics and the speakers are experts in their field. It is a way in which organisations can get up-to-date information. Organisations can run their own conferences for their workforce. Again the agenda is very short and concentrates on a few topics. It is a method by which an organisation can inform the workforce of new ideas and practices.

Departmental meetings

The frequency of these will depend on the alternative methods the management use to communicate with their workforce and the management's style of operating. It is usually an opportunity for the workers to participate in the running of the department. If the meetings are not structured they may merely be an opportunity for a general moan, or if the manager only speaks, the workers may become disillusioned.

Face-to-face conversation

This is the most common form of oral communication and is used by everyone in the organisation. Most take place between workers of equal status or between subordinate and line manager.

Induction

This usually takes place when a new worker joins an organisation. It is an opportunity for the new entrant to be informed about the organisational structure, policies and practices and about the organisation's products. It is from this process that the new entrant can quickly fit into the culture of the organisation.

Interviews

This refers not just to interviewing applicants for vacant posts, but also interviews which take place in the workplace which are not just social conversations. Interviews can take place regarding a grievance or for disciplinary reasons. These interviews will be very formal with a specific agenda.

If there has been an accident at work and an investigation takes place, people will be interviewed – perhaps to get a clear picture of the events leading up to the accident.

Other forms of interview may be concerned with worker performance and the assessment may be done in an appraisal interview.

Joint consultation

These are meetings made up of managers and workforce representatives. They provide an opportunity for the group to discuss areas of common concern. It is a forum where information can be imparted, awareness raised, and misunderstandings clarified.

Telephone

This is a common form of oral communication between people where distance is an irrelevance. A major drawback is the fact that the people in conversation cannot see each other and therefore non-verbal communication is lost. However, with the development of the videophone this disadvantage will be removed.

Non-verbal communication

This refers to all communications which do not use the written or the spoken word. Non-verbal communication (NVC) takes place without people realising it and can reinforce or contradict what a speaker is saying.

NVC can be:

- facial expressions
- body positions
- body movements
- gestures
- how we talk
- tone of voice used
- emphasis on words
- pauses in speech

NVC has been recognised for many years – Chinese merchants used it when trading in precious stones. Merchants would observe the pupil in the eye of a prospective purchaser to see how it reacted when the person was shown a piece of jade for sale. If it dilated the merchant knew the buyer was interested.

Business people and politicians are trained how to control their body movements and the way they speak so that they are consistent in conveying messages, both consciously and unconsciously. This is because people often reveal their true feelings through body language.

Non-verbal behaviour

Gestures

Individuals tend to use gestures to reinforce a message or communicate to someone who is difficult to talk to. We might beckon someone towards us or put a finger to our lips and we know what these gestures mean.

Other gestures are used to help to get the message across. To support speech, for example, people use their hands to describe what they are talking about. These gestures are called illustrations.

Some gestures give an indication of how a person is feeling. In an interview a person may be wringing his or her hands – an indication that he or she is under some stress. In another situation, someone may be twiddling his or her thumbs – which reveals boredom. When a person is nervous he or she may stroke the back of their head or fiddle with a small strand of hair.

TASK

Think about the situations where the following gestures might be used.

- hands over eyes
- hand over mouth
- clenched fist
- drumming fingers
- continually looking at a watch

Posture

The way in which people sit or stand will show how they are feeling. If someone is standing straight and stiff he or she is probably nervous, whereas someone standing with hands in pockets is relaxed.

The relationship between people can also be illustrated by the way they behave towards each other. If one person is standing stiff and the other appears more relaxed it may be that one person is the manager and the other is the subordinate.

What message may be being expressed in the following situations?

- somebody slouching in a chair
- a man leaning back in a chair with his hands behind his head
- a person sitting behind a desk and leaning forward to speak to another person
- a woman sitting on the edge of a table in a crowded room

Facial expressions

We use our face to express how we feel. The way we use our eyebrows and our mouth give clues about how we feel. The position of our eyebrows gives messages to the observer – if they are fully raised, this shows surprise, if they are lowered, this will indicate puzzlement or disapproval.

The shape of the mouth can illustrate feeling. Smiling shows friendliness or happiness, whereas lips turned down at the corners signify sadness.

DISCUSSION QUESTIONS

What other expressions can be made with the face?
Why is non-verbal communication often more powerful than verbal?

Eyes

What does it mean if someone 'makes eyes at you' or you 'catch a person's eye'? Eye contact shows communication between people. For example, when someone is talking to another person it is important that eye contact is made so that the person speaking knows that their message is being received. Eye movements give clues as to when to talk and when to stop, and the extent to which someone is listening.

Speech

The words spoken may give one message, but the *way* we speak clarifies to the listener what is being said. The way we talk can influence the message through:

- tone of voice
- speed of talking
- level of voice
- emphasis on words
- pauses in speech
- errors made

TASK

Practise saying these sentences and phrases in different tones of voice for different effects:

1 *George, don't do that.*

2 *Excuse me, but I think you're sitting in my seat.*

3 *I can offer nothing but blood, sweat and tears.*

4 *The Indian from Four Feather Falls felt furtively for his axe for a few minutes.*

5 *Would you come with me?*

Communication processes at Countryside Graphics

Lester Graf and Richard Uli started Countryside Graphics 20 years ago. It has grown into a very successful business specialising in commercial printing and employs 40 people. The offices are furnished and decorated like a well cared-for house. Carpets, wallpaper, pictures and ornaments, settee and magazines in the reception area, cakes and coffee in the kitchen. The atmosphere is very comfortable and family-like.

Each foreman has employees who report to him. Countryside Graphics also employ a print broker to increase sales. He acts an an intermediary between organisations who need a printing job completing and the different types of specialist printers.

Richard Uli, the president with responsibility for sales and the office, says that

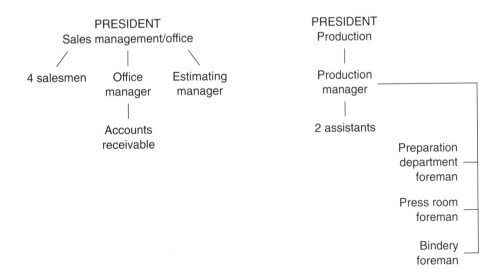

Fig. 3.16 Organisation chart

their objectives are to provide a very high quality product with a good service. He does not want the business to grow much larger because they can offer greater flexibility and keep in pace with a changing market if they stay fairly small. The company specialises in full colour printing individually tailored to customer requirements. The products vary from calendars to advertisements.

'Changes come instantly,' explains Richard. 'A customer gives us an order and the job can go on the press within half an hour. We can deliver next morning from an order received in the afternoon. Reactions have to be immediate.'

Having a workforce of 40 also helps communication. There is lots of face-to-face communication, and people speak to one another on the internal phones and have informal meetings as necessary. The four salesmen have bleepers to page them wherever they go and three of the salesmen have car phones. They also visit the office very frequently to keep in touch with events.

Written communication is used in the form of schedule sheets so that as the foremen arrive at work they can see from the sheet the jobs which are to be completed that shift. There are two shifts – 7 a.m. to 3 p.m. and 3 p.m. to 11 p.m. The schedules are put together by the production manager and the foremen also talk over the jobs with him when they arrive.

The bindery department has part-time staff as well as full-time. They are employed on an 'as-needed' basis and are supplied by employment agencies. Often the same people return to Countryside Graphics who have worked there previously. The bindery foremen give them instructions as to what is needed.

'The press room works like a family, they work well together and are all trained by our company straight out of school,' says Richard. 'They make sure that new people keep up the initiative and attitude towards the business. Morale is very good and the press room is kept clean.'

Good communication is a major reason for the success of the business. They could not provide the fast customer service if there were communication bottlenecks and hold-ups. 'Potential communication problems stop us from growing any further. Greater size can mean that information is lost and more mistakes are made. There is a demand for a very high level of service which needs a really effective communication system.'

Countryside Graphics is in Schaumburg, Illinois.

Communication processes at Motorola Inc.

Motorola is a manufacturer of telecommunications equipment and semiconductors. The firm is valued at around $13 billion and has 102,000 employees worldwide. It is based in Schaumburg, Illinois and has been voted 'most respected company' in the Chicago region. Products include: portable cellular telephones, pagers, computers, anti-lock braking systems and steering controls for motor vehicles, satellite communication systems and space communication systems for the government, and microprocessors for Sony camcorders.

Motorola is decentralised and organised around products. At their head office in Schaumburg there are around 6000 employees. Every year, each employee has 40 hours of training to update their skills.

Great efforts are made to keep employees informed of developments within the company. In October 1993, the chairman of the board resigned unexpectedly to work for Kodak. He left on the same day as he made the announcement. In order that the employees should be told of his departure before they heard it from the media, employees were called into their bosses' offices to hear it announced by a senior manager on speaker telephone.

There are difficulties in trying to keep such large numbers of employees informed. Dick Bruggeman, the manager of professional recruiting, says: 'Sometimes there's a new product released and I read about it in the newspaper at home.'

Senior managers make videos which are shown to employees of themselves answering questions asked by employees. 'This helps the troops,' says Dick Bruggeman. 'They can see it all over the world in Motorola factories and offices.'

People communicate with one another through teamwork. 'Teamwork is working, but it's not good,' explains Dick. 'When we can throw away all the managers and supervisors – then we're good!' There are appraisal interviews to monitor annual performance. There is a new programme called Individual Dignity Entitlement which is a series of six questions such as 'Do you feel you're contributing?', 'Are you happy with your career growth?', 'Are you being valued?'. The programme does not evaluate performance. Its objective is to encourage supervisors to help people to feel that they have achieved their career goals. The programme is done as an anonymous survey and it focuses on issues such as developing teamwork and empowerment of employees.

Senior managers have formal meetings and there are company newspapers and publicity releases for all employees. When the company has won a large contract, a town crier announces it in the dining-room, ringing a bell and announcing the news from a scroll. There are bulletin boards and job posting boards.

'You don't have to be small to be good,' says Dick. 'Empowerment will increase communication at all levels. Fewer layers of management mean less filtering of the information as it comes down.'

Documenting procedures is also a useful way of communicating with employees. The policy manual, giving directions to employees on what to do in various situations, used to be three inches thick. To encourage supervisors and managers to refer to it, it has been reduced to 20 per cent of its original size. 'Supervisors and managers are now more consistent and they have some discretion on how they should act.'

Employees have Macintosh computers and they can send one another messages through the computer network. The electronic mail part of the computer will fold up as small as a book and can be taken home and put on the home computer. It contains diaries and notes as well as mail. It will work by batteries standing alone, although it cannot receive or send messages alone. Dick thinks that they are so indispensable that everyone will have them within the next five years.

Employees also have voice mail which is attached to the telephone. This records messages electronically and therefore does away with problems of the tape running out or going wrong, as in the traditional answering machine.

People communicate with one another on an informal basis. 'Informal groups maximise our strengths and abilities to serve customers. People help one another on an informal basis to do their jobs. Informal leaders are often used as team leaders.'

There are also informal social groups such as sports clubs and chess and computer clubs. Events such as summer picnics and Christmas socials are organised for employees.

Motorola's excellent communication processes are one of the factors keeping the company foremost in its industry worldwide.

QUESTIONS

1 What different types of communication are used at the two companies?

2 What difficulties does Motorola have that Countryside Graphics does not?

3 How do communication problems, or lack of them, affect the product or service provided by the two firms?

4 How does communication affect the morale of the workers at both companies?

5 Would Countryside Graphics benefit from more technologically advanced communication systems such as voice mail and electronic mail?

6 What possible barriers to communication exist in the two companies?

Barriers to effective communication

Communications

Communication is the life blood of any organisation, as it is the flow of information from one party to another. Communication means that there must be a shared meaning and enables understanding and action to take place.

An organisation will not be able to function internally and operate in its external environment without communications. For example:

- Communication enables managers to carry out their function – they cannot plan, organise and monitor without receiving information from internal and external sources.
- Communication enables managers to share ideas or pass information on to their managerial colleagues.
- Communication enables managers to be in touch with their operatives to give instructions to them. Without this, subordinates would be unable to work.

Communication enables the organisation to be in touch with its external environment. For example, organisations need to know what is happening in their market, and the marketing department will obtain information such as:

- who their customers are
- what they are likely to purchase
- who their competitors are
- what their competitors are doing

Communication allows the organisation to send orders to their suppliers and be in contact with other organisations such as the Inland Revenue, Customs and Excise, and local government.

Good communications will also benefit the organisation in the following ways:

- Encourages interdepartmental co-operation and co-ordination.
- Gives the opportunity to identify and counter dissatisfaction.
- Facilitates more involvement in decision making/problem solving.
- Helps understanding and morale.
- Influences opinions, attitudes and creates better working relations.
- Keeps employees aware of their performance.
- Keeps employees aware of changes in the organisation.

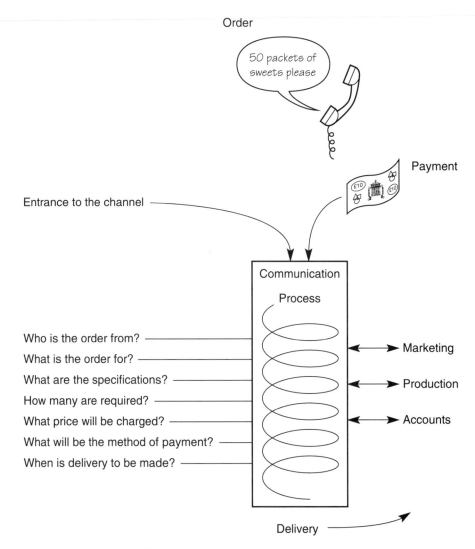

Fig. 3.17 Flow of information within channels of communication

Effective communication

To operate, the organisation must establish effective communication channels to enable a free flow of information. This information can be acted upon by institutions, groups of people and individuals. In order to set up effective channels of communication, organisations need to appreciate the complexity of the communication process. For example, when an organisation receives an order for its products it has to be able to execute the order. The organisation must be able to co-ordinate its operations, and people need to be in contact with each other inside and outside the organisation. Records need to be kept for future reference and various forms will have to be completed. The communication process needs to be such that everyone deals with their part of the order in sequence and there is no time delay between one section and another. People *need* to communicate with each other (*see* Fig. 3.17).

The communication process involves the **sender** of information, the **transfer** of information, the **receiver** of the information, the **understanding** of information, and finally, **feedback** (*see* Fig. 3.18).

The sender

The sender is the person who starts the process by sending out requests for information or issuing an instruction.

The transfer

The message has to be translated from the sender's idea into a form the receiver can understand, e.g. from concepts to words, numbers, symbols or charts. The actual physical form into which the sender encodes the information can be, for example, speech or written form. The method (or **channel**) used to transmit the message includes telephone, fax or letter.

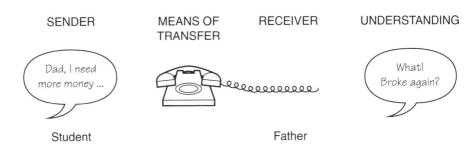

Fig. 3.18 The communication process

The receiver

This is the person who has to respond to the message, by translating and interpreting it. If the receiver is unable to do either activity, communication breaks down.

Feedback

For communication to be successful, there must to be a response. This means that there must be some sort of action which can acknowledge that the message has been received and understood. If a manager has asked for a file, it is necessary that the right file reaches him or her.

Barriers to communication

Factors which decrease the effectiveness of communication are called **communication barriers**. It is the receiver of the communication who determines the extent to which the message is understood. Unless the message is actually 'lost in the post', total blocks are rare.

Communication barriers may occur because of the following factors.

1 The increasing need for information

As the world we live in grows in complexity and is ever changing, there comes the need for more information. The demand for more information will overload the communication process and cause it to operate less efficiently.

2 The advances in information technology

Information technology has made the transfer of information in a variety of forms possible. The means of saving and retrieving information and the speed of transmitting it has been made easier by technology. However, the speed of operations can put people under increasing pressure to find the information and convey it to the people who need it.

3 The need for increasingly complex information

Information technology has enabled information to be presented in a variety of forms and this can cause problems of interpretation for the person who is receiving the information.

4 The globalisation of business

Businesses are becoming more international. In Europe there is a move towards a single trading block which may create communication barriers because of different languages and culture.

5 Time

Many managers now find themselves under increasing pressures as they have to deal with the rapidly changing business world. They have to master new and important ideas if they are to stay ahead of the field.

The greater the demands on their time the less time they have to communicate with colleagues in their organisation. Managers may find they are always in meetings which makes it difficult for them to be contacted. This may cause problems if a decision has to be taken quickly. Some decisions may be made without all the relevant information or without spending time to consider all the options.

Time can also be a barrier because it places constraints on operations. If people were allowed an infinite period of time to complete a task, either the task would never get done or each task would be completed to masterpiece standard. Time helps to concentrate the mind and forces people to work to a deadline. Lateness in completing forms may result in incorrect work or poor performance. The logistics manager, for example, may not be able to complete the scheduling of lorries because he or she is waiting for information. This means that he or she cannot distribute the work to the drivers.

6 Differing perceptions

People have varying educational backgrounds and experiences. This can mean that people perceive or interpret the same message in a different way. For example, if a manager tries to be helpful and supportive, the employees may see it as interference. The manager cannot expect people to understand unless situations are explained. The workers and managerial colleagues can completely misinterpret actions.

7 Language

Language is a major communication barrier. Language is a system of spoken or written symbols which communicate ideas, emotions and experiences. The greater the variety of symbols the more complex the language.

There are a number of languages – natural languages such as English or French and artificial languages such as algebra or COBOL.

The natural language is the most complex because of the number of words available for use, and this complexity can create barriers. Words can have more than one meaning – 'run', 'bank' and 'pack' are just three examples. In some cases a word may sound the same but be spelt differently, such as 'through' and 'threw', 'there' and 'their'. There are other situations where a number of words can be used to describe the same thing, e.g. 'shower', 'drizzle', 'rain'.

In conversation, the choice of words may send out the wrong message. *'I am watching you'* is not the same as *'I am monitoring your progress'*.

The natural language has so many words that no one person can know them all. Although the wide variety of words makes language a powerful tool for transmitting information, it can also cause barriers.

Speaking the language

Employees spend a lot of their time talking. This is a particular skill for which the majority of people receive no formal training. Our ability to speak a language usually depends upon our experiences learned from our home and school.

People's ability to communicate orally is often dependent on factors outside their control. If a person has received a high level of education and has enjoyed a wide range of experiences then he or she will have a wide vocabulary, an understanding of grammar, and the ability to express him or herself in both written and oral form. The people who have these language skills will probably be the managers. Managers can create problems by using language which may unintentionally confuse or intimidate the receiver. If managers have difficulty in expressing themselves, their subordinates may form a low opinion of them which will make it difficult to get their views across.

A further barrier associated with language concerns expressions. Regions of the country have different words or phrases for particular events or situations. 'Ow bin ya' is a friendly welcome from the Black Country, in the north 'nesh' means being overly sensitive to the cold and 'apple and pears' is Cockney slang for stairs.

In order to improve communications in organisations, abbreviations are used. In a bank 'BPV' refers to a 'branch payment voucher' but only those 'in the know' will understand this. Jargon is another barrier to communication as it is a closed language only accessible to certain people.

Hearing the information

It is the listener who hears and interprets the message. The mind has to absorb the symbols, see the relationship and then organise the information into a message. The mind has to conceptualise the information. If there are too many symbols, facts or figures, the mind will not be able to cope, and it becomes overloaded.

MEMORY GAME

Each member of the group starts off with the phrase, 'I went to market and I bought …'. Player 1 then adds the name of their purchase. Player Number 2 states Player Number 1's purchase plus their own, then Player Number 3 and so on, until the list is so long that no one member can remember it.

The mind can only retain a certain amount of information over a long period of time. Therefore, the person talking should keep the message as brief as possible and if necessary support what they say in written form.

8 The listener

The behaviour of the listener can create communication problems. He or she may not be giving his or her full attention to what is being said, or might be doing something else at the same time. The listener may try to interrupt the speaker, criticise, or become angry, or he or she may be thinking of a reply to part of the message and miss other parts.

Dividing attention means that messages are only partly heard or misheard completely. Nuances, hidden meanings and signals from body language, for example, may be lost by the receiver.

9 Noise

There are also barriers which make it difficult for the receiver to understand the message. It may be a poor telephone line, background talking in the office or some other distraction. Noise can distort the message or completely obliterate it.

Imagine a situation where a buyer of a company orders something over the telephone and promises confirmation of the order in writing. 'Please send 16,000 screws tomorrow, I'll confirm in writing' could easily be misheard as 'Please send 60,000 screws tomorrow, I'll confirm in writing . . .'.

Barriers to communication

This case study looks at communication problems faced by an engineer working for a television repair company in Telford.

'Getting the part number from looking at the exploded diagram of a television is tricky. Sometimes it is difficult to make out the number, or if we are distracted by the customer, we can misread or transcribe the wrong number. This can cause us frustration because of the time it takes to correct the error.

'Our suppliers can be a problem. We send in the right information on the right form. It is processed by the computer operator at the other end. The problem arises when the storesperson at the suppliers goes to get the spare part but goes to the wrong bin. We are sent the part and so when we get in touch with the supplier to say it is the wrong bit, they always ask for the part number and description and then assure us that is what they have sent. Unfortunately, we have problems from this point on because we have to persuade the computer operative who is not technically trained that there has been a mistake and we do have the wrong part. If the computer says we have been sent the right part then the supplier thinks we are the ones who have made the mistake. When we finally talk to someone who has the technical expertise, they know immediately from our description of the part that it does not correspond to the part number.

'We do a lot of sub-contracting for a large firm and sometimes we have to be mind readers. They don't always send us all the information. Sometimes we have gone to set up a television, but when we get there we have arrived days before the television. Sometimes the wrong address is supplied. Sometimes we get there and the people are out, so we leave a card saying that we've called and they get stroppy because they think we should have known that they were out.

'Sometimes a customer will leave a television with us to repair. They tell us to ring them when the set is ready. It makes me smile when they say any time after 6 o'clock as if we haven't got homes to go to. I get really annoyed with those people who say we can ring at any time. So we do and they are never in. You can't sit by the telephone and ring them all the time, so after a few attempts we wait for them to ring us. Normally, they are really angry with us, wondering why we haven't got in touch with them. You just can't win. Occasionally we might have a call nearby so I drop by to see if they are in. When they're not I leave a card to say we've called. They get upset because they have told us to ring them before delivering their TV. We try to explain that if they are not in we can't contact them. It doesn't matter how many times we ring, if they are not there we can't contact them.'

Good communication

Good communication will take place when the message has been easily understood and acted upon and the outcome is what is expected by the sender and the receiver.

Rules for good communication

Good communication can be established if the following rules are applied:

1 **Seek to clarify your ideas before communicating**. Before getting in touch with a person it is always best to work out what it is you really want the person to do. Clarification in the mind of the sender will make the message easier to communicate.

2 **Examine the true purpose of the communication**. Why is it you want to get in touch with someone? Is it to obtain information or ask for something to be done. Once this is decided select the right medium, the right language and tone. Do not overload the communication with too many ideas.

3 **Consider the total physical and human setting whenever you communicate**. The message to be communicated needs to be conveyed at the right time, in the right way and in the right setting. A manager should never reprimand someone in public. Sensitive communications should always take place in private. Managers can never be sure how people are going to react.

4 **In planning communications consult with others, whenever appropriate**. Help from others will give objectivity and direction to a message and will help commit people to the communication.

5 **While you communicate, think of the overtones as well as the basic content of the message**. The way in which the message is conveyed, the voice, use of language, the tone of the message will influence the receptiveness of the receiver. Shouting instructions by megaphone may not be the best way of communicating.

6 **Take the opportunity, when it arises, to convey something of help or value to the receiver**. The sender of the communication should attempt to look at things from the point of view of the receiver and emphasise the benefits which may accrue to the receiver. This is especially important during a period of change. People need to know the reasons for changes and how they might benefit.

7 **Follow up your communications**. If you assume that people are doing as you ask you may give the wrong impression to the receiver, i.e. the communication was not that important or that you are not a supportive leader.

8 **Communicate for tomorrow as well as for today**. Postponing difficult decisions may make matters worse. For example, if someone is always late or is not performing as they should, it is unfair on the subordinate not to point out their shortcomings. Putting off the communication makes it difficult to take action in the future.

9 **Be sure your actions support your communication.** One of the most important ways to communicate to your subordinates is by your own action. If you are continually late for work or meetings, subordinates will pay little attention to communications demanding better time-keeping.

10 **Be a good listener and seek to understand**. Listening is a skill which very few of us practise. Listening involves concentrating on what the person is saying to enable us to understand the message.

FORTUNE TELLER ACTIVITY

Aim
To build a fortune-telling pyramid and examine effective communication and barriers to communication.

Resources required
The fortune teller instruction sheet, one square piece of paper per person, pencils, rulers, crayons

Method
One person stands out at the front of the class with the fortune teller instruction sheet, and everyone else has their square piece of paper ready. The instructions are read out verbally to the class. The class make the pyramid, as instructed. The communication must be one way. No one is allowed to ask questions of the instructor, or communicate with anyone else in the class. If someone is stuck, they can tap the table twice in order to have the instruction repeated.

The instructor cannot move on until everyone has completed each stage.

Fortune teller instruction sheet
(references to steps are for the instructor's information only)

1 Take a square piece of paper.
2 Fold in half twice, corner to corner, and crease.
3 Open, then crease the four corners into the centre.
4 Turn over.
5 Write eight fortunes around the edges (Step 1).
6 Turn these new four corners into the centre and crease.
7 Mark numbers on the flaps (Step 2).
8 Fold in half.
9 Open and fold in half the other way (Step 3).
10 Slip your two thumbs and two forefingers underneath the flaps facing you (Step 4).
11 You will find that by moving your fingers and thumbs you open up the 'pyramids' in two directions, one showing numbers 1–4, and the other showing numbers 5–8.

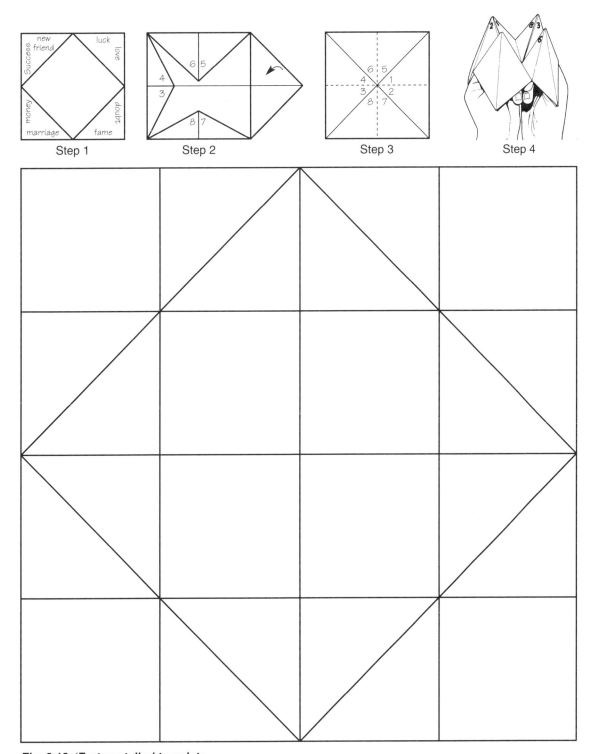

Fig. 3.19 'Fortune teller' template

Using the pyramid

1 Ask a friend to chose a number between 1 and 4.

2 If he or she chooses 3, open and shut the pyramid three times.

3 Ask the same person to choose one of the numbers showing, and again open and shut the pyramid.

4 Ask him or her a third time to choose a number, turn back the corresponding flap and read his or her fortune.

 QUESTIONS

In groups of four or five, discuss the following:

1 How easy was it to follow the instructions?

2 What common problems did you find with the giving or following of the instructions?

3 Would it have been easier if you had been able to ask questions?

4 Would it have helped to have a diagram to follow?

5 Did the instructor give any non-verbal clues?

6 How could the instruction process be improved?

Evidence Indicator

A case study examining the mis-management of a task over a period of time, examining the role of the leader and the communication channels used

Emma Ross is the newly-appointed manager of the Butchery Department in the large Skyline Store in Leeds. The store sells food and clothing. Emma has decided to use the meat suppliers she used in her previous job as she has always found them to be very good. That morning, when she arrives at work, the following letter from Skyline's current meat supplier is on her desk.

A B FURKINS & CO LTD
12 Standard Lane
Scunthorpe
SC2 7PJ

7 February 1994

Butchery Department Manager
Skyline Store
14 Main Road
Leeds L1 1BQ

Dear Sir or Madam

We are very pleased to welcome you in your new job as Butchery Department Manager. We had a long and friendly relationship with your predecessor Mr Eric Black. We hope to continue the relationship with yourself.

Our salesman, George Temple, will be calling in two weeks' time in order to meet you and discuss your future requirements. In the meantime, if you have any problems or changes you wish to make to the regular order, do not hesitate to contact him on 0724 589987.

We look forward to a long and happy working relationship with you.

Yours sincerely

Andrew Sinclair

Andrew Sinclair
Sales Manager

Emma throws the letter in the bin and writes a memo to the buyer for the department, Emma Singleton.

To: Emma
From: Emma
11 February 1994

In future, we are going to deal with a very good meat supplier called Zebra Meats. Please organise the necessary details.

Emma puts the memo into the internal mail basket and writes a letter to Zebra Meats.

SKYLINE STORE
14 Main Road
Leeds
L1 1BQ

11 February 1994

Mr T Cole
Manager
Zebra Meats
Factory Lane
Manchester
M24 9PN

Dear Tom

MEAT ORDER – WEEK COMMENCING 14 FEBRUARY 1994

I am pleased to confirm that we are working together again. Could you as a matter of urgency deliver the attached order by Thursday of this week?

Many thanks.

Best wishes.

Emma

Emma Ross
Butchery Department Manager

Emma sends the letter by fax so that it will arrive quickly. Later that morning, she receives a telephone call from Tom Cole acknowledging receipt of the order and confirming delivery on Thursday. She sends another note to Emma Singleton.

```
                                MEMO

To: Emma                                          11 February 1994
From: Emma


ZEBRA MEATS

I have ordered plenty of meat for the coming week, details attached. Ensure that the
order is cancelled from A B Furkins immediately.

Come up for coffee later and I can fill you in on the details about Zebra Meats.
```

Emma put the memo into the internal mail basket. The mail is collected by the post boy and taken to Skyline's own mailroom to be sorted.

FRIDAY

Emma arrives at work to find both her memos to Emma Singleton back on her desk with the morning mail. She picks up the phone and dials Emma's number.

Sally: 'Buyers.'
Emma: 'Is Emma there please? It's Emma Ross.'
Sally: 'Not at the moment, can I take a message?'
Emma: 'Yes. Ask her what she's doing putting these memos back on my desk that I sent her yesterday. Inform her in no uncertain terms that I want an explanation.'
Sally: 'OK Emma, I'll tell her.'

Emma is tied up in a management meeting for the rest of the day.

MONDAY

The morning mail brings a note from Emma Singleton.

```
                                MEMO

To: Emma Ross, Butchery Department Manager           11 Feb 94
From: Emma Singleton, Buyer


TELEPHONE MESSAGE:  11 FEBRUARY 1994

Sally Brown in the Buying Office informed me that you were under the impression that I
had put some memos on your desk. I assure you that this was not the case.

I could not get back to you as you were in a meeting. I will be available on Monday
morning to discuss the matter if you would telephone me on extension 2499 when you
are free.
```

Emma is annoyed by this memo and decides to ring Emma after her meeting with the cooked meat suppliers.

TUESDAY

Emma did not manage to speak to Emma Singleton on Monday. This morning there is a telephone call from Emma Singleton the moment Emma Ross gets into her office.

Emma S: 'Emma, a delivery of meat from some firm called Zebra Meats has arrived, it's absolutely huge – is there some mistake? We're expecting our usual delivery from Furkins tomorrow.'

Emma R: 'You should have cancelled Furkins.'

Emma S: 'When? I don't understand.'

Emma R: 'I told you in that memo to make the necessary arrangements to transfer over to new suppliers.'

Emma S: 'I didn't receive a memo.'

Emma R: 'So you say. You put it back on my desk.'

Emma S: 'I didn't do that. What are we going to do with all this meat?'

Emma R: 'Cancel Furkins.'

Emma S: 'That's unreasonable, they'll be getting the order ready today.'

Emma R: 'I said do it.'

Emma later receives a telephone call from the manager of the refrigerated stores, Peter Maxwell.

Peter: 'We can't store all this meat, there's another order coming tomorrow.'

Emma: 'There isn't another order coming tomorrow, that's cancelled.
Just do the best you can.'

Peter: 'We can't store it I tell you. There are regulations you know.'

Emma: 'I'll organise some discounts, that'll move it.'

Emma informs her Butchery Department staff that price reductions are to be made on many meats.

Emma Singleton has her coffee break in the staff canteen and while she is there, she mentions the problems with the two orders to the store manager. Steve Elliot, the manager of the vegetable department joins them and expresses his surprise at the price reductions in the Butchery Department which he has noticed that day.

During the afternoon, Emma Ross receives a telephone call from the store manager, Satinder Singh.

Satinder: 'I'm getting reports that we've got new meat suppliers Emma, and that the official buyer knew nothing about it.'

Emma: 'She is so incompetent, she can't do a simple thing like cancel an order.'

Satinder: 'It's causing problems. Apparently the refridgerated stores can't cope with the new supplies. Did you order such a large amount of meat Emma?'

Emma: 'Well, yes, I thought we would need that much, we always sold that much in my last job.'

Satinder: 'I see. Another disturbing discovery I have made is that the Butchery Department are putting large price reductions on the meat this morning.'

Emma: 'Yes, I thought that that would ease the problem of storage.'

Satinder: 'We don't have individual members of staff making these decisions alone, it's decided by the management team as store policy.'

Emma: 'Oh dear, I didn't realise.'

Satinder: 'Please be in my office at 9 o'clock tomorrow morning with a full report on the current situation in the Butchery Department.'

Emma: 'I'll be there.'

Within one week, Emma has upset a longstanding and reliable supplier, the buyer and the store manager, made a loss for the Butchery Department by reducing prices, and caused chaos in the refrigerated store.

QUESTIONS

1 Identify the communication channels used in the case study.

2 Were the appropriate channels used in each instance?

3 What barriers to communication existed during the time in which the problem occurred?

4 Which leadership style did Emma Ross adopt?

5 What role did Emma play in planning, organising and monitoring the task of ordering meat for the Butchery Department?

6 How did Emma carry out her leadership role in maximising her team's contribution, building on their strengths and recognising maintenance factors and motivators?

7 What were the key errors Emma made? What was the source of these errors?

SCALE MODEL ACTIVITY

Work in groups of six. Each group must elect a leader and an observer.

Aim:
To build a scale model of the room.

Materials required:
Large sheets of paper, A4 sheets of paper, glue, pencils, coloured pens, scissors, rulers, calculator.

Method
In a restricted time period of approximately 30 minutes the group has to make a scale model of the room they are in, using the materials provided plus any other materials they may find.

The role of the leader
The role of the leader is to plan, organise and monitor the group activity to complete the task and support the group.

The role of the observer
The observer watches the way in which the group operates, taking special note of the points on the observer sheet.

The role of the group member
To work as a team member, carrying out tasks which will see the successful completion of the task.

The Observer feedback sheet

During the activity the observer must watch how the group works and take special note of the following points:

1 Did the leader play his or her role?

_____

2 Did anyone else try to assume the leadership role?

_____

3 Did the leader explain to the group what their task was?

_____

4 Did the leader encourage and support the group, e.g. by thanking them during the activity, smiling at individuals, asking for suggestions?

_____

5 Were the tasks divided equally?

_____

6 Did members of the group elect to perform different roles or were members expected to perform particular roles? For example, who calculated the scale?

_____

7 Was there any member of the group whose contribution was not accepted by the leader or was accepted reluctantly?

_____

8 Were there any barriers to communications during the process, e.g. was anyone's view ignored by the leader and/or the group?

_____

9 How well did the group work as a team?

_____

10 Did the leader always perform their role and how much practical contribution did they make to the model?

_____

Reporting back

On reporting back to the group the observer asks the following questions of the group and then gives his or her own feedback:

1 *To the group*: Did the leader play the role of a leader?

2 *To the leader*: Did you feel you were always in control, planning, organising and monitoring?

3 *To the group*: Did the leader explain to you what the goal of the group was and what your individual task was?

4 *To the leader*: Do you believe you supported your group?

5 *To the group*: Did you feel the leader supported you and gave you encouragement?

6 *To the leader*: Did you think the tasks were divided equally?

7 *To the group*: How do you think the tasks were allocated, and could it have been done better?

8 *To the leader:* On what basis did you allocate tasks?

9 *To the group*: Did you feel at any time ignored by the leader, or by the rest of the group?

10 *To the leader*: Did you always perform your role and did you ever feel frustrated with your role and what you wanted to do?

11 *To the leader*: How successful was the group?

12 *To the group*: How successful were you as a group?

13 *To the group*: By the time the task was completed which stage in the life of the group (norming, storming or performing) were you at?

WORDSEARCH

Behaviour aspects of managing people which influence performance at work

```
O A L D E M P H B I F K L W R I T T E N
R L A H N O L A P F N J A L P B Q B R O
G D I A G N A C O M M U N I C A T I O N
A H S C J I N H G Q S R G T R R V K I V
N T S J B T N I O A N E U D C R W U W E
I K E H A O I E D S M T A B G I M G R R
S D Z E I R N V G R O U G V T E R T Y B
I R F P H I G E B S T L E J C R Y G Z A
N L A N N U M H C M A O T A S K R U L
G C I M L G D E D E M O C R A T I C D E
N I R Q P C O N T R I B U T I O N Y C Q
R J E U T F P T I M I N G L I R N X I N
L M O R V A F J M G E R A O H A B E T O
C R V U O N T C I B S C P A L L D Z A S
G N N S D L J P N T I F P A A W L J R E
R O N I U G D E R S F O M M W G Y S C X
C O K S B C L F Y E G R R O U P B C O N
C M N A G Y O H I N O M N C I V A N T O
L O S F T D P I N F O R M A L K W H U L
C O N S U L T A T I V E R Q S H U T A Q
```

STYLE	ORGANISING	COMMUNICATIONS
FORMAL	MONITORING	BARRIERS
INFORMAL	ORAL	GROUP
AUTOCRATIC	WRITTEN	TASK
DEMOCRATIC	NONVERBAL	ACHIEVEMENT
CONSULTATIVE	LANGUAGE	CONTRIBUTION
LASSEZ FAIRE	PHYSICAL	
PLANNING	TIMING	

Unit 3 Review test

Performance Criterion 1

1 List the different management styles.
2 What differences are there between formal and informal leaders?
3 What are the disadvantages of a leader having a democratic style of leadership?
4 What is the difference between the democratic and laissez faire styles of leadership?

Performance Criterion 2

5 What are the two main leadership roles?
6 What does 'planning' involve?
7 What differences does leadership style make to the planning stage?
8 What sort of activities are involved with 'monitoring' the work of the team?
9 Part of the leadership role is to 'maximise contribution' – how might management attitudes about workers affect this?
10 How can appraisal interviews help a leader to recognise strengths and weaknesses in individuals?
11 Name **three** maintenance factors.
12 What motivators can a leader use with a team?

Performance Criterion 3

13 What is the difference between formal and informal communication?
14 How can a manager use the grapevine?
15 What are the advantages of written communication?
16 Give **five** examples of oral communication.

Performance Criterion 4

17 What are the benefits to the organisation of effective communication?
18 Define 'barriers to communication'.
19 How might language become a communication barrier?
20 What physical barriers might there be to effective communication?

Further sources of information

Baron, R and I Byrne, *Social Psychology*, Allyn & Bacon Inc.

Bennett, R *Organisational Behaviour*, M & E Handbooks, Pitman Publishing.

Betts, P W, *Supervisory Studies* (1989), Pitman Publishing.

Davis, K and D Newstrom, *Human Behavior at Work: Organizational Behavior* 7th edition, McGraw Hill.

Evans, Desmond W, *People, Communication and Organisations*, Pitman Publishing.

Fletcher, Clive and Richard Williams, *Performance Appraisal and Career Development*, Hutchinson.

Gregson, Shaun and Frank Livesey, *Organizations and Management*, Made Simple Books.

Handy, Charles, *Understanding Organizations* (1985), Penguin Books.

Huczynski, Andrzej and David Buchanan, *Organizational Behaviour* (1991), Prentice Hall.

Jewell, Bruce R, *An Integrated Approach to Business Studies* (1990) Pitman Publishing.

Makin, Peter, Cary Cooper and Charles Cox, *Managing People at Work* (1989), the British Psychological Society, Leicester.

Matteson, Michael T, and John M Ivancevich, *Management Classics* (1986), Business Publications Ltd.

Riley, Michael, *Human Resource Management*, Butterworth Heinemann.

Salaman, Graeme, (ed), *Human Resource Strategies*, Sage Publications.

Stafford, Christopher E, *People in Business Organisations* (1990), Cambridge University Press.

Stoner, James A F, and R Edward Freeman, *Management* (1992), Prentice-Hall International.

Wainwright, Gorden R, *Body Language*, Hodder & Stoughton.

'Management Today', published monthly by Management Publications Ltd, 22 Lancaster Gate, London W2 3LY, subscriptions tel. 0858 468888

'Personnel Management', produced monthly on behalf of the Institute of Personnel Management by Personnel Publications Ltd, 17 Britton Street, London EC1M 5NQ

Index